D1554241

Life and Death in the Garden

Life and Death in the Garden

Sex, Drugs, Cops, and Robbers in Wartime China

Kathryn Meyer

ROWMAN & LITTLEFIELD
Lanham • Boulder • New York • London

Published by Rowman & Littlefield
A wholly owned subsidiary of The Rowman & Littlefield Publishing Group, Inc.
4501 Forbes Boulevard, Suite 200, Lanham, Maryland 20706
www.rowman.com

16 Carlisle Street, London W1D 3BT, United Kingdom

Copyright © 2014 by Rowman & Littlefield

All rights reserved. No part of this book may be reproduced in any form or by
any electronic or mechanical means, including information storage and retrieval
systems, without written permission from the publisher, except by a reviewer
who may quote passages in a review.

British Library Cataloguing in Publication Information Available

Library of Congress Cataloging-in-Publication Data
Meyer, Kathryn, 1947–
  Life and death in the garden : sex, drugs, cops, and robbers in wartime China /
Kathryn Meyer.
       pages cm. — (State and society in East Asia)
  Includes bibliographical references and index.
  ISBN 978-1-4422-2352-3 (cloth : alk. paper) — ISBN 978-1-4422-2353-0
(electronic) 1. Prostitution—China—Harbin—History—20th century. 2. Drug
traffic—China—Harbin—History—20th century. 3. Crime—China—Harbin—
History—20th century. 4. Japan—Relations—China—History—20th century.
5. China—Relations—Japan—History—20th century. 6. Manchuria (China)—
History—1931–1945. I. Title.
  HQ250.H37M49 2014
  306.0951'84—dc23

                                            2014008575

♾™ The paper used in this publication meets the minimum requirements of
American National Standard for Information Sciences—Permanence of Paper
for Printed Library Materials, ANSI/NISO Z39.48-1992.

Printed in the United States of America

Contents

Acknowledgments

This book has been long in the making and has taken me many times to the other side of the globe. During the process I have had the pleasure of meeting people who have made my life richer and the final product possible. I must extend special thanks to Norman Smith and Olga Bakich for their careful reading and suggestions that helped me improve the final draft. I want to thank Ron Suleski in advance for pointing me toward a new project, one that will keep me in Manchuria. No book of this sort is complete without the help of librarians. I will always be in debt to the supportive staff of both the National Diet Library in Tokyo, Japan, and the Library of Congress Asian Reading Room in Washington, DC. I give special thanks to Kiyoyo Y. Pipher, research librarian at the Library of Congress, who shared stories of her childhood in Harbin.

I could not have passed so many happy and productive hours in Tokyo without the encouragement of two dear friends, Yoko Maeda and Fumi-kazu Higashihara. I promise that the next time I come to Japan, we will do something a lot more fun than listening to my tales of trolling through the archives and getting thrown out of bookstores in Jimbōchō.

Closer to my home, I am grateful to Wright State University for several generous faculty development grants that made travel to Asia possible. Piper Martin, humanities librarian at Wright State University, has been an invaluable resource in getting me through the most obscure citations. John Oswald, of Wright State University's Urban Studies Department, did a wonderful job with the maps. I also want to thank friend and neighbor Wilmer "WoNo" Nussbaum, veteran of the War in the Pacific, for his enthusiastic reading of drafts.

It has been a joy to work with the staff of Rowman & Littlefield. I want to thank Susan McEachern for her patience and even encouragement over the months when I kept finding more details to add to the text. I am more than grateful for the careful editorial scrutiny that Jehanne Schweitzer and Jennifer Kelland gave the text.

Personally I have relied on the patience, support, and encouragement of my family, Helen Meyer, Betsy Meyer, Scott MacKay, and Sarah Meyer. Thank you all for putting up with my long silences and with forced readings of this work at the many early and unsettled stages of its slow emergence. Sorry for the mess Betsy, but your dining room table is still the best work space ever.

My career would not have been possible without the influence of many teachers along the way. I especially hold two of my own sensei dear to my heart. Both were superior scholars, and both were taken from this world at much too early an age. Therefore I dedicate this book to the memory of Shumpei Okomoto and Marie Jacqueline Mueller.

A Word about
Transliterations and Names

For Chinese names and places, I have used the *pinyin* transliteration system used in China. The exceptions to this are the names Sun Yat-sen and Chiang Kai-shek, both spellings more familiar to an American audience, and the place names Mukden and Manchukuo, as they appear spelled this way in English sources and texts.

For Japanese names and places, I have used the Hepburn transliteration system. I have left the diacritical marks off the spelling of Tokyo in the text, treating it as an English word, but included them—Tōkyō—in the citations when a Japanese language source has been used.

The original texts are written using Chinese characters. This means that most place names will have both Chinese and Japanese pronunciations. Manchukuo (滿洲國), for instance, is Manzhouguo in the Chinese reading and Manshūkoku in the Japanese reading. I have used the spelling familiar to Americans, Manchukuo.

Back in the day, Chinese would call the city Mukden "Fengtian," whereas Japanese residents would have called the same city "Hoten." Mukden is the Manchu-language rendering. Again, since it is most familiar to American readers, I have used Mukden.

Today the southernmost province in China's Northeast is called Liaoning (遼寧). It is much larger now than it was in the 1930s because part of old Rehe (熱河) Province has been merged into it. The name changed often. It started its political life in 1907 as Fengtian (奉天) Province, using the same characters as its capital city. It became Liaoning in 1929, changed back to Fengtian in 1932, and back again to Liaoning in 1945.

Japanese residents would have called the city Dalian (大連) "Dairen." Russians called it "Dalney." It is transliterated as Dal'nii in the formal Library of Congress system, but it appears as Dalney in the English texts of the prewar period. In Russian it means "far away."

Beijing, meaning "Northern Capital," became Beiping (北平), meaning "Northern Peace," in 1927 and remained so until 1949. During those years the capital of China was in Nanjing, meaning "Southern Capital." To avoid confusion I have let Beijing keep its original name through the text, as did many of the Japanese sources of the time.

In order to avoid confusion with transliterations that sound similar (the characters would be quite different), I have used the following convention:

The Japanese Army in Manchuria was named literally the "Eastern Pass Army" for the area in southern Manchuria just east of the Shanhai-guan (山海關), meaning "Mountain Ocean Pass." It is pronounced as the Guandong (or Kwantung in old texts) Army (關東軍) in Chinese and the Kantō Army in Japanese. I have used the Japanese pronunciation through the text so as to avoid confusion with names with similar transliterations. The Guomindang (國民黨; Kuomintang, or KMT, on Taiwan) is the party of Sun Yat-sen and later Chiang Kai-shek. The characters translate to "Party of the People of the Nation." To avoid confusion I have used the conventional "Nationalist Party" to refer to this organization.

Other than this, I have used the Chinese transliteration for place names in Manchuria, whereas I have translated the names of streets into English. This is to avoid confusion as often streets were named after cities. The only exception is New Capital. The city has long been called Changchun, as it is today. However, from 1932 to 1945, it was called New Capital, the administrative center of Manchukuo. It is pronounced Xinjing in Chinese and Shinkyō in Japanese. I have used the English because it conveys the fragile newness of the entire enterprise in China's Northeast.

Confused? You are not alone. In 1932 an American traveler to Manchukuo expressed his frustration with names. He dutifully learned to pronounce Changchun only to find he had to learn to say Xinjing, which he did. Then he was told to use the Japanese Shinkyō. He found the original name Changchun, or "Long Spring," to be a misnomer. One thing Manchukuo did not enjoy was a long spring.

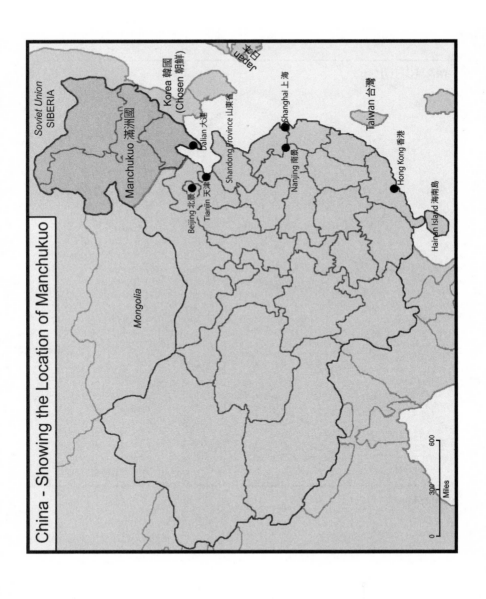

China - Showing the Location of Manchukuo

Soviet Union
SIBERIA

Manchukuo 滿洲國

Korea 韓國
(Chosen 朝鮮)

Japan 日本

Dalian 大連

Shandong Province 山東省

Shanghai 上海

Tianjin 天津

Beijing 北京

Nanjing 南京

Taiwan 台灣

Hong Kong 香港

Hainan Island 海南島

Mongolia

0   300   600
         Miles

Manchukuo

Prologue

As Americans we do not know much about the land war fought in China as part of the Second World War. Part of the reason is an American preoccupation with events in the Pacific. But another part of the reason can be found in the complexity of the participants who engaged each other in Asia. There is no larger-than-life personality like Hitler in Europe. Instead the Asian situation was a fluid, jellylike mixture of multifaceted civil war, anticolonial resistance, and regional struggles over land and resources, all of which had blended into the emerging global conflict by 1941. When we look closely at the clearly defined sides that emerged after 1927—Chinese Nationalists, Chinese Communists, and Japanese military—we find that they were riddled with factions, which makes pinning down icons of good and evil difficult. Briefly, the events break down as follows.

In 1911, the Chinese dynastic empire fell to a loosely organized group of revolutionaries who established a republic. While the new government tried to assert itself, the Chinese nation in fact fractured into areas dominated by regional warlords. In 1927, the Nationalist Party, led by Chiang Kai-shek, conquered most warlords, captured the coastal area of China, moved the capital to Nanjing, and began the civil war against the Chinese Communist Party led by Mao Zedong. A power vacuum in the North attracted both Japanese adventurers and the Manchurian warlord Zhang Zuolin. Japanese army officers knocked Zhang out of the game when they assassinated the man in 1928.

On September 18, 1931, officers in the Imperial Japanese Army placed a bomb on the tracks of their own rail line through Manchuria, blamed

1

it on Chinese terrorists, and used the event to begin the invasion of China's three northeastern provinces. On March 1, 1932, the occupation successful, the Japanese-sponsored nation called Manchukuo began its fourteen-year history. This Manchurian Incident could be considered the beginning of the Second World War. It certainly began sporadic fighting in East Asia as the boundary of Manchukuo moved steadily southward.

In 1936, two unrelated incidents ensured that simmering hostilities would come to a boil. On February 26, a small group of radical Japanese army officers attempted to overthrow the Japanese constitutional government, assassinating several cabinet members. The Japanese military itself ended this coup attempt. Afterward, the Japanese army, especially those who advocated a forceful Asian policy, gained political clout.

Meanwhile, in China, in December 1936, Zhang Xueliang, the murdered warlord's son, kidnapped Chiang Kai-shek. The generalissimo was only released after promising to fight seriously any further Japanese encroachment into Chinese territory. Two events in two different countries ensured that the low-level regional battles would soon explode into a major conflict.

On July 7, 1937, all pretense of uneasy truce ended when Japanese and Chinese troops began a skirmish that expanded into the full-scale invasion of China. On September 27, 1940, Japan, Italy, and Germany concluded the Tripartite Pact, linking war in Asia to the war in Europe. The scope of war expanded yet again on December 7, 1941, with the bombing of Pearl Harbor. Throughout the war in the Pacific, Manchukuo remained a bastion for Japanese military might. From the first invasion of Manchuria until Japanese surrender on August 15, 1945, Chinese men and women fought the Japanese invasion in any way they could. They joined with American forces, they fought with the Chinese Communist Party in the Northwest, they fought with Chiang Kai-shek's Nationalist Party in the Southwest, or they banded together, organizing impromptu and spontaneous resistance.

Many heroes fought in Manchuria and China. None of those brave men and women ever came near the building in the Harbin slums called the Garden of Grand Vision.

Introduction

People in the Garden of Grand Vision are driven lower and lower in the social order by the pressures of Manchukuo society. They have stopped just one step before destruction.

—Police lieutenant Gotō Reiji[1]

If one does not understand Fujiadian [the neighborhood around the Garden], one cannot understand Harbin. If one does not understand Harbin, one cannot understand Manchukuo; if we do not understand Manchukuo, we cannot govern. We need more Japanese people who can speak Chinese.

—Kagawa Tetsuzō, travel writer[2]

This is a story about living and dying on the lowest margins of society during the Second World War. It takes place in Asia, in Japanese-occupied Manchuria, where the Imperial Army of the Rising Sun based its military operations against China and the rest of the world. There are no heroes in this tale, no battles—nothing explodes.[3] The people we meet—men like Braying Mule Wang, Poor Mouth Liu, and Three Legs Guo or women like the pretty Chun Fang—earned what little they could through scavenging, grave robbing, prostitution, theft, or begging. They spent money as quickly as they got their hands on it, buying forgetfulness in narcotics, sharing a few moments with a prostitute, or risking it all on a game of chance. These folk lived in a dark world, becoming police informants for the Japanese enemy with no qualms or patriotic scruples.

Our Japanese guides into this dystopia are three police investigators. Gotō Reiji (?–1949) is their leader. The other men, Satō Shin'ichirō (1905–1999) and Katō Toyotaka (1918–), respect him as a mentor. These men studied Braying Mule Wang and his transient friends, hoping to understand the cause of poverty and to contribute to social reform. As Japanese police working in occupied China, they answered to the Japanese military intelligence apparatus. Like the infamous German Gestapo, the Japanese Kempeitai (military police), the Special Service Agency[4] (espionage), and later the Peace Preservation Bureau (Internal Security) acquired a well-deserved reputation for sadistic brutality. Yet Gotō and his colleagues were not searching for spies; nor were they cruel. In their own way, they harbored affection and concern for the subjects of their study. They met with Braying Mule and his friends in a flophouse complex with an improbably poetic name, the Garden of Grand Vision, located in the slums of wartime Harbin.

Harbin is not a familiar city outside Asia. It rarely appears on the itineraries of American charter tours to China. Located in Heilongjiang Province, China's northernmost territory, it shares the harsh winter climate associated with Siberian Russia, its immediate neighbor to the north. Harbin has little to offer in the way of classic Chinese culture, history, or the traditional architecture loved by travel poster makers. The little it has—a weedy Confucian temple, a busy Buddhist temple complex—is a product of the 1920s.[5]

The year is 2004. From my eleventh-floor hotel window I can see a bleak panorama of industrial, ferroconcrete sameness. The city has now been under Chinese government control for over sixty years, half of its short history. Newly built glass-and-steel buildings, trimmed in neon, appear here and there, lending a postindustrial hopefulness to the tableau of Soviet-inspired housing blocks thrown up during the 1950s, a time when the city was the center of China's heavy industry. The dark green bulb of St. Sophia's cathedral dome intrudes smack into the middle of the view, a reminder of the imperial Russian origins of Harbin.

Perhaps readers have seen the spectacular photos from the annual Harbin winter festival, where gigantic ice sculptures light up the night sky with neon brightness. I fear that readers who may have heard of Harbin think of massive pollution. Dramatic November 2005 news stories described one hundred tons of benzene spilling into the Songhua River. The eighty-kilometer pool of floating toxic chemicals fouled Harbin's drinking water for a week, threatening the health of the city's residents. Grim news clips showed people of an industrial city lining up for water trucked in from elsewhere. In October 2013 pictures of coal-induced smog showed a city smothered in gray, toxic fumes, a few bemasked residents braving the man-made elements on bicycle, all transportation and business brought to a halt.[6] The newscasters did not go into the Harbin streets where a rich architectural past lies beneath the grayness of a concrete present. Harbin boasts Russian churches, a mosque, a synagogue, examples of twentieth-century Chinese baroque style, Russian dachas, and the world's third-largest collection of art nouveau buildings. To find them a traveler needs to walk through the city.[7]

The eclectic architecture betrays a past when the wealth from a thriving international trade attracted people to the city from around the globe. From its founding in the late nineteenth century by Russian railroad engineers putting through the Asian connection of the Trans-Siberian Railway, it attracted trade and commerce from Europe and Asia. Money came in; buildings went up. Whatever was new appealed to builders in Harbin. In the early 1910s, art nouveau was popular, and so there it remains today. Harbin became the little Paris of East Asia, a city of nightclubs, easy money, stylish clothes, and beautiful women. Fashions from the real Paris showed up in Harbin in a matter of weeks.[8]

The profusion of post-1949 utilitarian housing comes from more recent times when Harbin was a beacon for state-run heavy industry. In the 1950s and 1960s, Manchuria, with Harbin as an urban center, nurtured China's heavy industry. The Daqing oilfields, held up as a model industry, are located to the east of Harbin. Toward the south is a wealth of coal and steel, industries that attracted Japanese capital in the early twentieth century. After 1949, in the days of five-year plans, families relocated to Heilongjiang Province and Harbin to work in the factories there.

The benzene photos capture the sad truth that today's Harbin lags behind in the twenty-first century Chinese economic boom. Without international accessibility, the city's industry did not reap the immediate benefit from the economic reforms of the 1990s. It lagged behind while coastal areas like Shanghai and Shenzhen turned into financial and manufacturing powerhouses. The Manchurian area is only slowly catching up with the economic boom south of the Great Wall. Once celebrated as model industries, state factories have laid off workers in recent years. The region has become China's rust belt. It is only recently catching up with the Chinese boomtowns to the south.[9]

I did not come to Harbin to dwell on recent industrial hardships. I came to walk the streets, following a route made familiar to me by Gotō Reiji and his colleagues, who described the underbelly of the city in a time of war and occupation. They produced a three-hundred-page police report titled *Autopsy of the Garden of Grand Vision.* In 1941 they labeled the report "top secret," turning it over to the Japanese Manchukuo military intelligence authorities on the eve of the War in the Pacific.

I had already familiarized myself with the Harbin of the past by reading in the Tokyo library where I first encountered Gotō's remarkable report. I pored through memoirs of Japanese expats who once lived there. I studied maps of the city from days gone by and read reviews of those Harbin hotels recommended for Japanese tourists of the 1930s. The Hotel New Harbin was then one of the tallest buildings. The Yamato Hotel (today the Longmen Hotel) included instructions to Japanese tourists to keep up appearances in the international city: Behave well in public. Always look neat when leaving the hotel, collar straight, socks clean. I knew the route that I should take even before I stepped out of my modern Holiday Inn—straightening my collar.[10]

I walked along Center Street. Russians called it Kitaiskaia Street—Russian for China Street. In the early 1900s, this was a show place. In 2004, Center Street still is. The cobblestone roadway is blocked to traffic. It is lined with the European architecture—much of it baroque or art nouveau—that gives the city its exotic European quality. The buildings house boutiques, bridal shops, restaurants, and Russian souvenir shops. A sign promises that one establishment is the "best dance club in China." A coffee shop calling itself USA-Bucks looks for all the world like the Starbucks it is not. Guidebooks recommend the Oriental King of Dumplings. Across the street, the Tyrant of Dumplings offers brave competition.

At each intersection beer gardens offer brews from around the world, from the local Harbin Beer (from the oldest brewery in China and actually pretty tasty) to Corona (Mexican music and blow-up plastic cacti) to Pabst Blue Ribbon. At night stages light up along the street, drawing crowds to watch singers, dressed to the nines, performing every musical genre from Western rock to Chinese patriotic. Comedians do routines; magicians amaze the children. Over and over again, there are beer-drinking contests. People in Harbin like their beer.

Center Street ends at a large open plaza overlooking the Songhua River. Here the crowds stroll along the promenade that stretches along the riverbank. Families sit on benches watching the water. Turning to the left brings me to Siberian-style wooden-frame buildings painted green, yellow, and white, where children buy ice cream or water toys or rent in-line skates. Skaters of all ages move smoothly among those enjoying an evening walk. They are keeping in shape for winter skating on the river. The short Manchurian summer is the off-season for skaters in training. This city is home to gold-medal-winning speed skater Yang Yang. In the plaza, many younger Olympic hopefuls learn basic moves from a watchful trainer. They are picking up a sport with a long tradition here. Manchurians have been skating and skiing for centuries—long before the coming of the West.[11] In July, when the river runs liquid, skaters move onto the promenade.

Turning to the right, I walk among the crowds passing under the iron railroad bridge, a landmark mentioned in all of the memoirs. I come to Daowai, the area of the city once considered the Chinese section, exotic and frightening to Japanese residents in the 1930s. Here crowds still gather to enjoy the cool evening along the river, but the atmosphere in the park is not as commercial. Two elderly train spotters call out the destinations of trains rumbling across the bridge. Chess players set up boards under trees; a cricket seller tries to talk me into a new pet; the bird and fish market blossoms among stalls of fruit and vegetable sellers. Impromptu street musicians without the benefit of stages, lights, or amplification play folk songs on traditional instruments. On one corner a man hides a pea under one of three cups, inviting the crowd to place their bets. He could be the descendent of gambler and police informant Braying Mule Wang. On another corner a group of elderly men and women dance to a recorded drumbeat.

This is the area in which Gotō and his colleagues worked. Few Japanese ventured into the Daowai section of Harbin in those days. Even now, when I told my Chinese friend Annie that I was going to Harbin, she warned me against venturing too far off the main roads. Yet, when I asked my cab driver if Daowai was safe, he answered that of course it was. He lived there. After many walks through the comparatively narrow back streets of Daowai, the worst I have encountered is a yappy little dog—its owner a kindly old man—and a ruined pair of shoes after crossing a large mud puddle.

I walk away from the main roads, around the market, until I come to 59 Rich Brocade Street, once the address of the Garden of Grand Vision. The cave-like building is long gone, replaced by a ferroconcrete apartment complex—a clone of others in the neighborhood. A pedicab company office occupies the first floor where the main gate would have been. On the corner, a China Petrol station stands ready to fuel the Chinese love affair with the car. If only Gotō Reiji could see the place now. Many brick, courtyard-style buildings, constructed in the same style as the Garden of Grand Vision, still line other streets of Daowai, but I fear their days are numbered. The tyranny of the wrecking ball and urban renewal is changing the neighborhood. A massive construction site spilling over onto the road created my shoe-destroying mud puddle.

Gotō Reiji comes alive in the pages of his police report, which I have translated line by line with the plodding determination of a tortoise. About the man himself, I know little. He was a Japanese police lieutenant serving in Harbin. As such he helped to oversee a multiethnic force made up of Chinese precinct police who worked along with divisions of Russian and Korean officers. His special assignment began in 1940, in the same year that the Manchukuo authorities conducted a nationwide census. He worked with two junior men, both of whose family names also ended in *tō*, the character for wisteria. Within the force they were known as the "Three *Tō* Group." They were considered a bit strange for their fascination with the slums.[12]

Gotō liked proper Japanese cooking. He ate at a Japanese-owned restaurant called Little Warrior's Storehouse. He had a mistress there, a
woman who could be jealous. At times he treated the police informant
Braying Mule Wang to a meal there as well, but sliced raw fish did not
appeal to Wang, who claimed that back home fellow villagers fed such
food to cats.[13] Gotō Reiji died in August 1945 as Harbin fell to the Soviet
army. He is remembered in the memoirs of Katō Toyotaka, his youngest
assistant.[14]

Born in Matsuyama in southern Japan, Katō Toyotaka came to the
Harbin police force at the young age of twenty-two. Katō survived the
war. He returned home to Japan after spending five brutal years in Soviet
prisoner-of-war camps with his fellow Russian Harbin police officers. In
the 1960s, his memories drove him to write about his experiences. He
completed a lengthy three-volume work, which he ingenuously titled
A Short History of the Manchukuo Police.[15] The second volume, devoted
to clandestine police activities, includes a chapter about the Garden of
Grand Vision.

Not content with the police history, he added to his work a novelette
about the people in the Garden.[16] In the introduction he cautions his readers that the work is fiction, but not really fiction. Indeed, he follows the
narrative of the original police report, at the time still tucked away in the
archives, adding touching little details of the sort that a young assistant
would notice—the vivid red color of a hand-painted sign, the treachery
of a landlord's wife, the interest that his boss has taken in the welfare of
a pretty prostitute.

Satō Shin'ichirō was the scholar among the three. In the 1920s he went
to China as a young man to study language. He lived with Chinese in the
dorms at Beijing University in 1927 and again in 1934. This was a time
of aggressive anti-Japanese boycotts and demonstrations. Satō could not
have missed the passion of his classmates who took to the streets calling
for Japan to leave Chinese affairs to the Chinese. Living in the dorms at
Beijing University, he could observe the dynamics of a growing grassroots
nationalism from a nerve center of the movement.[17] Was he a sympathetic
fellow student caught up in the passions of his classmates? Was he working undercover, reporting what he saw to Japanese authorities? Was he an
agent provocateur? This we do not know. In all likelihood, neither did he.

We do know that Satō came back to Manchuria in the 1930s. When
the Japanese military used Chinese agitation to separate the northeastern provinces from China, Satō went to work for the newly established
Manchukuo government. He mingled with some of the highest-ranking
Japanese officials. In 1940 he brought his experience to the research group
investigating conditions in the Chinese slums. Satō's educated hand
penned most of the body of the report.

After the Japanese defeat in 1945, Satō returned to Japan. He became a professor of Chinese history at Shokutoku University, where he is remembered as a popular teacher who gave riveting lectures based on his own experiences. His postwar writings describe Communist Chinese land reform programs of the 1950s and 1960s but become critical of the abuses of the Cultural Revolution. Perhaps for this reason, his connection with the earlier *Autopsy of the Garden of Grand Vision* remained unacknowledged until after his death in 1999.[18]

Three colleagues—two police officers and one scholar—produced a document that is sophisticated in its analysis of the conditions of the slums. At the same time, it is blatantly racist in its portrayal of Chinese society. The report contains data and analysis that a criminologist today would find useful, often using terms that we consider cutting-edge. I have presented their information for them several times at meetings of the American Society of Criminology. But in telling the tale, they also play up the grotesque, a temptation modern scholars strive to resist. People in the Garden become a freak show. As readers, we join in a voyeurism of the worst sort. It gives the reading a guilty sort of fascination.

Why should we care about a slum so far removed from our own twenty-first-century world? Aside from the lurid descriptions the *Autopsy* provides, the place, the people, and the police who conducted the survey offer an understanding of conflict and occupation on three levels. On the micro level, the Garden of Grand Vision provides a wonderful platform from which to observe Japan's complex experience with colonial empire and war. The Chinese residents of the Garden had continual contact with the basic mechanisms of Japanese social control. Some of them found ways to manipulate the system for their own benefit. Gotō, of course, represented that control organization. Yet there were times when he allowed himself to be used by the people he studied.

As Americans, we know the details of the naval battles in the Pacific after Pearl Harbor. Our Second World War lasted four long years against a Japanese enemy we picture as an imperial monolith. For Japanese people, the War in the Pacific with America came only at the end of a fifteen-year conflict. Military and civil institutions, riddled with factions and often at odds with one another, took on enemy after enemy as war spread from Manchukuo through China and into the Pacific. Gotō and his colleagues had to work with and around a complicated command structure under increasingly difficult circumstances. They had to be careful in their wording and obscure some of their sympathies.

On a macro level, Gotō, his companions, and his supervisors grappled with problems that continue to plague modern societies. They posed questions that still puzzle psychologists, criminologists, and anyone else studying the darker side of human behavior. What are the causes of crime? How should addiction be treated? Does prostitution have a place in society? Should gambling be outlawed as a vice or taxed as a recreation? What is the role of a modern police force in molding society? The *Autopsy* touches on each of these problems.

Moreover, an existential problem is embedded in the document. What is an idealistic person to do when a cherished project turns bad? Gotō and his friends wrote their document for their superiors, not for the public. As such they presented facts, as they were required to do, within the shared assumption that the Japanese military mission in Manchukuo, indeed in all of East Asia, was just. They were openly proud that Japan was the only modern East Asian world power. A well-organized, efficient police bureau added to modernity. They assumed that failed states like China needed Japan's stern guidance. For Japanese patriots like Gotō, Manchukuo was a laboratory for a bright Asian future.

Autopsy of the Garden of Grand Vision describes a harsh warren of crime seen through the eyes of two policemen and one scholar trying to make sense of social disorder. In following them around the Harbin slums, we come to understand the predicament of good cops—who are clever criminologists—serving a dysfunctional organization. A careful reader will find a few cautiously worded reservations about the Manchukuo experiment. Many years after the war, Satō, the scholar, confessed to a time, right in the midst of the Manchukuo experience, when he discovered clear evidence of just how brutal his organization could be. But how much did he dare say while the conflict continued? Gotō and his colleagues were, after all, writing for bosses known to react harshly to criticism.

Gotō Reiji and his colleagues despaired of the Chinese lack of social order. They keenly felt that the promise of Chinese modernity had been wasted in the early twentieth century as the Chinese republic, established in 1912, fell into the chaos of an endless civil war. But they were clearly men who shared a sense of adventure, a good command of Chinese, and a feeling for the tragedies that can lead people to desperation. With the help of Braying Mule and others like him, Gotō and his colleagues painted a vivid picture of a forgotten aspect of war in the modern world. They do not describe the heroes, the villains, the battles, or the camps that we all know so well from history and films of the Second World War. Instead, they bring us into the lives of men and women who fell through the cracks of a world torn apart.

Gotō Reiji was something of a flaneur of the slums. As I followed the policeman and his colleagues through the rabbit hole of time, I joined them strolling the streets of the city. In school I learned about Manchukuo briefly as a drab prologue to world war. What I found was much more exciting. While fixing the men and their document in their social context, I met an odd assortment of folk crossing the path of the Harbin police, all attracted to the city by its wealth and international intrigue, all misfits in their native places. Manchuria was a frontier. It attracted adventurers from around the world: a pistol-toting American consul, an Italian spy who became Chinese, and a Japanese spy with murder on his resume who ran a film studio.

These men found in Manchuria a comfort zone that eluded them in their homelands. In the end, however, each man met with tragedy as he ran head-on into the violent forces of history that defined Manchuria. This book is not simply about the slum. It will introduce an array of characters who helped to make the strategic city the dangerous place that it was in the 1930s. It will tell stories about people struggling in a forgotten war zone.

1

In the Garden

Is this place akin to the human world? Is this not the only verdict to reach? In this world we hear limitless gory episodes of people driven to the wall. Before the many wonders of this world we grow pale. Our intellect and sense of morality cannot help but shudder. Here the customs spreading out into the street are nothing but nihilism and emotional void.

—Gotō Reiji[1]

Hey, hey, I play the bones, I'll tell you something good. Come on into the Garden of Grand Vision. The Garden of Grand Vision is a wonderful place. Japanese girls have small noses [vaginas]. Russian girls have big ones. Big or small, Gentlemen, Gentlemen, roll right on in. . . . Japanese women have small ones, Russian women have large ones. Small is best, but in the Garden there are only large ones. Too bad! Quick! Come on in.

—Poor Mouth Liu's song of welcome[2]

Gotō Reiji, police officer with the Harbin Central Police Administration, invites his readers to join him on his commute to the Garden of Grand Vision. Leaving the comforts of his office in the police bureau, a granite building in the solidly middle-class area of Harbin, we join him on a late winter day as he boards the No. 16 trolley. Together we ride from the Harbin station north toward the Chinese section of town. Gotō names the streets as we pass: Baron Xu Street, Bright Sun Street, Righteous Sun Street, Great New Street.

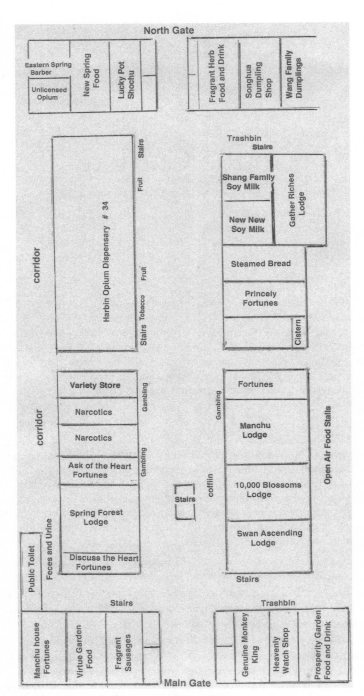

Garden of Grand Vision, Layout, First Floor

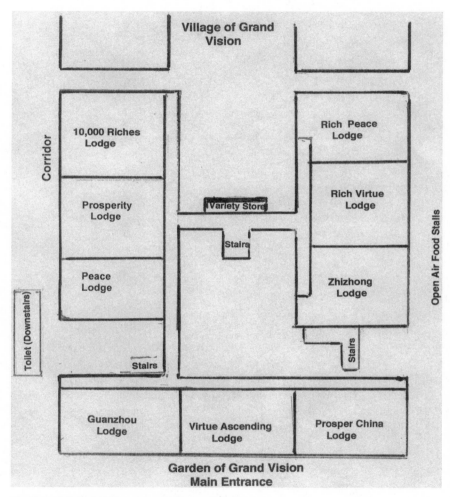

Garden of Grand Vision, Layout, Second Floor

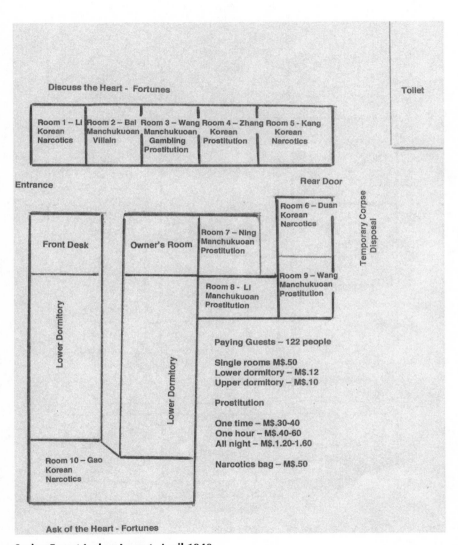

Spring Forest Lodge, Layout, April 1940

The year is 1940. Merciless war grips the world. Tentacles of violence spread deeper into Asia and Europe, soon to threaten the United States, even as we ride along the Harbin streets. Gotō's assignment is secret. His orders: study the slums of Harbin, a perfect hiding place for spies and enemies of the state, an area the Japanese-run government finds difficult to control. As he fulfills his duty, however, he is drawn into a more perplexing riddle. His personal quest: discover the causes of poverty and crime.[3]

From the trolley window Gotō shows us a scene bursting with life. The crowd grows chaotic as the trolley moves on its way north toward the wide Songhua River. This is the Chinese section of town. On one side of the street is a police box; across the road, peddlers clog the streets. Baskets heavy with wares hang from shoulder poles. On one corner Gotō points out a tattered sign. It reads, "Flower Shop." Lest we be fooled by the name, he tells us it is a cheap flophouse.[4] On the opposite corner, a variety store owner has clearly marked his shop wall with characters reading, "Public urination prohibited." Below the message traces of urine stain the alley wall. The owner has added the ironic comment "Rabbit piss" to the collage, "rabbit" being local slang for "fool." The joke is lost on most of the crowd. Few on the streets can read.[5]

Along the road Gotō shows us impromptu street stalls where merchants sell cheap goods, probably the spoils of pickpockets. Women follow their pimps into the shadows. Pickpockets, fortune-tellers, and gamblers work on the street. Along a fence, day laborers wait for odd jobs. It is, says Gotō, a dirty, immoral crowd. We can almost feel him catch his breath as he leaves the trolley.[6]

Walking now, we follow him into the narrow Rich Brocade Street. Gotō leads us to the door of Number 59, which opens into a deep vestibule. In a happier past, an artisan carefully carved the characters for "Garden of Grand Vision" in a classical hand. The sign hangs elegantly over the lintel. The door faces south, a lucky direction in the Chinese practice of feng shui. The name itself, Garden of Grand Vision, evokes a scene of rich beauty. It refers to a pavilion in the romantic novel *Dream of the Red Chamber*, a place where children of privilege came of age amid poetry and opulence.[7] The name would be familiar to those passing by, just as the word "Camelot" conveys a sense of fantasy in the West. Yet the entrance under the sign is cave-like. The light is dim, nurturing the "sprouts of crime."[8]

The building itself is brick. Inside the main gate is an open atrium. A stairway separates the east and west halls. Two more stairwells are in the rear. Along the east hall we find Swan Ascending Lodge, Ten Thousand Blossoms Lodge, and Manchu Lodge, all flophouses, intermixed with fortune-telling businesses. Along the west hall, beyond the public latrine and a dustbin, we find more fortune-tellers, several morphine shops, a variety store, and the Spring Forest Lodge.[9] At the top of the stairs: two more halls, more shops, more flophouses.

The Garden of Grand Vision is a skeletal version of a Chinese baroque courtyard house. We can find many lovely examples of the style elsewhere in the city. On the surface a Chinese baroque building displays European ornamentation. But look more closely. At the top of that Corinthian column, Chinese cabbage leaves replace laurels; at the base, an artist has placed details from Buddhist temple designs. On the roof arabesque balustrades are in fact plaster, giving the building a feeling of height. Inside the main gate, we find a courtyard with shops. Rental flats make up the top floor. Or we may find a second building of rentals behind the first. Inside, as more people migrate to the city, units are subdivided, and rooms are rented out for extra income. The central hall area, usually open to the air, becomes a place where people living in the units can gather, carry on daily activities, or just relax outside. The Garden of Grand Vision offers shelter, community of a sort, but little aesthetic value.[10]

We pass through the building, out a back door, where we cross a small alley into a rear addition—the Village of Grand Vision. This building mimics the first. It is brick and has two stories with three staircases, a dustbin, shops, and flophouses along the halls. The Manchukuo government sponsors Harbin Opium Dispensary Number Thirty-Four in the rear building, catering to registered users. Outside the rear door of the second building, Long Spring Street stretches out in a filthy sprawl like a pig's intestine, to use Gotō's words.[11] We follow the policeman into a bustling thieves' market surrounded by several brothels. Gotō's young assistant warns us to beware of pickpockets. He points out beggars, pimps, and Korean morphine sellers.[12]

The pleasures of opium and heroin dominate the lives of the residents of the Garden. This may lead an American reader to confuse the Garden of Grand Vision with today's crack houses or shooting galleries, deserted by all but those seeking a fix. Such places are a far cry from the economically vibrant Garden complex. The buildings are not abandoned; nor can they be likened to a squatters' community. They house nineteen flophouse franchises, thirteen in the front building, six in the rear. Altogether there are eleven food shops, three of which cater to the Muslim diet. Signs in front of the door have the Chinese characters indicating *halal*, crudely written. Gotō explains that these places do not sell pork. A *shochu* liquor brewer keeps a shop in the rear building. Small businesses set up stalls along the north wall of the Village of Grand Vision. We find a tailor, a tinker, a man who repairs artificial legs, two medicine shops, and a watch-repair shop.[13]

The Garden of Grand Vision was registered with the Harbin City government. The income was taxed. The owner, Zou Xisan, subdivided the building into spaces all rented out to subcontractors, showing enviable entrepreneurial talent in such dire circumstances. Each of the flophouse owners paid Zou up to three hundred Manchurian yuan (M$) in franchise fees to take over a portion of the building. In addition they paid as much as M$100 in monthly rent. Quarterly business taxes went to the local government tax office.[14] Along the hallways between the flophouses, a hungry fellow could find bean curd sellers, fruit stands, steamed-bread shops, and snack shops selling fish, pork, and rice. Prices ranged from M$0.02 for a steamed bun or a piece of fruit to M$0.10 for a bowl of rice and fish. Before trying his luck, a gambler could consult a fortune-teller. The Garden was alive with economic possibilities catering to the needs of the desperate.[15]

As Gotō takes us back inside the tunnel-like doorway, he warns us that we are coming to a dark, fearsome place filled with stench and vulgarity. As we enter we face the main stairway. Here we meet a cluster of prostitutes waiting for customers. Their eyes show a white muddiness, a sign of syphilis. We are lucky. Usually several naked corpses litter the stairwell, but today the stairs have been swept clear of the dead. Gotō ushers us into the Spring Forest Lodge, a flophouse in the western hallway of the main building's ground floor. Gotō uses this area as a sort of operational base. Many of his informants live here.[16]

The Garden complex was not intended for squalid flophouses. Its owner, Zou Linchang (courtesy name: Xisan), purchased his packet of land to build on in 1927 for M$36,000. The next year he spent M$90,000 to put up a two-story building for a motion picture theater and rental property. (The prices are estimates. The actual payments were made in the confusingly eclectic currency of the 1920s, in this case money from the Jilin Provincial Bank.) Katō Toyotaka claims that Zou extorted the property. Nevertheless, the area was ripe with possibilities that attracted Zou's speculative instincts. In the 1920s a tramline went from the center of Harbin into the outskirts of Daowai. This created a building frenzy, attracting capital from all over Manchuria. Zou realized the potential of a growing area. His choice of the name Garden of Grand Vision reflects the opulent future he pictured for the building. He built a movie theater on the site with a rental property in the rear. But Zou mismanaged the theater. At the same time the area failed to prosper in the way Zou expected. Unskilled laborers flocked to Fujiadian. Korean heroin sellers soon followed. The area grew in population but deteriorated, becoming the slum of Gotō's report.[17]

Zou himself lived in a better area of town, along with a wife and a concubine. At the time of Gotō's research, he worked for a Harbin newspaper, the Japanese-owned *Binjiang* (Harbin County) *Daily*. He held the title councilor but did little in the way of actual work. He showed up at the office on occasion. His real wealth came from his building and a money shop he owned in the area.

In 1929, Zou's theater burned down. Zou cashed in on insurance to the tune of M$45,000. He used the money to rebuild the Garden for a new purpose. One of Gotō's informers claimed that Zou had hired a thug to torch the building. Whether he did or not, the fire was timely. The ensuing renovations reflected the changing status of the neighborhood. Zou added apartments in place of the theater, intending to house working-class families. Instead, over the following decade, the facilities appealed to a growing, drug-addicted underclass. Resourceful builders further reworked the inner structure, adding rooms and lowering ceilings to create the bunkrooms in the flophouses. Zou profited from the changing arrangements. Formally, he received M$1,100 per month in rents, paying the Harbin government M$700 in yearly taxes. Katō estimated Zou's real monthly income to be M$8,000.[18]

Thirteen flophouse businesses lined the halls of the Garden of Grand Vision building; another six could be found in the Village of Grand Vision. Scattered about the surrounding neighborhood were thirty-four more belonging to different landlords. Each enterprise sported a hopeful name that clashed oddly with the dark atmosphere of the building. Inside the Garden, a needy fellow could find a bed at Virtue Ascending Lodge, Prosperity Lodge, or Prosper China Lodge. Each franchise followed a similar business pattern. Since Gotō has connections to the Spring Forest Lodge on the first floor of the main building, it is to this lodge that he takes us.[19]

A staff of three or four managed each of the flophouses. The typical franchise owner employed a desk clerk, an accountant, and an enforcer. In 1940, the time Gotō takes us on our tour, Lin Jitang owned the Spring Forest Lodge. Like many we will encounter in the Garden, including the landlord, Lin hailed from Shandong Province, just a boat ride across the Yellow Sea from Manchuria. He came north from his family home in 1935. Lin has been running the Spring Forest Lodge for three years at the time we meet him in Gotō's investigation. Although Lin came from the same county in the same province as Zou Xisan, the Garden's owner, he arrived in Harbin with no money and no contacts. He found work as a boatman for the North Manchuria River Authority, earning M$20 per month.[20]

River work did not suit Lin. He got the job because he could read, but the flat-bottomed freight boats that plied the shallow Songhua River offered little in the way of comfort. Lin soon tired of sleeping in a dark area near the keel of the craft. He tried his hand at running a variety store, but in a short time the business failed. He ended up in the Harbin slums because he could claim a connection to Zou the landlord. As they came from the same county, Zou helped him buy into the flophouse franchise. Lin had a complicated relationship with his benefactor. Behind Zou's back, Lin bad-mouthed the landlord. To Zou's face, Lin was polite.[21]

When we meet Lin Jitang, we see his polite, even servile side in the way he treats Gotō. Lin is not ordinarily a kindly man. He lives with his concubine, a woman he picked up in the alleyways near the Garden. Gotō calls her an owl. She perms her hair and uses liberal amounts of flour on her face in lieu of makeup. The money to buy into the Spring Forest Lodge franchise, Gotō tells us, came from the earnings of this prostitute concubine. Lin's wife and two daughters remain at home in Shandong Province.

Lin rarely smiles. He keeps in good standing with local ruffians and the precinct police. He survives by being personally obsequious to those in authority, like Gotō, while sending his concubine to handle any local thugs who might pass by. He augments his income when he can by helping those who kidnap women for prostitution, offering them space to hide their victims until they can be sold. He accepts stolen goods from his customers when they cannot pay cash for their nightly stay. He is a fence and a procurer, and he helps embezzle narcotics from the government monopoly. On top of all this, he is a police informant. Clearly Lin is not a man of character.[22]

Gotō's young assistant swears that Lin is a rat. He tells us that it was Lin who provided the information that Zou hired an arsonist to torch the Garden in order to collect insurance money. Zou the landlord and Lin the flophouse franchisee have a love/hate relationship. Although from the same county in Shandong Province, they are not from the same town or the same class. Whereas Zou came to Manchuria with connections, Lin struggled. Lin was able to use their common origins to buy into the Garden business at a time when he was hard up, but the friendship ends there. Lin keeps up his barrage of complaint and rumor about Zou. Confronted with Lin's evidence, such as it is, Gotō only remarks that he is glad prosecuting fraud is not his jurisdiction.[23]

Lin spends most of his time in a small back room where he smokes opium. His concubine joins him at the pipe—when she is not turning a trick. He leaves the day-to-day running of the business to his cousin and counter man, Lin Yuming. Men who work the counter have a position of relative power in the Garden's social hierarchy. Customers politely call them sir. Lin's counter man is a thin, hawkish-looking man with a mean temper. Once, out of the blue, he hit a prostitute, fourteen-year-old Sun Jinzi, with an abacus, raising a welt on the girl's head. He handles the day-to-day affairs of the franchise with a curse for all who pass his desk. He greets one and all with the words "You! Raised by a stinking cunt!" When the Garden residents talk among themselves, they call him "stinking cunt." To his face, though, they politely address the cousin as "second boss" or just "sir." "Such two faced behaviors are a practical survival strategy in this society."[24]

Over the year that Gotō studied the Garden, several enforcers came and went from the Spring Forest Lodge. The enforcer, officially called the "boy," was never a child. When Gotō began his survey, a certain Feng Daren held the post at the Spring Forest Lodge. Feng's fellow lodgers politely called him Feng Dàren (大人), or Feng the Great Man. Among themselves and in their minds, they heard Feng Dǎren (打人), or Feng Beats People. A slight shift in accent transforms the honorific into an insult. Feng had once made a rough-and-tumble living through blackmail and extortion. It was said that he first came to the Garden for a rest. At the time he paid for one night's lodging, after which he merely glared at the desk attendant whenever the question of payment arose. Instead of leading to his ejection, his talent for intimidation received recognition.[25]

Lin, the owner, saw that Feng had useful abilities. He hired Feng to throw troublemakers out of the Spring Forest Lodge. Feng also did a job called "guiding across," which involved dealing with those who were about to die or, in the language of the Garden, to pass into Buddhahood. Feng's job involved stripping them of their clothing and dumping them in a mud room outside the building where a few hours of exposure to the harsh Harbin climate would finish them off. Feng might be seen carrying a man gasping for his last breath, looking like a bundle of rags and stinking of vomit. "Oh, you have not yet become a Buddha," Feng might say, giving the rag bundle a swat on the head to hurry the process along. Gotō comments that a sick person, tossed naked into the Harbin cold, could survive no more than three hours at best. Lin, like other owners, did not want anyone to die in his establishment. A death would require procedures, such as filing a police report. Questions might be asked. And so, the barely alive went to the dirt room, out into the alley, or into a public latrine on the first floor of the Garden. Their clothes were stolen and sold.[26]

Feng was a sturdy fellow who strutted around with a puffed-up chest and a lethal kick. He had a sense of humor as well. The residents of the Garden called him the Scorpion. He earned little from his job, but he also collected a percentage from the prostitutes and gambling games run on the premises. His life would have continued comfortably in this job were he not a drug addict. Within the year, his health went from robust to frail. He fled the Spring Forest Lodge so as not to be "guided across" himself. Feng was replaced by an even more ferocious character lacking any sense of humor but with an equally healthy narcotics habit.[27]

The flophouses shared a similar layout. They offered three types of lodging accommodations—single rooms, lower bunkrooms, and upper bunkrooms built under the eaves. The single rooms had dirt floors and were divided from one another by wooden partitions. They were no more than six feet square. The door was fashioned from a warped board. They were small but did offer a measure of privacy. Each room had a small *kang*, or heated platform, to serve as a sitting area during the day and bed at night. The daily rate for such luxury was M$0.50. Prostitutes and Korean heroin dealers favored these rooms. Few others could afford them.

The lower bunkrooms accommodated many more lodgers at a lower price. M$0.20 provided a bunk in the long room. The bunk was really no more than a board covered with a dirty quilt, usually in the process of shedding its stuffing. Lice, roaches, bedbugs, rats, and vermin of every sort plagued all of the accommodations.

The upper bunkroom was little more than a ledge built over the flophouse, under the eaves. It was only three feet high, with no bedding provided. Men packed into the room, keeping each other warm. They used each other's legs and shoulders as impromptu pillows, covering themselves with discarded newspapers. The entire room stank of sweat and vomit. However, at M$0.10 per night, this was the most popular and affordable lodging available. In the summer, people could sleep out of doors, along the riverbanks or in parks, but when the long, icy Harbin winter set in, the upper bunks provided a service to the homeless.

The flophouse itself had windows in the east or west main walls, but they were so grimy that little light passed through them. Forty-watt bulbs cut the darkness as best they could, but the establishment was quite dank. A barrel of drinking water appeared in the lobby three times a day. Any heat provided radiated from the flophouse owner's personal cooking stove.

All customers seeking a room in the Spring Forest Lodge would first encounter Lin's caustic cousin at the counter by the door. Each would be greeted with a sneer and the snarled, "You! Raised by a stinking cunt." Lin the counter man was never polite, even though, Gotō adds with wonder, he came from the same area of China in which Confucius was born. Lin rudely questioned all guests about who they were and where they came from. If granted a room, they had to pay in advance. Flophouses never extended credit. Objects of value—most often stolen goods—would be accepted. Anyone too sick to pay could expect no mercy. He or she— no kindness was extended to women in the Garden—would be thrown out of the building and any clothing stolen.

After receiving payment for the night, the counter man assigned a bunk or a spot under the eaves to the newcomer, whom fellow bunkmates sized up as he settled into his spot. A clever fellow would know to tie his shoes and meager possessions to his body before drifting into sleep so as to prevent theft, for clothing and shoes were important to the residents of the Garden. With winter temperatures reaching minus thirty degrees

Fahrenheit, adequate shelter and warm clothing meant survival. Clothes could also be loaned or shared. A warm coat was a kind of capital.

Harbin was a city known for up-to-the-minute style, but not in the Garden of Grand Vision. Clothing reflected both poverty and national origin. Gotō made a catalog of the styles of dress. It was hardly a fashionable display. In the 1920s and 1930s, the Chinese gentleman might wear a long silk gown over trousers, an adaptation of Chinese tradition to Western style. Or he might show up to formal occasions in a suit and tie. The silk long coat of the Chinese elite rarely appeared in the Harbin slums. Instead Chinese men wore padded half jackets, always black, grey, or navy blue in color. The result only added to the drab atmosphere in the neighborhood. Baggy trousers held up with a sash completed the ensemble.

Gotō tells us, with some glee, that these pants have no front or back and so do not need to be donned in any particular way. Gotō attributes this style to the lazy nature of the Chinese working classes. In a whispered aside, he informs us that Chinese men wear no undergarments. When the men of slums argue, he says, the arrangement of their trousers makes it easy for them to moon each other. To a Japanese gentleman, such behavior would seem outlandish, foreign, and shocking. Gotō would not have been happy in an American frat house.[28]

Underwear may have been lacking, but in the arctic weather, no one went without shoes and socks. In every case the shoes were dirty, as were the socks inside them. The residents of the Garden slept in the clothes they wore all day. At night they either kept their shoes on or bundled them into their bedding for fear that they might be stolen.[29]

The wives of the Korean morphine dealers wore nicer Korean-style clothes. But it was the prostitutes who brightened up the streets and hallways of the Garden area. Their colorful—Gotō calls them gaudy—outfits added color to the drab gray, blue, and black of the Chinese crowd. Gotō only saw one person dressed in the Japanese style. This was an old man with a limp who visited the Korean morphine dealers from time to time. What his business might have been, Gotō does not tell us.[30]

Korean morphine dealers and beggars both wore Western-style clothing. Beggars wore their coats with pride. There was a reason for this. The Chinese charity known in English as the Red Swastika Society ran soup kitchens, infirmaries, and donation centers for the poor of the city. The jackets were substantial, with long, puffy sleeves. Stamped on the back, bright red characters read, "Donated by the Red Swastika Society." Gotō points out that a beggar's coat will have any number of hatch marks on it, indicating that it has been pawned time and again to pay for drugs. Korean morphine dealers often showed up wearing these coats as well. They took the coats in exchange for drugs. In such a cold climate, no one had any qualms about wearing another's coat. If the garment provided warmth, it would do.[31]

Despite the sinister wording of the English name, the Red Swastika Society bore no relation to German fascism; nor was it part of the Japanese enterprise in Manchuria. "Red swastika" is a misleading translation of *hong wan she*. The character *wan* (卐) looks somewhat like a swastika but is oriented on the page differently from the icon that Adolf Hitler made infamous. It is an ancient symbol for balance in the universe, for universal peace, and therefore for charity. An observer in Harbin would no more confuse the *wan* with the Nazi symbol than we would mix up a cross and an ankh. Now called the World Red Swastika Society, the charity still operates in Taiwan, Hong Kong, Malaysia, and Singapore.[32]

As part of the Morals Society, the Red Swastika Society provided charity to the poor of North China. It modeled its organization after the Red Cross. The charity had its origins in Chinese religion, especially Daoism, but added a missionary element of Western origin. Manchukuo officials tolerated the Morals Society and the Red Swastika Society because they were not political. Zou Xisan, owner of the Garden of Grand Vision, served as a director of the Harbin Morals Society and the Red Swastika Society as well. Gotō found the pious charity of the landlord, who grew rich from the suffering of the poor, jarring.

Gotō classified people living in the Garden into three types. The first he called the "floating population," which included the orphaned, the sick, the deformed, and imbeciles, all creatures of ill fortune with no social safety net. The second, and largest, group included those people who fell through the cracks of a rapidly changing world, such as peasants who lost land through drought or bandit activity and gentry from the imperial order who failed to change with the times. Such people became migrants who created an endless supply of labor in Manchuria. The backbreaking work most newcomers found paid low wages. Those who could not adapt to the conditions ended up in the Garden of Grand Vision. Gotō despised the third group, which comprised the villains who made life in the Garden hell on earth; he called them worms and parasites.

Gotō introduces us to some of the residents of the Spring Forest Lodge. Most living in the better rooms would belong to his third category of scoundrels. Each of them earns an income high enough to provide a measure of privacy. Rooms one, five, six, and ten house Korean morphine sellers. In private room number one, we meet a sixty-year-old gentleman named Mr. Li, who supports two women—a wife and a concubine—by selling the drug. Mrs. Kang in room five, a single mother, is able to raise a son and a daughter through unlicensed morphine sales. Duan the Korean sells morphine in room six. Mr. Gao in room ten only arrived three months ago with his wife and two daughters. When he first showed up, he looked like a beggar. Now he wears a new suit of Western clothes and nice shoes. In room two we meet the thirty-something Mr. Bai, who is Chinese. Gotō does not know how he earns his living. Mr. Bai sleeps all day and is gone every night. Room four belongs to the Zhang family. Mr. Zhang lives there with his wife and mother. Put aside the happy family image. Zhang is a bully and a scoundrel. His wife and mother fight constantly.[33]

In room three we meet Wang San, aka Braying Mule Wang, nicknamed for his unpleasant-sounding vocal chords. He associates with two other local villains. Wang himself runs a gambling operation on the street. His only capital is a pair of dice that he uses to earn what could be a comfortable living by local standards. Wang's villain friends often show up in the Spring Forest Lodge. These men serve as shills and lookouts, helping to lure customers and to bid up each game. They also act as police spies. Braying Mule Wang and his crew ply their craft in the open at the side of the roads in the vicinity of the building.

Rumor among the residents of the Garden has it that Braying Mule Wang can earn up to M$100 on any given day. Gotō watched Wang run his game one day and made his own estimate. The bets came in as low as M$0.20 and as high as M$3. Gotō calculated a take of M$40 to M$50 on that day. From the day's winnings, Braying Mule Wang must pay his henchmen. He sends a hefty bribe to the local precinct police. Braying Mule Wang lives with a prostitute, whom Gotō refers to as his wife, although the relationship is not so clear. Both are morphine addicts.

Between his street games and her prostitution, Braying Mule Wang and his wife earn a good income. Unfortunately Braying Mule often loses what money he acquires plying his dice during the day to other gamesters in the neighborhood at night. When this happens he returns home at the crack of dawn, waking everyone in the Spring Forest Lodge by pounding on the door, waking the poor woman who is exhausted from a night selling sex in the halls of the Garden. His braying voice carries to all corners of the flophouse. He and his wife spend a lot of money to feed their morphine habits. Braying Mule Wang gains this needed cash by providing the know-how and equipment for giving shots of morphine to the other residents of the lodge. He is the only resident of the lodge who knows this craft. He charges M$0.05 for each injection. If an addict has no morphine, Wang will supply the drug as well, charging a commission for his trouble. He can clear between M$2 and M$3 each day.

Braying Mule Wang dresses up and carries an umbrella each time he visits Gotō at his midtown office. It is a moment of importance in a shattered life. Wang brings Gotō scraps of information scribbled in pencil: Zhou Chengting of the Prosperity Lodge has no real income; he often visits the Soviet consulate. Or Li the bean curd seller has recently brought into the Garden the Japanese widow of a soldier killed in action.[34] Gotō pays Wang for all such information. He even buys the man an occasional meal. Yet he finds the scribbled revelations to be based more on rumor than evidence. Each time Wang leaves his office, Gotō tosses the slips of paper into the trash, usually unread. For Gotō's purposes, Wang is much more useful as an entrée into the gloomy social life of the Garden than as a witness to particular crimes.[35]

These are the well to do of the Spring Forest Lodge. A different sort of boarder lives in the lower and upper bunkrooms. Gotō introduces us to several of these transient folk. We meet Blind Man Wang, aka Sticky Bean Cake, who earns a living by sitting at the door of a store near a busy intersection. He has a morphine habit and so is thin as a rail. This is an asset in his pandering business. He stands by the door without moving. Gotō tells us that even a lever will not make him budge. He has no money in his hand, but when people gather, he falls to the ground in a pile of worn out rags. Is he hurt? Wounded? If poked, he will howl, threatening to bite, promising that death will strike his victim. Any store owner would pay to get him to move. He is so fearsome that even the beggars in the charity home fear him.

We could chat with Zhang En, aka the Frozen Ghost. He seems not to feel the cold. He wears only the thinnest rags even in subzero weather. He threatens people who pass him on the street, demanding money or valuables. He can earn M$3 to M$4 each day, which he augments by lending his winter clothes to a poor old man who is too feeble to run off with the clothes. Frozen Ghost earns M$0.10 a day renting out his clothes. Everyone hates him. No charity will take him in. Or there is Yang Fulin, who owns a syringe, red with rust. Yang earns money giving heroin shots to his fellow addicts. At M$0.10 a shot, he can earn M$6 or M$7 a day. He spends it all on opium or heroin, so he is frightfully poor.

We may not want to meet Feng Tiger Two. Once he was an informant for spies, but his morphine habit put him out of commission. He steals money from gamblers returning to the lodge with their meager winnings. People avoid him. They also avoid Jin the Korean, who was once a translator for the Kempeitai. Now he works as an informant. He also earns money through extortion. He is full of himself. He struts around the neighborhood wearing Western clothes and a Chinese long coat as though he is a scholar.[36]

Gotō Reiji was very much the Japanese gentleman, fastidious about personal hygiene, even when abroad. He closes his discussion about clothing with a gut-felt reaction to the habits of his subjects. They did not bathe. Not one of them. Only the Korean morphine dealers and the prostitutes may have washed their faces now and again, but that was the limit. No one bothered to really get clean. There was a notion floating about the Garden that if a person's hands were to touch a bath, it would kill the effects of drugs. Since most of the residents of the Garden spent most of their day drugged out or looking for ways to pay for their habits, washing was not part of the daily regimen. Gotō does not need to tell us that the place stinks of body odor, but he does. Even so he has grown used to the place.

Kagawa Tetsuzō, a Manchukuo bureaucrat turned travel writer, wanted to see the real Harbin. To understand the place one had to visit Fujiadian, he said. So he followed Gotō through the neighborhood into the Garden of Grand Vision. The poor man was overwhelmed by the stench, by the noisy disorder of the area, by the proliferation of thieves' markets. Following Gotō to a flophouse on the second floor, he noticed a shill beckoning to him, inviting him to patronize a fortune-teller. At the top of the stairs, he found a man calmly eating corn in the filth and confusion. Kagawa could hardly keep his stomach from turning. But, he commented, his police escort would calmly take a meal from the local eateries. Fearing for his life, Kagawa would not follow suit. In fact, he quickly cut the tour short to head for the train station. How Gotō must have laughed. Food poisoning was the least of the deadly possibilities for people living in the Garden of Grand Vision.[37]

The cost of staying at a lodge in the Garden of Grand Vision was low. The comforts were few, but in the frigid winters of Harbin, even rough, filthy shelter was a life-saving necessity. Yet these folk did not come to the Northeast seeking addiction in freezing poverty. They came to a new city filled with the vitality of growth. They escaped a home province crippled by flood and civil war. Men like Zou Xisan or Lin Jitang hoped that in the northern frontier, a clever fellow could make a fresh start, help his family back home, or strike it rich as the wilderness developed. In doing so they added to a growing and volatile mixture of people from Asia, Europe, and beyond who gave Harbin its international quality. For the city was not so much a melting pot as an ethnic stew.

2

Ice City

Harbin is a city a person yearns for, both beautiful and ugly, controlled and free . . . like an easy chair when you are tired.

—Nagano Sei'ichi[1]

Harbin, green city of elms
International trains arrive each day
A rainbow bridge between
the flower of Tokyo and the sky of Paris
Take a carriage to Fujiadian
Sweet young girls like pussy willows
Kitaiskaia Street around noon
dimples on their cheeks

—Yanagida Momotarō, "Ode to Harbin"[2]

What kind of city produced this ghastly slum? Why would people seek their fortunes in the frozen North in the first place? True, Harbin occupies a harsh piece of real estate for a major commercial and cultural center. But there the city sat, an international gem shivering away through long subzero winters. Its central location in the resource-rich Manchurian plain transformed it from a fishing village into a hub of global commerce in the early twentieth century.

Manchuria is a rugged environment. In winter, when arctic blasts blow in from Siberia, the temperature can drop to as low as minus thirty degrees Fahrenheit in the North. Harbin Januaries average nine degrees Fahrenheit. Winters are long and summers humid, but the brief spring

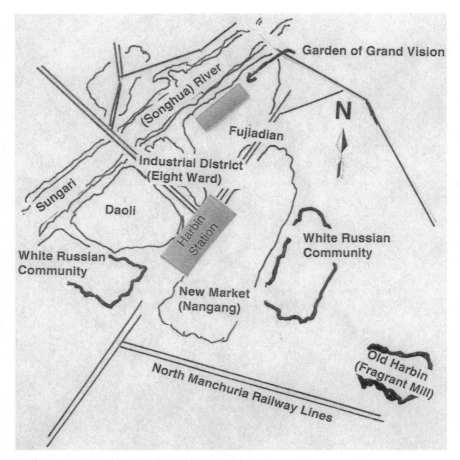

Harbin, Location of the Garden of Grand Vision

and autumn bring clear, balmy weather. Despite the climate, the landscape is beautiful. The central plains, sandwiched between two mountain ranges, are fertile and support robust agriculture, even in the long cold. Corn, sorghum, and wheat grow in abundance. The medicinal herb ginseng is native to the place. But the primary crop is soy. In 1930 Manchuria was called the "Land of the Bean," supplying half of the world's soy. The crop continues to flourish in northeastern fields.[3]

Rugged mountains of the Changbai Range to the east and north border North Korea. Here one finds lakes and waterfalls that are a travel agent's delight. The area produces abundant timber. Today ski resorts cater to the adventuresome traveler. To the west of the plains, rolling hills give way to the Mongolian steppe. China's Northeast attracts wildlife lovers, for here they will find the habitat of Siberian tigers, red-crowned cranes, and Amur leopards. In days past Chinese emperors used the territory as a summer hunting ground; now it features nature preserves.

The real wealth of Manchuria rests underground. The Daqing oilfields lie less than a hundred miles northwest of Harbin. Developed in the 1950s, the enterprise became a model socialist production unit. Now it provides petroleum for China's newfound capitalist love affair with the family car. Had Japanese industry had the time to develop this resource, the Second World War might have lasted longer. The Fuxin Mining group in central Manchuria operates the region's coal mines, including the large open pit mine founded with Japanese capital earlier in the twentieth century. Manchuria has gold mines as well. This mineral wealth attracted foreign attention in the early 1900s. In Japan, politicians, industrialists, and military leaders alike took note of the region's bounty. Manchuria became a needed supplier for Japan's rapid modernization, especially as the home islands are small, cramped, and resource poor.[4]

As a complement to rich resources, the region is blessed with two river transportation systems. The Amur River (Heilongjiang or Black Dragon River), into which Harbin's own Songhua River feeds, flows north; the Liao River system moves south. Both river networks are enhanced by rail. By 1930 rail networks laced through the territory like a web. Competition in rail building between Russian, Chinese, and Japanese companies spurred the rail boom, while rivalry among the competing systems increased international tension in the area. Ownership of a rail line became a territorial marker in this open frontier. In the 1920s and 1930s, when conflict brought Manchuria to international attention, track and rolling stock inevitably featured in the news coverage.

The southernmost Liaoning Province[5] ends as a peninsula jutting into the Yellow Sea. At its tip are two ports: Dalian and Lushun. Both cities changed their names several times over the first fifty years of the last century. This naming complexity speaks to the international interest the area attracted in the early twentieth century. As one example, the Chinese city Dalian began the twentieth century as a Russian port called Dalney (Dal'nii, meaning "far away"). In 1906 the city became Dairen, center of Japanese military activity and enterprise in Manchuria. Today it is Dalian, a busy Chinese port sending the goods from Chinese workshops to the rest of the world. The city is now a beach resort, a soccer powerhouse, a shoppers' mecca, and a port of supply for Walmart and the world. Yet, in the city center, Japanese-made trolleys with wood-paneled interiors clang their way through the downtown traffic. The trams are old enough to have made the transition from 1930s new, to 1970s antiquated nuisance, to present-day retro chic.

Close to Dalian is Lushun. Once called Port Arthur—a name that speaks to its brief British origins—it became a Russian concession before falling to the Japanese navy in 1904. In Japanese hands it became Ryojun. Today it is Lushun, a Chinese naval base open to the curious foreign tourist only by permit, although I am told Japanese citizens can travel there permit-free.

Manchuria is located outside the Great Wall of China. For most of China's long history, the area's harsh climate supported a sparsely populated homeland of nomadic peoples. Living outside the Wall—built to keep them in their place—tribal peoples of the region seemed beyond the reach of civilization to Chinese observers. The harsh climate made them tough. To Chinese eyes, all lands beyond the Wall belonged to ferocious peoples who knew nothing about Confucian legal traditions, literature, or settled agricultural life. They were hunters, nomads, and tent dwellers. They excelled at horsemanship and mounted archery. Technically speaking, they belonged to the Jurchen ethnic group. Chinese people, living in warm homes surrounded by farmlands, called the horsemen to the north "barbarians."

Barbarian is a loaded term, one that can blind the speaker to changing conditions abroad. In the late sixteenth century, the tribal people in Manchuria began to make money from the wealth of local resources: ginseng, minerals, pelts, and pearls. Their settled neighbors on the other side of the Wall provided a ready market. Commerce is hardly a savage pursuit. In the 1600s those known to us as the Manchus reorganized their society to meet their new income status. They created an efficient military machine, identifying hereditary units by colored banners under which soldiers lived and fought. Many a town or village in China's Northeast includes the word "banner" in its name. These rugged Manchus had their own prejudices. They worried that living among the settled Han people would make them soft. They maintained extensive hunting grounds in the Northeast for bannermen to stay tough. Examples of the banners and Manchu warrior armor are on display in the Harbin museum, along with moth-eaten specimens of local wildlife.[6]

The Manchu leader Nurhaci (1558–1626), ancestor to a line of ten Manchu emperors who would rule China until 1911, had aspirations beyond the frozen North. Under his leadership his people welded the Chinese bureaucratic organization and the Confucian belief system onto their own successful military organization. In 1644, when the Chinese Ming Dynasty (1368–1644) collapsed, leaving the empire in civil chaos, the Manchu banner armies easily crossed through the Wall. They filled the political vacuum left in the wake of a deposed emperor. The Japanese armies would repeat this pattern in the 1930s, using the chaos following the collapse of the Manchu Dynasty as a strategic opportunity. In the

1600s it took Manchu emperors thirty years to reestablish a unified China. Japan would not have so much time.

Applying Chinese political know-how to their own frontier toughness, the descendants of Nurhaci moved into the palace, the Forbidden City in Beijing, took over the mantle of government, and created the Qing Dynasty (1644–1911)—China's last. Within thirty years, the whole of China was pacified. The new emperors settled into Chinese life in the palace in Beijing. They put aside nomadic ways. Horsemanship and hunting became training and sport, not livelihood. They spoke the Chinese language as their own. They became patrons of the arts.[7]

The Manchus ruled according to Chinese law and custom. They maintained the bureaucracy, based on an extensive examination system that was the millennia-old hallmark of China's political success. Yet they were conquerors. They imposed their own look on the Chinese people. They forced all Han Chinese men to wear their hair in a long, braided queue with the front of the scalp shaved—Manchu style. The clothing that we in the West consider quintessentially Chinese—coats with high-necked Mandarin collars and side closures—originated in Manchuria.

The original Manchu jacket was quite utilitarian. The sleeves were wide, the hem long. The side closure protected against wind when the wearer was riding in the cold. Later the pattern could be made in silk and embroidered with symbols of power or beauty. In the early 1920s, fashionable women modernized the style. The sleeves and waists tightened; the hemline shortened; the dress became a sheath. A slit on the side of a tighter skirt made walking easier. We know the style best as the sexy look of the *cheongsam* (Cantonese for "long shirt")—the body-hugging dress made famous in the West by Suzie Wang or Madame Chiang Kai-shek. It is called a *qipao* in Mandarin; as the *qi* refers to the banners, a *qipao* is literally a banner gown.[8]

The second Qing emperor, Kangxi, who wore robes embroidered with ancient Chinese symbols of power but fashioned in the Manchu style, was a capable horseman and archer, as were his ancestors. Hardly the barbarian, he was a lavish patron of Chinese arts who subsidized Confucian learning, Buddhist studies, encyclopedia collections, and a comprehensive dictionary. Artwork and ceramics produced by the artists and craftsmen he patronized can be found in museums worldwide. He had a lively interest in astronomy. He hired a Jesuit tutor and set up an observatory on the city wall so that he could observe the heavens.[9]

It is difficult to reconcile this long-lived, vigorous leader with his grandson to the seventh power, the sad little boy Puyi, who in 1908, at the age of nine, became the last Chinese emperor and in 1932, at the age of twenty-eight, became the first (and last) emperor of Manchukuo. Puyi's formal Manchurian enthronement ceremony in 1934, on a freezing March day, made the cover of *Time*. The accompanying article called him a life-long "helpless tool of one agency or another."[10] Both Gotō Reiji and his colleagues lived under the reign of Henry Puyi as the Kangde emperor of Manchukuo. Yet when they spoke reverently about His Majesty, the emperor, they referred to the sovereign in Tokyo.

This, then, is the background of an area that would become a cradle of conflict in the early twentieth century. It was a developing frontier, but one that had already supplied pivotal figures in Chinese history. Harbin sat in the middle of the rich and fertile land. It was a natural transportation hub. More to the point, it was a port of supply with easy access to China, Russia, Korea, and Japan. Given the needs of the modern world, conflict was sure to follow.[11]

In 1932, when Harbin began its Japanese chapter, the city was little more than thirty years old. Yet it already had a strong international identity and a thriving Chinese presence. In that short time it grew from a fishing village among the reeds of the Songhua River into an urban complex of beauty and sophistication. Situated at the point where the river met a trunk rail line, it prospered as a commercial center and transportation hub. In 1896 Russian diplomats representing the tsar negotiated the right to develop this rail line. Its construction was part of the larger strategic rail plan to link European Russia with its Far Eastern territories. As an extension of the Trans-Siberian Railway also under construction at the time, the line would run from Chita to Vladivostok and extend south to Dalian, on the tip of the Liaodong Peninsula. Dalian is a warm-water port—that elusive object of Russian diplomacy. A Russian rail company formed to capitalize and build the rail line. Russian warships appeared in Port Arthur within a year.[12]

Cities along the southern part of the rail line—Dalian, Mukden, Changchun—already had established residential centers, although the presence of a rail line changed their size and appearance drastically. There was no comparable foundation city in the North. In 1896 China gave then tsarist Russia treaty rights to build a rail line through the Northeast. Surveying teams showed up soon after. In 1898 construction got under way. This line would be called the Chinese Eastern Railway Company (CER). It was set up as a joint Russian-Chinese venture. Joint ownership did not guarantee an easy relationship between the two nationalities. In 1929, for example, China and Russia nearly went to war over rail ownership.[13]

The first Russians arrived at the point chosen for the rail crossing over the Songhua River in the spring of 1898. They discovered that what had seemed solid riverbank was in fact swamp. Thus the first buildings went up near an abandoned distillery—the Fragrant Mill that is a district of Harbin to this day. In no time, however, the swampland filled in, and Harbin began its vibrant growth. Originally called Songhua Station, the city soon changed its name to Harbin, which convention holds is Manchu for "a place to dry fishing nets."[14]

Development of the rail line and the city moved quickly. In 1901 the first trains began to move on temporary tracks; by 1903 the line was up and running. The city followed suit as railroad engineers developed areas closer to the river. The Harbin Station, which would become the art nouveau heart of the city, appeared in New Town. By 1900 the name Harbin showed up on maps. By 1901 enough Russian families lived in the area to require the first schools and churches. To meet the need for civic administration, the Chinese Eastern Railway Company gained the right to settle legal disputes in its own community. This right, always contested by China, soon included administering the entire area of land ceded to the company. Russian soldiers policed the area as railway guards. In its earliest stages, the rail company became a colonial institution as it developed Harbin.[15]

Railway building attracted labor. Chinese migrated to the area. By 1905 enough Chinese lived in the areas outside the CER right-of-way for the Chinese imperial government to create Chinese city and county governing bodies, one of which was Fujiadian. Japanese merchants also moved in, opening stores to supply the growing population.

Not all Japanese businesses were innocent of intrigue. Russian engineers had no sooner set up camp in the area that would become Harbin than the Japanese army's general staff officers took notice. Military men would naturally be concerned about the construction of a rail system planned as a direct link from European Russia to the warm-water ports at Vladivostok and Dalney. Once finished, the trans-Siberian route could easily supply men and materials to a battlefront close to the home islands. By 1900 the Japanese embassy in Beijing reported to the home government that a European city was under construction in northern Manchuria.

In 1901, Captain Ishimitsu Makiyo, working for the Imperial Japanese Army, disguised himself as a common laborer. He went to work in Manchuria laying down rail in the countryside. His goal was to reach Harbin. He arrived on the banks of the Songhua River with the help of a Japanese woman who ran a small eatery in the Manchurian countryside. A former prostitute, the woman had become the mistress of a local Manchu bandit. Ishimitsu joined the bandit in his travels to Harbin. There, Ishimitsu worked as a coolie in a laundry while he studied the layout of the city under construction. By 1903, the Japanese military had the beginnings of a map of Harbin.

Russian military police grew suspicious of Ishimitsu, forcing him to flee to Vladivostok. Yet the Japanese army still needed intelligence. Ishimitsu returned to Japan and retired from the military. He changed his name to Kikuchi Shōzō. With a new name and identity, he traveled back to

Harbin, where he set up the Kikuchi Photography Studio. Not only did the shop become a safe house for spies, but Kikuchi managed to send lovely photographs of Russian military-supply installations and railroad equipment to his former employer, the Japanese army.[16]

There are many photographs of Harbin at every stage of its growth, not all taken by spies. The earliest convey the same look and feel as pictures of the boomtowns and mining camps along the growing rail lines of the American West. One picture, taken in the early years of the building frenzy, shows a group of Chinese laborers—men, women, and children—eating a meal in front of a tent. Crude wooden storefronts, laden with goods, line muddy thoroughfares. Within a few more years, photos of the port area show the beginnings of the business district. Wooden buildings form an outline of Kitaiskaia Street; they will transform into the banks and department stores of the international business center. The Harbin Station, soon to become the busy hub of the city, sits alone surrounded by dirt roads. Leafing through the photos leaves an impression of a building frenzy in progress.[17]

Jurisdictions in Manchuria and Harbin grew more complex after 1905. As a result of the Japanese victory in a war with Russia, the newly built rail line split into sections. Ownership of the southern rail shifted to Japanese hands. In that year Japanese victory in the Russo-Japanese War and triumph at the negotiating table put Russian concessions in southern Manchuria in Japanese hands. The South Manchuria Railway, a Japanese company, met the Chinese Eastern Railway, the Russian company, at Changchun, a city that would become the capital of Manchukuo under the name New Capital (Shinkyō in Japanese; Xinjing in Chinese). This relationship would become further complicated after the Russian Revolution in 1917. By 1924 the northern rail line came under Soviet control. Through a program of police harassment and negotiation after the Japanese occupied the territory, the northern section of the line passed into Manchukuo (in fact, Japanese) control after 1935. One observer, reporting on Manchuria for a Western audience in 1932, as the area became a point of global tension, described the awkwardness of the rail situation. He took the train to New Capital (or Changchun) on his way north. There, he explained, a person traveling through to Harbin had a choice: take the Chinese Eastern, the most expensive in the world, or fly.[18]

The Japanese military policed the South Manchuria Railway. Japanese capital developed economic interests along a swath of land on either side of the tracks. The mineral-rich and fertile Manchurian territory became a supplier to Japanese industry. As a result, although Harbin's section of the rail line remained under Russian control, Japanese residents developed a noticeable presence in the city. By the 1920s, a Japanese consulate, a Japanese Residents' Association, a branch of the Yokohama Specie Bank, and a Shinto shrine had added to the international character of the city.

Harbin attracted residents from all over northern China and as far away as Paris and Los Angeles. From their rural beginnings, several early settlements grew into a city with distinct sections. Each section had Chinese and Russian names, confusing the uninitiated but reflecting the cosmopolitan contributions to the city's growth. The oldest section, called Old Harbin or Staryi Kharbin, was the first area of Russian settlement. It appears on today's maps as Fragrant Mill in honor of a workshop that made incense and a local distillery that quenched the thirst of the hardy Russian engineers and Chinese builders who pioneered the railway line. Closer to the river was New Town, Novyi Gorod, or, as it still is known, Nangang (South Hill). The CER management headquarters and Harbin Station were located there, and in the 1930s Gotō Reiji and his colleagues would live and work in this district. Two more major sections soon appeared. Next to the river was the business center known as Pristan, the wharf. In Chinese the area was and still is called Daoli, or the Inner City (inside the tracks). Crossing the rail line along the river leads to Daowai, or the Outer City (outside the tracks and, in fact, outside foreign jurisdiction). This was the Chinese residential section. It sat sandwiched between an industrial section surrounded by railroad sidings, the industrial Eighth Ward, and the Songhua River. Although separated from Daoli by only tracks and a road, it was a separate city with a discrete governing system until it was taken into a reorganized Greater Harbin by Japanese order in 1932.

Daowai had no Russian name; locals called it Fujiadian. The neighborhood turned from suburb into growth area with Chinese businesses along its main streets. The name Fujiadian could be translated as "domain of the Fu family." Its origin is obscure. Japanese sources merely state that a certain Fu family ran an inn and food shop as the area developed. Chinese sources give more detail but are often at odds with one another.

One story tells of a man named Fu Zhenji who moved to the banks of the Songhua River in the 1740s. Fu worshiped the Chinese god of war, Guanyu. Once, while fishing, Fu came close to dying in a dangerous storm. A dark-faced stranger appeared out of nowhere to save Fu's life and bless him with a bountiful catch. Fu credited his luck to Guanyu. His family prospered along the banks of the river as one of four clans living in the area. Or it is said that a man named Fu Zhenji worked as a cook for a Manchu general, also in the 1700s. Fu's culinary skills were so appreciated that the general granted Fu a plot of land in an area known as Horse Field Gulch. Fu set up shop there, and the area took his name.[19]

Another, less romantic, foundation story for Fujiadian credits a certain Fu Baoshan (1864–1937) with opening a traditional medical clinic and supply store in the area early in the 1890s. At that time the character *dian* in Fujiadian indicated the common word for "store." In 1907, when growth brought the area into the urban organization, the city council replaced the prosaic character for "store" (店) with the flowery homonym "royal suburb" (甸).

Any or all of the foundation stories for Fujiadian may contain kernels of truth that have sprouted into urban legend. They all share the theme of national pride. Fujiadian existed before any Russian engineers appeared on the scene. Japanese sources, including Gotō Reiji, may claim the area consisted of swamp and open fields. Chinese remember that a market town occupied the spot and included as many as four families, one called Fu. Nevertheless, if Fujiadian marked a traditional Chinese town, by 1903 that town had been swallowed up as the Chinese population soared to 10,000.[20]

Fu Baoshan himself died in the midst of the Manchukuo experiment. His was not the death of a heroic patriot. Instead, Fu fell victim to toughs who murdered him in the street for his pocket money. His own family sold his estate, hoping to use the money, which they hid in a gunnysack, to relocate back to China proper. With the end of the war and the beginning of a new regime, however, the hoarded money was utterly worthless. One detail comes through in the Chinese versions: whereas the Japanese assumed a wilderness, Chinese stories always tell of a settlement predating the 1898 arrival of Russian engineers.[21]

Within twenty years Harbin grew from a plat of muddy road grids and construction sites into a stately urban landscape of wide tree-lined avenues that provided the addresses for offices of businesses from around the world. As it was a city created from scratch, architects followed the latest designs. In 1900, art nouveau was all the rage in Europe. The style lasted little more than a decade in Europe, but in Harbin builders modified and adapted it well into the 1930s, giving the city a European air with a distinctive, eclectic look. Harbin ranks along with Paris and Nancy in France as a treasure trove of art nouveau buildings.[22] This makes walking through the city's neighborhoods a delight. In Fujiadian architects lined the roadways with courtyard-style buildings embellished with Chinese folk designs, creating Chinese baroque. One of these structures was the Garden of Grand Vision.[23]

Most representative of Harbin's European display was Kitaiskaia Street (today, Center Street) in Daoli. The cobblestone avenue runs from the town center to the Songhua River. Strollers could study the rich department store display windows, offering the latest European fashions, on their way to a bank, an office, a tearoom, or a cabaret. The buildings—art nouveaux and baroque—still stand, interspersed with modern glass-and-steel constructions sporting postmodern domes. Ignored during the years of revolutionary fervor, the dilapidated buildings have been refurbished. Harbin has a Russian/European appeal that makes it a tourist draw. The original Russian Harbiners are gone. Many fled during the Manchukuo period; others left in in the postwar period. By the 1960s most had found homes elsewhere. Today Center Street features Russian restaurants and souvenir shops whose windows offer nesting dolls, vodka to put inside Lenin flasks, and Soviet army knives for tourists. These stores are staffed by a new generation of Russians who have come to Harbin to find opportunity in the new China.[24]

Kitaiskaia Street ends at the long promenade along the embankment of the Songhua River (today, Stalin Park). Wealthy residents could enjoy the water as members of the Harbin Yacht Club (today, a senior center). In the summer boats filled the wide river, taking people to Sun Island on the opposite bank; swimmers and sunbathers enjoyed Sun Island's sandy riverbank. In the winter horse-drawn sleighs, iceboats, and skaters replaced the boats, but the riverside was still a source of diversion. Residents liked to say, "If you have not been to Sun Island, you have not visited Harbin."[25] Russian émigrés built dachas there. The buildings remain, all in various stages of disrepair and renewal.

Nangang (South Hill) begins at the Harbin Station. This station, the gateway to the city, sits regally at the head of an open square where taxis and buses joust for space in the chaotic traffic. Today a nondescript grey slab has replaced the splendid original art nouveau facade. A broad boulevard runs south from the station (then called Station Road, today it is Red Army Road). It connects the station with Nangang's central district. Within a few blocks, the road intersects Great Straight Street at a large traffic circle once dominated by St. Nicholas Cathedral. Built soon after the first Russian engineers took up residence, the wooden structure, with its angular spires, became the symbol of the city. The cathedral's distinctive image is preserved in photographs and on the covers of Japanese tourist pamphlets and posters from the 1930s.[26] Unfortunately, the building itself suffered from its imperialist origin. In the 1960s, Red Guard youth destroyed it during the height of the Cultural Revolution. A futuristic pyramid and entryways into a vast underground labyrinth of shopping take its place. The green-tile dome and turrets of St. Sophia Cathedral—harder to demolish than the older wooden church—are now the icon of Harbin.

Nangang was, and still is, the center of government. It was a residential area for senior and mid-level railway employees and later Japanese personnel. The government building where Gotō worked was located here, only a few blocks away from St. Nicholas Cathedral. When so inclined, Gotō might enjoy cakes purchased from the Nangang branch of the Autumn Forest Department Store, a Russian-owned emporium famous for its pastry.[27] The store is still there, open for business and bustling with shoppers on rainy Saturday afternoons. Or he might have stopped by the museum or the Shinto shrine located across the way from St. Nicholas Cathedral. The museum is still open; the shrine, of course, is long gone.

Daowai was the Chinese section, outside the foreign concession area and open to development. Chinese came in numbers to help build the city. In 1904, when Russia and Japan went to war, Harbin became a barracks and supply city for Russian troops. Fujiadian merchants profited, and the population continued to grow. Daowai expanded eastward from the railroad tracks like dye on cloth. By 1910 the grid of Fujiadian proper was laid out and developed. Gotō would describe the numbered streets running north-south from Fifth to Eighth, bisected in the south by Righteous Sun Street (today, Jingyu Street, so named to commemorate a war hero) and flanked by the riverbank to the north, as the heart of the slum. Work began on the riverbank, where enterprising farmers were pushed out to make way for the levee and promenade. By 1916 the area, once swampland, had become a city of 4,534 houses and 22,613 people. In the 1910s, businesses on Righteous Sun Street thrived.[28]

Population growth brought with it Chinese institutions. By 1907 the Chinese imperial government south of the Wall appointed a district head for Fujiadian. This man, we are told, changed the *dian* character from "store" to "domain," hoping to give the area an air of elegance. By 1911 a shrine to the god of war, beloved by merchants, appeared in the neighborhood; by 1916 migrants from Shandong Province in North China had established a mutual-aid association to comfort those far from their homeland. This would include Zou the landlord as well as Lin and many other flophouse owners and their clients.[29]

Growth in the area continued apace. In 1917 a certain Fu Juchuan headed a construction company to plan new development further east. The new area would include more housing, a theater, and a park. The Chinese government at the time set aside a section of the new area to become a red-light district. The area, designated Pingkangli, or the Peace and Health Alley, became the most famous of the many brothel districts in Harbin. Patrons called the area Huifangli, or Lush Flowers Lane.[30] During this construction burst, the first tramline connected Daowai with the rest of the city. European-style buildings sprouted along Righteous Sun Street. Fujiadian was not meant to be a slum.

Japanese had lived, worked, and traveled in the city from the days of its Russian inception. Harbin gave both tourists and expatriates a taste of Europe without the need for a difficult journey halfway around the globe. A 1910 guidebook for Japanese business adventurers capitalizes on photos of Russian meals and samovars. The book is peppered with ads with copy in both Japanese and Russian. Much later, the poet Morigawa

Yūko, who accompanied her husband on a tour in 1941, wrote haiku about the cold and the Russian quality of life in the city. The Japanese military sent language officers to Harbin to study Russian. One writer remembered Harbin like a dream. He recalled swimming in the river and walking along streets lined with elms. Yachts and motorboats filled the wharf at Sun Island. Women with chestnut-colored hair strolled past the signs for Russian restaurants and shops on Kitaiskaia Street. The evening sky turned from a bright vermillion into rose madder. His memory of the city was filled with church domes, bells, and cream-colored houses with red roofs.[31]

Perhaps the best snapshot of the city is given by Yanagida Momotarō, who came to Harbin as a young clerk for a shipping company and served six years with the Harbin planning commission. In his memoirs, Yanagida plots an imaginary tour of Harbin of the 1930s, the city of his youth. Yanagida meets us as we get off the luxury *Asia Express* at Harbin Station. We stand on the steps of the art nouveau building, looking out at the broad square bordered by elms and willows. Here, amid the trolley stands, horse carts and cars wait for fares. The Chinese and Russian drivers call out the virtues of the hotels they represent. The cars could make a museum of automotive history. Clever Russian mechanics keep their junker Fords and Chevys patched together, their motors purring, often jump-started using vodka. They have the skill to breathe new life into the most decrepit rust bucket, even in the deepest winter. We will probably want to stay at the Yamato Hotel, formerly owned by the Chinese Eastern Railway. It is pricy but conveniently close to the station. This hotel represents the best in European luxury. Russian architects built the hotel for luxury in the early days of the city. We may have heard of the poor service that accompanies the beautiful rooms, but we are assured that the management has changed—Japanese have taken over—and service is much improved.

After freshening up, we are ready for a tour. Yanagida assures us that the Russian cars are quite safe, and we can trust the drivers. Yet he recommends that for the best tour of the city, we hire a horse cart, or a troika if we arrive in winter. Be sure to get a Russian carriage. Chinese cartmen use sickly old ponies, but the Russian carriage horses prance along the streets, the drivers' whips cracking in the air.

Starting from the hotel we travel over a broad bridge—Harbin's viaduct—to the cobblestoned Kitaiskaia Street. In the domed buildings we can buy furs, gold watches, and other luxury items. We may stroll along Songhua Park, now Stalin Park, a green promenade by the river. Along this walkway we can stop for a Russian meal at the Yacht Club. Perhaps we will sip coffee, heavy with cream, and nibble on cake while we watch the yellow-brown water of the river flow by. If it is winter, we can watch skaters and iceboats while we eat. If it is summer, we can plan to cross the river to enjoy the banks of Sun Island. We will certainly return at night to enjoy a show at one of the cabarets that open at ten, just after the Japanese restaurants close for the evening.

Back in our carriage, our host takes us to another park on Third Street, green with willows and elms. The park, built by Russians, is filled with amusements for the children, paths through lush greenery for adults, and ice cream vendors for everyone. Around the corner we find the reassurance of home: the Japanese elementary school, a Japanese market, a veterinary hospital. A little further to the east, we come to the Japanese licensed-brothel district. Our host takes us through the Eighth Ward, the industrial district, with its soy processing plant and flourmill. He notes with pride that the area once was a swamp, unfit for human habitation, but under Japanese urban development—he does work for the city planning department after all—the water has been drained, and the area has improved.

As we approach Fujiadian, Yanagida points out the many steam ships at the public docks. All sorts of boats are carrying food and opium from the fertile grounds of the North, he tells us. Our destination is the main street of Fujiadian, lined with two-story buildings selling all sorts of cheap goods and exotic treasures. Our host warns us, though, to avoid the back streets. Pointing in the general direction of the Garden of Grand Vision, Yanagida lists the kinds of depraved characters lurking in the alleys: opium and heroin addicts, revolutionaries, beggars, thieves, unregistered people—the sorts of characters who became the informants and friends of Gotō Reiji. The area once was prosperous, he tells us, but in the 1920s the drug trade brought decay.

We travel back to Nangang along a main road, past the police bureau where Gotō Reiji and his crew worked on their report, the city hall, and the Japanese-Manchurian Cultural Association. We can visit the Russian-owned Autumn Forest Department Store before we continue on to the Russian St. Nicholas Cathedral. As we ride along, we are perhaps comforted to notice, amid the Russian churches, a Shinto shrine built on St. Nicholas Square, a testament to Japanese control of the city. About 1,000 meters north of the store, we can visit the Buddhist Temple of Extreme Joy.[32] In the temple monks seek release from this world of suffering by enduring the harshest of austerities. Each spends many hours in deep meditation on the coldest winter days wearing only a thin robe. When tempted by feelings of greed or desire, they burn their arms with hot tongs. The head monk shows us his arms covered with scars.

The temple, one of four major temples in Manchuria, is still active to this day. About eighty monks, secluded behind a wall, are sheltered from crowds of lay folk of the new China, all burning incense at an altar and seeking charms to make them rich. Today, over the opposite wall, a day-dreaming monk can watch the top of a revolving Ferris wheel. In Yanagida's time, this amusement park had yet to be built. Yanagida would have taken us to the Russian Cemetery instead. A graveyard may not excite an ordinary traveler, but this one was worth the stop. Monuments to the dead were large and exotically European in design. The site was recommended in every guidebook, noted in every memoir.

Throughout Yanagida's tour, the city's European Russian quality is emphasized but rendered safe by the presence of home—a Shinto shrine, the Manchukuo government buildings, the Japanese grade schools for Japanese children. Russians as Europeans are depicted as remarkably poor, victims of their Revolution. For Japanese, like many Asians, the sight of Europeans working at menial tasks—drumming for the hotels, fixing junker cars, dancing in chorus lines—reinforced the feeling of Japanese modernity associated with empire expansion. Although all visitors wrote at length about the Russianness of the city, they referred to Harbin as the Paris of the East. Many Russians were poor, but Japanese living or visiting Harbin enjoyed a style of living that they could never have afforded at home.[33]

In 1898, only eight Japanese citizens lived in Harbin. The population grew to 10 by 1900 and 519 by 1902, after which it blossomed. After the Russo-Japanese War, the first of several companies appeared in Daoli when the Kumazawa Trading Company opened on Barrier Road. Many followed thereafter. The First World War saw Japanese banks, pawn-shops, and insurance companies pop up throughout the city. These included branches of Mitsui Trading Company, the Yokohama Specie Bank, the Chosen Bank, and a Harbin Bank founded with local Japanese capital.[34] By 1937, according to official publications, Harbin supported a population of 457,980 people. Of these, 393,145 were Chinese, 26,347 were Japanese, 4,355 were Korean, and 34,133 were foreign. The surrounding Binjiang County, 87,110 square kilometers in scope, included 743,558 households with a population of more than 4.5 million souls.[35]

The Chinese had nicknames for the sections of Harbin. Nangang, where the wealthy resided, they called "Heaven." Daoli, the business district, they called "Earth." Daowai, where the Chinese population resided, of course, became "Hell."[36] In the center of this hell stood the building known as the Garden of Grand Vision.[37]

Main entrance to the Garden of Grand Vision (Hara Shobō).

Interior stairway of the Garden of Grand Vision (Hara Shobō).

Courtyard house under renovation for preservation (photograph taken by the author).

Crowds inside the Garden (Hara Shobō).

Prostitutes in the hallway (Hara Shobō).

Outside the Garden (Hara Shobō).

59 Rich Brocade Street today (photograph taken by the author, July 2013).

Rich Brocade Street today (photograph taken by the author, July 2013).

3

Settlers

Forty years earlier Fujiadian was grasslands. The Fu family came and developed it. It is now home to 400,000 Chinese. A flood of labor came from North China. They came looking for work so they could send money home to their families. Some lost hope. They ended up in Fujiadian.

—Gotō Reiji[1]

Ice dappled blue vapor
Like an incense offering
The fragrant steam of the samovar
Freezes on the window pane

—Morikawa Yūko, 1941[2]

Chengde is a beautiful city of palaces and temples perched at a crossroads between China proper and Manchuria. In books, maps, and dispatches of the 1930s, the city and its region were called Jehol (Rehe), meaning "warm river." The area, although still north of the Wall, is far enough south that its small stream never freezes, unlike the waters of Harbin's Songhua River. Further north and west, a traveler can find the ruins of Shangdu, the palace of Kublai Khan, known to us in English as Xanadu. No pleasure dome can be found there now, only crumbling walls and the hills of Inner Mongolia. When the Japanese military captured the territory in 1933, their armies sat poised to enter North China proper. At the time of Gotō Reiji's study, the region thrived on profits from the poppy trade. For Chinese people at the beginning of the last century, it was the gateway to a frontier. For Mongols, then Manchus, and then Japanese soldiers, it was a point of invasion.

In the 1600s, the Chinese emperors built a grand summer palace, hunting lodge, and temples in Chengde. To the north of the city lay their homeland, a region they tried to keep closed to Chinese migration. Chengde served as their refuge from the summer heat of Beijing. Legend has it that in 1820 the imperial family abandoned the property after lightning struck dead the fifth dynasty emperor, Jiaqing (1760–1820). Officials took the mishap as a heavenly sign. The city, once a haven, became inauspicious.

In the same year as the emperor's misfortune, a darker portent of a worldly sort loomed along the South China coast: foreign ships selling illegal drugs to Chinese smugglers. Calling opium "foreign mud," "crow slices," or just plain poison, Qing Dynasty legal codes banned the drug beginning in 1729. Yet smugglers continued to supply a growing number of eager Chinese addicts. From 1820 to 1839, a rising tide of illicit drug use spread from the southern coast, through the Chinese river system, even into the imperial palace in Beijing—all this despite increasingly harsh Chinese laws against opium.

The drug problem worried officials for both moral and financial reasons. Chinese Confucian officials, like many politicians in the West today, charged that addiction weakened the moral fiber of the empire. Smokers became unproductive. Addicted soldiers lost the will to fight. Wealthy smugglers corrupted the bureaucracy by tempting underpaid officials with generous bribes.

By the early nineteenth century, fiscal concerns eclipsed moral anxieties. The empire based its currency on silver. During the two decades following the death of the Jiaqing emperor, foreign merchants traded such large amounts of foreign opium for Chinese silver—off the books and away from official eyes—that the empire experienced currency fluctuations. By the 1830s, opium sales had noticeably depleted China's silver reserves, causing inflation in the South.

Opium and its derivatives played such an important role in financing the civil unrest of the early twentieth century—and ruled as the important daily necessity of the residents in the Garden of Grand Vision—that it should be mentioned here. Simply put, China in the 1820s and 1830s, under the Qing emperors, became the first nation in the modern world forced to deal with a foreign drug cartel—in this case British merchants working between India and Canton on the China coast. Qing officials appointed modern history's first drug czar, the ill-fated Lin Zexu (1785–1851). Theirs was the first government, though by no means the last, to find the task of sealing off borders against drug smugglers impossible. Lin did not know that he was struggling in only one corner of a growing worldwide trade in products we cannot seem to live without: coffee, tea, chocolate, sugar, rum, tobacco, cocaine, opium. One scholar has called this development the global psychoactive revolution.[3]

In China, the drama itself was short. In 1839, after twenty years of an expanding illicit traffic in opium, the sixth Qing emperor, Daoguang (1782–1850), appointed Lin Zexu as imperial high commissioner with full powers to do what he could to stop the illicit traffic on the coast. Lin captured all opium, destroyed it, and forced the merchants to sign pledges giving up their criminal activities. His actions caused the First Opium War (1840–1842) with England. China lost, Lin went into exile, and China opened its ports and territories to foreign merchants. Thus began a long decline into revolution and civil chaos. Today, Chinese scholars call the period from the Treaty of Nanjing (1842) to the Chinese Communist victory in 1949 "one hundred years of humiliation."

The Opium War was the first in a series of short, humiliating wars, all lost by China, that gave Europeans, Americans, and finally Japanese the right to reside, trade, and eventually station troops in China under preferred conditions. Starting with the Treaty of Nanjing, Western nations signed increasingly unequal treaties with China that granted a mixture of commercial and territorial rights to foreign powers and gave their citizens special status inside the Chinese Empire. These treaties gave no such rights to Chinese nationals traveling abroad in return, and their terms destroyed the fabric of Chinese sovereignty—the ability of the Chinese government to enforce its own laws within its borders.

Extraterritoriality figures most in the story of the Garden of Grand Vision. This long word has a simple application. Foreigners had immunity from Chinese laws. The citizen of any nation with extraterritorial rights was subject to the laws of his or her own country. If accused of a crime, a person protected by treaty would face his or her own consul and courts. These institutions could be lenient with citizens living abroad. Extraterritoriality proved a clause made in heaven for smugglers. Japanese acquired extraterritoriality in China in 1895. After 1910, when Korea became a Japanese colony, Koreans, as Japanese subjects, also enjoyed treaty protection. In Fujiadian, Koreans dominated the morphine market. In 1937, when Japanese officials ended extraterritoriality in Manchukuo, Zou the landlord opened the Garden of Grand Vision as a haven for those enterprises no longer protected. Japanese and Korean traffickers flourished in China.

A second treaty institution peculiar to China was the concession area. Gradually, over fifty years, foreign enclaves expanded from an original five treaty ports to include more than 130 cities. Treaty ports allowed foreign nationals to live and trade in particular cities. The original treaty ports lay along the China coast, Shanghai being the most famous. The peculiar relationship between Harbin and Fujiadian, two distinct cities separated by a rail line, owes its complexity to this kind of treaty arrangement.

Entire swaths of land called "spheres of influence" expanded the treaty port concept. Nations enjoying a sphere of influence were free to develop commercial institutions, extend loans, and exploit resources for their own benefit. In 1896 Russia gained the right to develop rail and minerals in Manchuria. The privilege passed into Japanese hands after 1905, after which the Japanese military moved into the northeastern leased territory and concessions.[4]

Japan was not one of the original treaty powers in Asia. In 1842, when China signed the first unequal treaty, Japan was a feudal country closed to foreign trade and residence. Ruled by a shogun and samurai warriors, the country was united as much by feudal bonds of loyalty as by a legal system. Japan resisted contact with the world until 1853, when the American commodore Matthew Perry forced the issue with gunboats. Not until a new government replaced the shogun in 1868 did a younger group of Japanese leaders begin restructuring the nation's political system, military, and society in a modern fashion. Once these changes began, Japan's modernization was rapid and thorough. Being both Asian and modern became a point of Japanese pride.

As treaty concessions chipped away at China's sovereignty, the Qing Dynasty began to modernize its own military. Early projects produced a handful of Chinese arsenals and shipyards. These attempts created a patchy armada of gunboats, mostly castoffs from European navies. They were the projects of a handful of dedicated officials. Government support came in a superficial, sporadic fashion.

Nothing and no one coordinated the array of China's modern projects into a national effort with a central command. Instead, a battery of conservative officials, along with remnants of the once ferocious and now opium-addled Qing banner army, frustrated attempts to modernize where they could. They rightly felt that reform threatened their traditional privileged status and way of life. When put to the test, China's modern military failed miserably.

The test came in 1894 when the Chinese modern military fought a short war with Japan and lost. Although Japan adopted European military techniques slightly later than China, the country had produced, in twenty-five short years, a coordinated, efficient army and navy, fully supported by both the government and the people. Winning a war against China made Japan a world power overnight. It acquired treaty rights in China. It gained the first piece of its empire: Taiwan as a colony. By 1902 Japan had entered into a naval defense treaty with Great Britain.

Japanese woodblock prints celebrating victory in China make a visual statement about the rate of progress of the two Asian nations. In one picture, Japanese officers sit tall on horseback wearing European uniforms, sabers aloft, leading well-armed soldiers into battle. Their mutton-chop whiskers make them look European. The Japanese battle flag flutters red in the foreground. The distinct lines of a Chinese city wall place the action squarely in Asia. In another graphic, a Japanese soldier, astride a prancing war steed, uses his saber against Chinese soldiers in centuries-old costume. In another, three Chinese naval officers, pigtailed and wearing flowing robes unsuited for modern combat, beg for peace. Japanese admirals, again in Western uniforms, stand tall, officers and honor guard alike holding themselves ramrod straight.[5] These pictures capture a theme repeated in Gotō Reiji's writing: stagnant China, mired in tradition, in contrast to virile, adaptable, and modern Japan.

Success in China brought Japan onto the world stage. The Chinese defeat opened the doors to international activity in Manchuria. Imperial Russia came first. The Russians gained concessions in Manchuria and began to build a railway system toward the warm-water port they called Dalney. But when they became active on the Korean Peninsula, Japanese politicians took notice. The tip of Korea lay perilously close to Japan's southern islands.[6]

In 1904–1905 Japan went to war with Russia, a European power, and won. The ensuing treaty granted the Japanese a concession area based in the city they called Dairen (today Dalian) and including the entire southern Liaodong Peninsula. Japanese capital and engineers took over the southern portion of Russian rail projects. Japanese prospectors excavated for minerals along the rail line. This short war may seem distant to us now, but it has an American twist. President Theodore Roosevelt facilitated a negotiated end to the conflict, bringing both sides to treaty talks held in Portsmouth, New Hampshire. He received the Nobel Peace Prize for his efforts.

The rail line that Japan received as part of the Treaty of Portsmouth became the South Manchurian Railroad Company (Mantetsu). Japanese owned and operated, the system became an instrument of empire. It did what rail companies do—put down track, maintained stations, operated the railroad on schedule—and much more. It included a research wing with experts compiling reports on every aspect of Asian life, from Russian milch cows to the resources of central China to fur export figures. The bibliographic index of these experts' hard work is a seven-hundred-page doorstop of a book. The survey of the Garden of Grand Vision, although commissioned by the military, fit into this information-gathering obsession. The functionaries of the Japanese Empire excelled at collecting minutia.[7]

Japanese police guarded the rail line, trunk line cities, and Liaodong concession area itself. This police force was, in fact, an army of one division stationed in six garrison cities along the tracks. It was called the Kantō Army, or the Army East of the Pass. The name designates the area just on the other side of Shanhaiguan, the entryway to the lands beyond the Great Wall. Holding a command in the Kantō Army was a crucial posting for ambitious Japanese army officers. The Kantō Army was also far from the prying eyes of Japanese commanders and politicians. From the ranks of this Manchurian military branch, radical young officers created their own defiant national policy in the late 1920s and early 1930s.[8]

Modern European nations of the day had empires, along with industry, commerce, and laws. In like manner, the Japanese Empire grew. After 1910, Korea became Japan's second colony. In 1915, the Shandong Peninsula, located to the south across the Yellow Sea, became a Japanese concession area. As mentioned, many of the Garden's residents, including its owner and the Spring Forest Lodge's landlord, came from Shandong Province. Thus, twenty years after its first war with China, Japan controlled strategic areas in Asia, backing by colonial possessions and active trade networks in China.

When Gotō Reiji talks proudly of his Japanese patriotism, he is thinking of these events. Living in Harbin, he must have gone many times to the Tower of Loyal Souls, an obelisk erected by Japanese living in the city to commemorate several of their compatriots who died during the Russo-Japanese War. The men gave their lives while planting explosives meant to blow up a section of the Russian railroad track near Harbin. They were also spies. The memorial stood in a park, near the Harbin racetrack, in a space of green between Nangang and Fragrant Mill. The tower was a favorite stop for Japanese touring the city. Needless to say, the memorial is now gone. Its loss should not be mourned. It was a rather ordinary cement tower that looked much like a miniature Washington Monument. Today, the Chinese Martyrs Cemetery takes its place.[9]

Russia's loss to Japan in 1905 did not mean that Russian residents left Harbin. The city became the administrative center for the Chinese Eastern Railway. The growing presence of Russian émigrés gave Harbin an exotic quality that thrilled Japanese visitors and residents alike. By the 1920s Harbin had become a tourist destination. The South Manchuria Railway guidebook to Harbin characterized the city as evocative of northern Europe. One resident fondly recalled celebrating the new year three times each year: by the Western calendar, the Chinese lunar calendar, and the Russian lunar calendar. He claimed that Russian women liked wealthy-seeming Japanese men far better than poor Chinese men. A Japanese expat confessed to loving the cabarets, where he found beautiful women dancing on stage or with patrons, tapping out the latest steps from America. No one headed home until the early hours of the morning. Happiness was everywhere. Yet, he confessed, the place gave him a hint of sadness, as though he were watching the last days of Rome.[10]

The Japanese dead of the Russo-Japanese War are remembered as heroes who sacrificed their lives for the glory of Japan. Sacrifice it was, for the Russo-Japanese War was a hard-won victory. Had Europeans been paying heed to the battles far away, they might have rethought their strategy in the Great War of the next decade. The land battles of the Russo-Japanese War took a huge toll in human lives. Soldiers fought in trenches. Young men became human bullets as they charged against machine-gun fire. Yet the Japanese Empire emerged victorious from the war, claiming a place among the world powers. From the Russo-Japanese War onward, Japanese migrants began arriving in Manchuria in larger numbers. Even more Chinese followed in their wake. One of these was Zou Xisan, owner of the Garden of Grand Vision.

Zou Xisan was a newcomer who made out well in the frontier territory. Zou's success came in part from his early arrival. He also benefited from family connections that made adjusting to life in a new land easier. Mostly, though, his success stemmed from an adaptive instinct. He quickly grabbed any advantage that came his way. This last quality appalled Gotō Reiji, who felt the man had shifting loyalties and questionable morals.

Zou Xisan was from Yellow County on the northern coast of Shandong Province, just across the Yellow Sea from Manchuria. His family was comfortable enough to provide him with an early private classical education. In 1887, when he began school at the age of six, an elite curriculum required memorizing the ancient *History*, *Poems*, and *Ritual* books, each dating from 1000 BCE, as well as the four Confucian classics. Zou would learn these books by heart in a language as far removed from the Chinese he spoke at home as Latin is from Italian. He would learn to mimic their style in essay form. Zou would have also studied poetry and perfected his penmanship. We know that he excelled at calligraphy. His scholarly hand provided the style for the Garden's entryway sign.[11]

Zou, like many young boys throughout China, endured the difficulties of such an elaborate education—and his family bore the expense—hoping he could pass the grueling, three-tiered civil service examinations to qualify for a bureaucratic post in the Chinese imperial state system. The examination system had served China well for many hundreds of years. It created a literate bureaucracy with a common educational base. It brought together the brightest men to be found throughout the empire, all of whom shared the experience of the examination hall.[12]

The system worked too well, in fact, for when challenged by modern Western nations, which soon included Japan, the Chinese bureaucratic state, founded on classical Confucian education, failed in every way. Yet older bureaucrats had a hard time imagining that any system could work better. They were not entirely wrong. In the years of chaos that followed the end of imperial rule, old relationships continued in the countryside if not the cities. Japanese in Manchuria would find rural areas hard to administer.[13]

For China, the 1800s brought crisis and failure. The Chinese Empire lost a series of foreign wars, the most traumatic being the 1895 defeat to Japan. Military loss followed military loss despite unsuccessful attempts to create a modern Chinese military. Conservative Confucian bureaucrats paid lip service to modernization, but change came hard despite repeated military and diplomatic losses at the hands of the West. The desperate national situation created a younger generation of students searching for radical solutions to China's problems. Education would be at the forefront of change.

In the 1880s, just when Zou must have been learning his first characters, one member of the Chinese gentry began to question China's outdated political and education methods. Kang Youwei (1858–1927), a Confucian scholar, exam passer, and political thinker, advocated restructuring the Confucian imperial government to include democratic institutions. He took Japan's constitutional monarchy as a model. He had no intention of overthrowing the dynasty or the emperor he respected. Instead he proposed introducing modern subjects—math, science, geography—into the education system. In doing so he attracted a younger generation of scholars to his way of thinking. Under such conditions, the classical education of Zou's childhood became obsolete.[14]

Kang Youwei did manage to gain the trust of the Chinese Guangxu emperor (1871–1908). Over one summer in 1898, Kang, his emperor, and a handful of allies rearranged the Chinese political structure. They introduced democratic processes into the imperial structure, reforms to strengthen the military, and a new education system based on practical subjects, leading to revamped content for exam questions. Such drastic reforms threatened too many powerful people. After little more than one hundred days, the reaction was swift. Conservative elements in the government sent troops to the palace. Kang Youwei fled into exile, several of his colleagues, including his brother, were executed, and the Guangxu emperor spent the rest of his life under a glorified house arrest. The emperor died in 1908, leaving the throne to a young nephew, the unlucky Henry Puyi.

When Zou Xisan was seventeen years old, his life changed course. Perhaps the ideas of Confucian reformers influenced his family. It could be that the young Zou did not show the talent or drive required to pass the rigorous exams. Gotō's young assistant boldly states that Zou had done no more than superficially gnaw on the classics. In fact, Zou came to Manchuria because his family, like those of Braying Mule Wang and

Poor Mouth Liu, had fallen on hard times. Shandong farmers faced difficult conditions in the best of times. The soil was poor, the weather harsh. In the years of Zou's youth, peasants in his province took to violence to redress their grievances. By 1900 a full-blown peasant revolt shook North China.

Peasant revolts punctuate China's dynastic history. All of them targeted the dynasty and bureaucracy—all, that is, but the Boxer Rebellion. In 1900, the dynasty backed this peasant uprising, which had turned antiforeign. Riotous peasants, armed with spears, farm implements, and a religious certainty that they were impervious to bullets, attacked every sign of foreign presence. They burned foreign-made goods, attacked merchants, and slaughtered Christian converts. They swarmed into the capital from Zou's native Shandong Province. Peasants surrounded the foreign embassies, holding the residents hostage in Beijing over two desperately hot summer months in 1900.

By the fall, a joint expedition of foreign armies, including a Japanese battalion, had captured Beijing, liberating all hostages. In English the episode is known as the Boxer Rebellion, although the so-called rebels supported their dynasty, instead attacking anything foreign as an unwanted intrusion. The Chinese name, Yihetuan, or the Righteous Harmonious Militia, captures the sense of a movement bent on righting wrongs rather than rebellion. The Boxer Rebellion accomplished nothing but to bring foreign forces into Beijing. Building in what would be Harbin halted only briefly. The movement's failure was a nail in the coffin of the Qing Dynasty, which would wither away along with the traditional political arrangement of emperor and exam-based bureaucracy.[15]

Zou's family suffered like so many others in Shandong Province. But Zou was no righteous fighter. Instead he sought opportunity in the developing northern territory. In 1901 the family sent Zou to seek employment in the growing Manchurian business sector. Leaving his home province behind, Zou wrapped up his belongings in a sleeping mat, piled on layers of clothing, and joined a boatload of migrant laborers on their way north seeking work. He may have shared deck space with fellows who would end up in his building. Zou arrived with other migrants in Yingkou, a port in southern Manchuria. There the similarity in their circumstances ended. Zou lived with a merchant family; later he apprenticed with a Chinese business with Japanese connections. This allowed him to spend a year in Osaka. Zou's career began to flourish.[16]

In 1909, at the age of twenty-eight, Zou moved north to Harbin. There he finally entered the official world, when he became an appraiser in the Harbin Land Office. He achieved a coveted government position without passing through the dreaded examination halls. In 1905, during the years of Zou's Manchurian education, Chinese imperial officials had bowed to the inevitable. They instituted educational reforms called for and refused in the 1890s. Zou no longer required the status of examination passer to get a government post.

Zou Xisan worked for the imperial government for only two more years. In southern China, Dr. Sun Yat-sen (1866–1925) plotted the downfall of the Qing, drawing to him a new generation of dissatisfied Chinese. Sun rejected reform. He called for nothing less than complete revolution. Unlike the classically trained Kang Youwei, Sun had spent three formative years with an elder brother in Hawaii. There he went to high school, where he learned firsthand about Western institutions. He returned to Hong Kong, where he studied medicine (hence the "Dr." before his name). During the same years that Kang Youwei promoted a constitutional monarchy, Sun devoted himself to plotting the overthrow of the Manchus. His activities did not go unnoticed. In 1895 he forged an intricate plot to begin a revolutionary uprising. Dynasty agents discovered the intrigue before it could begin. Sun, knowing an excruciating death would certainly follow his capture, fled into exile.

Sun Yat-sen was one of many young men of his generation who dreamed of overthrowing the Manchu rulers. Revolutionary outbursts, like Sun's failure in the South, punctuated the last years of the dynasty. These plots were sporadic and uncoordinated by necessity. The Qing would not easily bow out of Chinese history and had informants. Plotters, when caught, faced a slow death by slicing. For this reason Sun went to England, where he had friends from his school days in Hong Kong. In London an incident made the name Sun Yat-sen synonymous with revolution in Chinese communities worldwide.

In 1896, agents working for the dynasty kidnapped Sun Yat-sen, holding him prisoner in the Chinese embassy for over a week. He escaped only through the intervention of a friend and former teacher. His adventure made it into the British tabloid press. Sun capitalized on his sudden fame. In 1897 he wrote a riveting account of his ordeal, *Kidnapped in London*. The monograph brought him instant recognition. He became the best known of the many leaders and groups working to overthrow the Manchus. He could not return to China, but he could organize and raise money for the cause. In doing so he gained the support of several Japanese ultranationalist adventurers who became his friends.[17]

Sun Yat-sen appealed to a younger generation than Kang Youwei. His followers were not interested in reforming the imperial structure. They demanded total change: destruction of the incompetent dynasty and its replacement with an American-style republic. On October 10, 1911, skirmishes broke out in Wuhan, an industrial city on the Yangzi River, initiating the fighting that would lead to the end of the Chinese dynastic tradition. In 1912 China became a republic. The last emperor of China began a lonely phase of his life. Like his emperor uncle before him, he lived as a prisoner inside his palace until 1924, when a warlord expelled him to Tianjin, where he lived a playboy's life.

Zou's appearance would have changed drastically in 1911. Whether by force or by choice, he would have cut off the long queue of hair that he, along with all Chinese men, wore as a symbol of submission to the old dynasty. He did not, however, lose his job. Zou was a lucky man. He came of age while China collapsed around him. Even as he learned to read, write, and cipher, the larger society experienced failure in both war and government reform, peasant and revolutionary uprising, and dynastic collapse. Meanwhile, Zou moved from one lucky break to the next well-paying position.

Zou understood that governments came and went, but the Chinese people and their need for local order would remain. By 1940, when Zou sat down for an interview with Gotō Reiji, he had lived in a Manchuria transformed from a monarchy into a Chinese republic, then into a province run by a warlord, then into a Japanese-inspired state. Yet, unlike his tenants, he continued to survive and prosper. He admitted as much to Gotō Reiji, saying that dynasties rose and fell, but the Chinese people would continue to thrive. The Japanese were there now, but if the Russians were to come in later, Zou assured Gotō, he would find a way to work with them as well.[18]

Such a bold admission made Gotō uneasy. He was, after all, a Japanese police officer personally willing to die for a Japanese emperor whose lineage stretched back into the mists of time. Gotō's imperial family had no surname, no dynastic name, only the boast of its origins with the Japanese sun goddess. Gotō saw, in this difference, the source of Japan's strength and China's weakness. In Gotō's eyes, men like Zou were cynical. In his introduction to the police report, Gotō presents Zou and his view of survival as evidence of the Chinese people's innate stagnation, lack of patriotic vision, and, by extension, need for strong Japanese guidance. He included Zou on his personal black list of people to watch.[19]

Nor did Gotō care for Zou's personal morals. As mentioned earlier, Zou served as a director of the Harbin Morals Society and the Red Swastika Society as well. He donated money according to an elaborate monthly schedule based on the Chinese almanac. This perplexed Gotō. How could a person who grew rich from the misery of the poor embody virtue? Gotō asked the slumlord point blank, "Do you not think that earning money from a den of evil like the Garden of Grand Vision is a moral wrong?" The landlord answered, "I give alms to people of the world, so I am not concerned."[20]

Zou's almsgiving proved to be a complicated affair. Each day on his Chinese calendar was marked with a black or a white circle. On the black-circle days, Zou gave between M$0.30 and M$0.40. On the white-circle days, he donated between M$2 and M$3. He did not tell Gotō where the money went but assured him that the amount came to more than M$50 each month. Zou donated more than M$700 to the Morals Society and its affiliates. He also supported a friend, a mendicant Daoist hermit, with M$1,000 each year. Zou gave his money to worthy causes, but he avoided walking along streets filled with beggars. He took a rickshaw instead and felt that there was no economic benefit in handing out alms to the beggars.[21]

Zou assured Gotō that all Manchukuoan police were corrupt and suggested that the government should order them into the Morals Society. After all, he said, controlling one's social privilege was the essence of virtue. Gotō, the Japanese officer, suggested that the Concordia Society, a Manchukuo-government-sponsored political group, might serve just as well. The society had quickly become a propaganda brigade for the government that any Manchukuoan of importance was pressured to join. Zou had to be careful in his answer.

The slumlord made a distinction between merit, or deeds done for compensation, and virtue, or donations made seeking no reward. The Japanese, he said, had organized the economy and politics of Manchuria to benefit Japan; therefore the action has merit, not virtue. In the same way Zou offered cheap housing in the Garden of Grand Vision for merit. After all, someone had to do the job. Merchants who offered goods for a lower price than their competitors became more successful. This too was considered merit. The Concordia Society, therefore, would not teach virtue the way the Morals Society would.[22]

Gotō looked down on Zou in general. Although Zou spoke Japanese, his accent had a western drawl, reflecting the year he worked in Osaka. Gotō was as conversant in Chinese and the Confucian classics as Zou. Yet Gotō's school-learned Chinese carried the crisp diction of the elite, while Zou spoke with the regional lilt and cadence of a Shandong peasant. Moreover Gotō could not but condemn a man who gained substantial wealth from the misery the police officer personally investigated during his trips to the Garden of Grand Vision. Even Zou's assurances that he gave money to charities on a regular basis did not erase the stigma of such ownership in Gotō's eyes. This very adaptability made Gotō despise the slumlord.[23]

Zou did not possess the patriotism, elocution, or livelihood that pleased Gotō. Still, Zou was a survivor. He had a knack for investments. He proved more than willing to use his Japanese and underworld connections. His career followed a successful path, even as the country of his birth convulsed with military failure, thwarted reform, peasant uprising, and revolutionary violence. He ended up in Harbin with money in his pocket and the opportunity to invest at just the right time.

Zou's experience with the Garden of Grand Vision paralleled the booming growth of Manchuria, of Harbin, and of the Fujiadian area. Zou was only one of 3 million Chinese migrants who by the end of the 1920s had made Manchuria their home. They joined 54,000 Russians, Japanese, and other foreign nationals. Each of these migrants, coming from all directions and quickly filling up the empty land, arrived in search of new opportunities to earn a living. Most did not find the comfortable occupations that Zou enjoyed.

4

Dirty Work

The pilferers can be classified into two kinds of groups. The first kind have been harshly beaten up by society, and all have been locked out of the larger land. They become tramps, gadding about on the edges of society when in the end they meet others like them in these lodgings. The other kind enjoyed the taste of the vibrant life in the Garden of Grand Vision from the start.

—Gotō Reiji[1]

For the urban scrounger, street life unfolds like a series of practical opportunities. . . . Day after day, I and other scroungers negotiated the porous boundaries between private property and discarded public resource.

—Jeff Ferrel[2]

L ife in Fujiadian was hard. People who wandered into the Garden of Grand Vision found cheap shelter from the harsh climate. With their lives in disarray, they could not—or, out of shame, would not—return to the comfort of their families and villages south of the Wall. At any rate, given the turmoil in early-twentieth-century China, those hometowns could not afford to take them back.

Residents of the Garden had all fallen out of the mainstream economy; yet their lives were neither idle nor unproductive. A vibrant, if squalid, work ethic thrived in the shadows of the slums. Gotō Reiji titles his chapter about working in the Harbin slums "Stolen Goods and the Distribution of Stolen Goods."[3] In fact, the boundary was blurred between

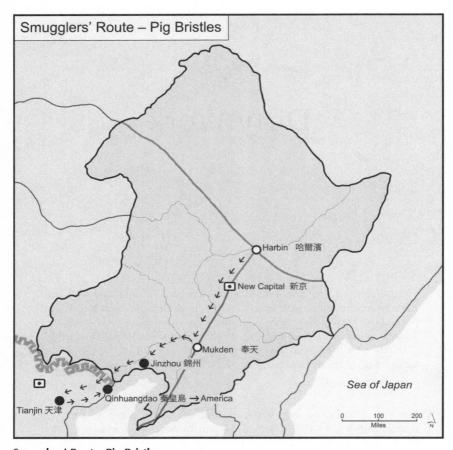

Smugglers' Route, Pig Bristles

pilfering and what we would call rag picking, or dumpster diving, or recycling. The Garden was alive with industry, some of which merged seamlessly into the mainstream economy of the Manchukuo world.

Our twentieth-first-century world abounds with gigantic slums. In recent years, academics, journalists, and artists have discovered unexpected community and enterprise in the impromptu neighborhoods of tin and tarpaper that surround many major cities. Danny Boyle's film *Slumdog Millionaire* captured global attention and a host of awards in 2008. In the same year Sudhir Venkatesh brought South Side Chicago slums alive after working and socializing with a gang leader. Most recently Katherine Boo won the National Book Award for a study of slum life and enterprise in Mumbai.[4]

Academics who study urban squalor in today's world call the kind of activity found in the neighborhood of the Garden of Grand Vision an "underground economy." The term includes any and all pursuits that help people survive in the cramped poverty found in the favelas of Rio de Janeiro, Brazil, or in the squatter communities of Mumbai, India, or in the Kibera megaslum of Nairobi, Kenya.[5] Such scholars talk about "autonomous subsistence activities."[6] In articles, books, and conference papers, they describe active slums, each with a social hierarchy within what seems at first to be a mass of poverty. This hierarchy includes a group of informal entrepreneurs—the upper class of the lower class—who employ and cater to the needs of the poor. Slum life is both complex and productive.

With their wealth of data, Gotō Reiji and his colleagues, had they lived today, could have joined the conversation. The three men described in detail the moneymaking activities they observed with an eye to discerning the trade networks that made the Harbin slum businesses thrive. Today's writers could provide Gotō with terminology he did not have— phrases like "informal economy" or "subsistence entrepreneur." Today's scholars emphasize the surprising amount of community that exists amid crushing poverty. They would not care quite so much for the graphically disparaging tone Gotō uses in places to make the Garden residents seem grotesquely alien. On the other hand, today's scholars attend conferences and appear on talk shows. They do not have to turn their studies over to Japanese military intelligence.

RECYCLING FOR PROFIT

Gotō Reiji's research shines as he details the activities of the slum. He takes us to Fujiadian to show us how goods, services, and money move from the streets of the poor into the better neighborhoods and back again. He introduces us to men living in the Garden who work as pilferers, grave robbers, and beggars. He tells us that pilfering alone keeps this neighborhood afloat. A pilferer's job fell somewhere between theft and recycling. These individuals would collect or steal—often both in the same evening—everything from cloth to pig bristles to rat pelts. They sold the fruits of their labors to the many variety stores and small-scale manufacturers in and around the Garden, whence these items found their way back into the mainstream economy.[7]

Pilferers collected animal carcasses, rags, cigarette butts, anything they could get their hands on and resell. Some worked in crews of three or four. One crew Gotō studied entered factories at night to steal scrap metal or burlap bags. Each thief had a quota of at least four or five bags per night. The bags could be resold for M$0.10 the next day. Some men traveled the streets carrying baskets of wastepaper, a handy prop for hiding ill-gotten lucre. Gotō describes them all as they move from shadow to shadow.[8]

Gotō introduces us to the Garden's most successful pilferer, who lives in the Spring Forest Lodge. The man looks helpless, gloomy, and old, although he is only in his fifties. His sorry appearance is his capital. It helps him in his work. He regularly returns from his forays with sacks of chicken, pork-filled buns, fish, clothing, even furniture. He cheated a rich man's wife by pretending to be in Harbin searching for a lost son. He needed money, he said, to return home to China. The wily old man was such a clever actor that he drew a crowd of onlookers from those passing by in the street. The woman felt sorry for him and gave him money. How could she do otherwise? With such an audience, the poor woman was afraid to lose face. The old man's story was, of course, totally false.[9]

Gotō dwells in gruesome detail on the men who steal from graves. Wang Huixiang, a ferocious man in his forties, is just such a person. As expected, he works at night. His place of business is the Circle River Cemetery, a public graveyard near the Peace Bridge. He finds a fresh grave, pries off the coffin lid, and takes the clothing off the corpse, along with anything else of value. Wang has bragged that he can make up to M$20 on a good night, selling the clothes to a secondhand shop. He has also implied to Gotō that he enjoys contact with the corpses of young women. Gotō attributes this unhealthy sexuality to the man's morphine addiction.[10]

Wanting to learn more about Wang the grave robber, Gotō visited him several times. Needing lodging, Wang represented himself as a beggar and secured a spot at the Twelfth Street Benevolent Home in Fujiadian. Feng Dengdiao, one of Gotō's informants, a man Gotō considered something of a friend, also found lodging at the same charity. Gotō worried that Wang would entice his friend Feng to take part in his bizarre pursuits. Indeed, Feng joined Wang in robbing a grave. He described the trip to the graveyard where the two men dug up and pried open a coffin.

The trip did not turn out as planned. The weather turned unseasonably warm that day. The body in the coffin, already rotting, had swelled to such an extent that they could not strip off the clothing. Undeterred, the two men chose a second coffin. Finding a more suitable corpse, they took the clothes, which stank of death. They easily sold them to a secondhand clothing store, earning M$16 for their labors. The two men spent what they earned on women, drugs, and gambling in the Garden of Grand Vision. Wang Huixiang died shortly after this incident. Although he kept a place at the benevolent association, he moved into a hospital room. Just before his death, some impatient fellow inmate managed to steal his clothes.[11]

Gotō Reiji is at his scholarly best when walking us through the networks by which stolen goods travel from the black market to the everyday street. He points out the many variety stores doing business throughout the Fujiadian neighborhood. Each day any of these stores might buy between M$60 and M$80 worth of goods, all of questionable origin. To make his point Gotō introduces us to Zhang Junshan. We find Zhang's shop at 13 South Eleventh Road, just to the rear of a school. Nestled in the street with several competitors nearby, the business consists of a two-room building and a large yard for which he pays M$12 a month. He and his family of eight people work all day long in filthy conditions. He employs an old man who earns M$0.40 a day. Zhang will buy anywhere from M$30 to M$70 in a given day. His scales hardly get a rest from the coming and going of the beggars and the pilferers. The clothing, shoes, and hats taken from graves sit piled in their own corner of the property. Stacks of other goods litter the yard. Zhang's workers go about the business of cleaning these items up for sale.

Zhang claims to be a legitimate businessman, but he has had his problems. He has told Gotō that as a junk dealer he pays taxes of M$6 each month to the city office. In fact he has been entrusted with the job of collecting the monthly payments for all the variety store owners in his area. He has a voucher signed by Hosokawa Takuyoshi of the city office. He even received an invitation to a Chinese meal to celebrate the new year, although he did not attend. However, this Hosokawa person also collected M$12 in what he called "guarantee money." Other variety store operators in the area made payments to the same fellow. These arrangements sounded wrong to Gotō, who made a note that the situation should be investigated.[12]

Stolen goods circulate through Harbin hoisted on the shoulders of basket carriers. Vendors carry goods in two baskets suspended from a long shoulder pole. Basket peddlers are so much a part of the traditional Chinese market street that they will hardly be noticed. Gotō has pointed them out to us already from the trolley window as we came into the Fujiadian neighborhood. The basket peddlers claimed to be buying and selling junk. Gotō suspected that in fact they were using their common appearance to roam through the better neighborhoods of Harbin to pilfer as well as do business.[13]

In addition to the basket peddlers, open-air stalls pepper the streets of Fujiadian, stolen goods among their wares. "Stall" is not the right word. A person need only spread out a board or a canvas on the side of the street, pile it with goods, and he or she is open for business. Small shops around the area buy pilfered goods. Iron foundries operate to melt down old metal. The goods come to them from all sorts of places, like rail yards, and even include manhole covers. Lumberyards, brickyards, foundries, and used-clothing stores all take what comes without asking too many questions about origins.[14]

People living in the Garden buy their daily necessities in stores near their location. These variety stores buy their wares as often as not from the local scavengers and pickpockets. The ghost market—the open-air market where anything might appear for sale—provides an even cheaper place to buy almost anything at all. A short walk along Long Spring Street brings us to a small alley between the New Jade Hair Dresser and the entrance to Warm Fragrance Alley, a red-light district. Here we find the ghost market. If something has been stolen, a person might come here to buy it back that evening. The market convenes here every night between 7 and 10 p.m., weather permitting. Gotō walks with us through the crush of people.

What an assortment of goods. On display along the street we find empty cans, an odd shoe, filthy rags, dirty towels, empty makeup tins, bowls, a rat corpse, bent nails, chicken feet, gloves with missing fingers, a rather elegant brass door lantern. A fellow from the store in the area comes by with a crate of mandarin oranges. He is selling them for M$0.02 each, but as he glides through the crowd, hands attack the carton from all sides, snatching away free oranges. A second fellow circulates among the crowd. He carries a square whiskey bottle. For M$0.05 he will proffer a swig. Of course, in no time arguments erupt. The buyer took too much; the seller allowed too little.

Many of the peddlers are children. One child shouts from the curb, "A good Japanese padded jacket—M$20, not a penny less." Another child is selling bundles of cotton thread. He is not a thief. His father owned a cotton shop, but he became seriously ill and could not keep up the business. Now the father works as a seller for a cloth merchant group. His son helps as he can. Not all of the goods are stolen. Some of the merchants are selling family capital to get by in a crisis. Gotō finds yet another group of children selling pure cotton yarn for M$3 a bundle. He tells us that they are not thieves. Rather they are the family of a cloth merchant who has come down with a sudden illness. He cannot work, and his children are raising money for medicine.

On one corner a small boy offers the crowd a lovely leather briefcase. Gotō is attracted to its obvious high quality. The boy is only asking M$5. Just as Gotō pushes his way through the crowd toward the boy, a fellow grabs the briefcase. The poor boy chases after the thief, who tosses back a M$0.50 note. What can the boy do? He takes the money, makes a brave face, and wanders off. At that moment Gotō spies a police officer rattling his sword in the crowd. He has been totally useless to the boy.[15]

Aside from the stores, markets, and street vendors, any of the flophouse owners can fence pilfered goods. The franchise owners do not openly buy stolen goods, which they instead accept in pawn for a day's rest if a fellow runs out of money. Of course the goods are valued well below their street price. The custom is to hold the goods for three days. The working girls in the building also valued stolen goods, especially if a customer has brought her makeup or pretty clothes.

The best example of the seamless merger of the Manchukuo economy and the enterprises that thrived around the Garden was the trade in pelts. Trade in valuable fur is part of our own American frontier history. Manchuria was no different. During the dynastic period, tribes of hunters trapped the fur-bearing creatures of the North, everything from squirrel to fox to tiger. Sable was most desired. Foragers turned pelt quotas over to government agents as tribute. Manchurian fur graced the robes and headwear of emperors and empresses, all worn according to a strict seasonal calendar.[16]

Gotō gives us exquisite detail about a different Manchurian fur trade. His foragers are not the hearty mountain men of myth. Pilferers from the Fujiadian slums collect rat, cat, and dog corpses. If they are lucky, the cat or dog fur will be glossy and fine. Each rat can be sold to the variety stores for M$0.02. Dead cats bring M$0.10 to M$0.15; dead dogs can be sold for M$0.05 to M$0.10, the price dictated by quality. The variety store owner, acting as middleman, sells the skins to a tannery for M$4 to M$10 per pound, the price depending on the quality and color of the fur. The tanner makes the skins into eight-inch squares—two squares sewn together became a "scroll." A good worker can create five scrolls from one pound of pelts. The tanneries can be found along Lucky Street between Eighth and Twelfth streets, near the Shandong Province Benevolent Society.[17]

Thirty-nine-year-old Li Xiangchen from Hebei in North China owns one of the tanneries. He invested M$200 to buy the enterprise. He employs four professional tanners who earn M$0.10 for each scroll. He is also training four apprentices who are not paid for the three years of their training. In addition to paying the salaries, Li feeds all eight of his workers. In one day a person can produce between twelve and fifteen scrolls. Li pays quarterly taxes of M$11.25.

The scrolls go from the tannery to a dye shop. From there they find their way to the workhouses of topflight fur companies. They are made into hats, gloves, and scarves, which will be sold to the best shops in Harbin. By this route, a dead rat from the Harbin slums can easily make its way to the show window of a trendy shop on Kitaiskaia Street.[18]

Pig bristle and pig hair provide a good livelihood for some of the pilferers. Pig bristle is tough. Gotō tells us that in the old days in China, authorities used pig bristle to get confessions from felons. The bristles have sharp, barbed points. Inserting a pig bristle into a fellow's urethra would have him talking in no time. Gotō claims that in the countryside the method is used in personal vendettas.

Pig bristle has more humane uses. It produces high-quality hair-brushes and is sold as such even in today's world of synthetic goods. War made the coveted Chinese boar hair scarce; thus it commanded a good price on the international market. Pilferers who gathered pig bristles sold their findings to the variety stores. The owners sorted the bristles from the hair, turning the valuable bristles over to brokers. These middlemen bundled the bristles into straw bags. Because the trade in pig bristles was illegal, the brokers labeled their packages "wool." In collusion with partners who worked for the South Manchuria Railway, the jobbers smuggled the pig bristles through the Wall into China proper. On arriving in Tianjin they sold their goods to an American merchant house. From Tianjin the bristles traveled to First Emperor Island City, a port on the Yellow Sea just south of Shanhaiguan. From there the goods went on to America. This was a popular smuggling route for other strategic material, especially gold and tungsten. The pig bristles in this case would go to make brushes, not to untangle the hair of American beauties but to clean military equipment.[19]

People also collected scraps of cloth, selling them through jobbers to local felt makers. Workmen in felt shops shredded the cloth, mixed it with flour paste, and left it to dry on boards in the sun. Felt had all sorts of everyday uses, serving as everything from the soles of Chinese cloth shoes to lining for coats to pillow stuffing to insulation.

Gotō takes us to a felt operation on South Eleventh Street in Fujiadian. There Zhang Junshan has a variety store. He buys rags and resells them to a neighbor who runs a felt factory. Zhang Fengshan, forty-seven years old from Hebei Province, owns the factory, which he, his wife, and his four children have been running for four years. He buys rags, paying from M$0.50 to M$2 per pound, depending on the quality. Ten pounds of rags will create fourteen feet of thin felt. The neighborhood has thirty felt makers.[20]

Gotō explains that the scavengers have no problems finding animal carcasses of every sort. Nothing is turned down. If the fur is not of fine-enough quality for the pelt trade, the rejected hide can be sold to mat makers. The mat maker's workshop becomes the destination for all of the pig hair that, more often than not, is mixed in with the pig bristles. Every kind of hair—horse, donkey, mule, dog, cat, monkey—can fetch a price even if a pelt proves useless.

Mat makers collect the hair during the winter and pull it from the animal hide. In the spring they wash the hair they have collected, beating and stirring it into a kind of pulp-like wadding. They dry this mixture in the April sun. The resulting pulp can be formed into mats of five by three feet. Each mat sells for between M$0.40 and M$1, and each person makes about seven mats per day. Such mats have many uses, serving as anything from insulation to hat lining. They meet a basic need in the cold Harbin climate.

Any leftover skins from the pigs, horses, and dogs end up in factories. Gotō has talked to the owner of the Yihe Glue Factory on New Market Street, who claims to be able to render three hundred pounds of skins in one day, although he can only work during the mild weather in the spring and fall. He puts the skins in a cauldron to boil down for twenty-four hours. He buys skins for M$1 for one hundred pounds.[21]

Recycling operations include burlap, pig bristles, and animal hair; scavengers glean what they can from trash heaps and sell what they find to middlemen in the variety stores, from which it will return to the legitimate market. Even tobacco supplies a lucrative recycling industry. Scavengers roam through the town, picking up cigarette butts and empty packages. Gotō reminds us that we may have seen them around the tram stops throughout the city. They sell the leftover tobacco to nearby factories, such as the aptly named Nimble Finger Company located just inside the north entrance to the Garden. A pound of tobacco will earn a fellow M$0.60. He receives a penny for each reusable cigarette package.

The workshop near the Garden produces Patterned Waist brand cigarettes. Workers in the room unroll used butts, pile the tobacco on boards, and chop and reroll the tobacco into white paper on the dirty floor. The product is then repackaged. A pack of ten repurposed cigarettes costs a mere M$0.06. If that is too expensive a person can buy three for M$0.02, a bargain for the residents of the Garden of Grand Vision.[22]

Nothing in the Fujiadian area goes to waste.

THE SERVICE SECTOR

Gotō Reiji describes men and women who are thin as rails with bones showing through their skins, folks who die of exposure and malnutrition. Yet this is not for lack of affordable food in the area. In the mornings along Long Spring Street a hungry person can find all sorts of makeshift stalls selling *shaobing youtiao* and soybean milk—the standard Chinese breakfast. (*Shaobing youtiao* is a flat piece of fried bread wrapped around a cruller. It is actually pretty good on a cold morning with a bowl of freshly made, piping hot soybean milk.) In the evenings merchants sell rice, vegetables, and fish. Inside the Garden of Grand Vision or the rear building the Village of Grand Vision, a range of restaurants offer food at reasonable prices. The restaurateurs inside the building have bought their franchises, and they pay rent to Zou the landlord and taxes to the Harbin City Office. Gotō has made a study of these businessmen with all his usual attention to detail.

Li Xuejing, for instance, a man from Shandong Province, is a Chinese Muslim. In 1928 he migrated to Manchuria. He opened a fish store in Dalian before he and his brother moved north to Harbin. They opened the Increase Fortune Food Shop in the Village of Grand Vision, paying M$200 for the franchise and M$16 monthly rent. Each year they pay M$37.50 in taxes. Each day they bring in M$40 selling food. They use thirty pounds of flour and twenty pounds of rice each day. They get their flour from a cooperative at the local mosque where each month they can buy seven bags at reduced rates. When they need more, they buy on the black market for one pound at M$0.30. They buy rice for one pound at M$0.32. These supplies, ordered from a warehouse, are delivered at night. The Li family employs two people who are paid M$20 and M$12 a month, respectively.[23]

On the same floor, a hungry resident of the Garden of Grand Vision can stop at the New New Soy Milk Shop. Here Yang Zhongyin, also from Shandong Province, his wife, and his three children earn their living. Yang came to Manchukuo in 1936. He began by selling juice, tobacco, and breakfast foods from a pushcart in the streets of the Fujiadian neighborhood. In the spring of 1940, he pulled together the M$100 that allowed him to settle into a commercial space in the Village of Grand Vision. He pays monthly rent and M$33.40 in yearly tax to the city. Every month he uses three bushels of soybeans, 150 pounds of soy oil, and 120 pounds of sugar. The Yang family is Muslim.[24]

In the front building, sixty-five-year-old Shang Youwen owns the House of Shang Soy Milk Shop. Shang Youwen came to Manchukuo in 1934. Like the others he came from Shandong Province, where he could find no work. He sold breakfast foods in Mukden before coming to Harbin. Like Yang, he paid M$100 for the franchise and pays M$20 for monthly rent. He buys eight bags of flour each month, 150 pounds of soy oil (which he gets for one pound at M$0.65 on the black market), 120 pounds of sugar (which he gets for one pound at M$0.40), and fruit. He supports a wife, a child, and three employees.[25]

That Li and Yang would be Muslim is not as rare as it might seem. A Muslim minority lives in China. Most belong to ethnic groups, the Uighurs of West China being the most conspicuous. There are Han Chinese families who have adopted Islam. They would be more comfortable living in the multiethnic border region. Harbin restaurants signal their cuisine by placing a lantern by the door: red for regular Chinese cuisine, black for food that is *halal*, green for vegetarian Buddhist food.

Shops like the House of Shang Soy Milk Shop are decent places where a person can sit down to enjoy a meal. The food is nourishing and cheap. Offerings include steamed meat-filled dumplings called *shaomai* (M$0.02 each), a breakfast of *shaobing* (M$0.03), varieties of fruit (M$0.05 each), a bowl of rice (M$0.10), fish (M$0.10), or soy milk (M$0.06). Outside, along the road in back of the Garden complex, we find a different sort of food being offered.

Along the sides of the road, food stalls appear each day, making a temporary food court. A hungry fellow can buy tea, fruit, salted dried fruit, corn porridge, fried bread, rice gruel, watermelon, and corn cakes. One dish, called "deep-fried devil," is actually a deep-fried corn cake. The name commemorates an evil bureaucrat who met his fate at the hands of an angry mob that treated the official in much the same way the cook handles the corn batter.[26]

One old man sitting in the sun by a fence has a bucket, a cup, and five bowls. He pays M$9 each month for the right to collect leftovers from area restaurants. The food is passed to him each evening by bus boys working in the better restaurants of the city. The old man cooks these scraps together in a stew to sell on the street. One portion of the stew costs M$0.03. People line up to buy their cupful, pushing against the person already drinking his portion to hurry him along. One beggar laps up the oil in the bottom of the bowl like a dog. Needless to say, the bowls don't get washed between customers.

BEGGING

Of all of the laborers to be found in the Fujiadian neighborhood, Gotō Reiji considered beggars the most professional. They have a guild with an organization centered in Beijing. They have local bosses to whom they contribute dues and from whom they collect in times of hardship. They help one another. They perfect their personal presentations to maximize public sympathy. Despite their sorry appearances, they are often better off than others in the area. They are known as the Begging Gang.

The local bosses are the center of the begging profession. In Fujiadian they are called "sitting in the square," indicating that each one reigns over a specific turf. They are also called "top of the staff," which is better translated perhaps as "holder of the staff." The title refers to a rod in the leader's possession. The rod represents both the beggar chief's authority and imperial will. It is said that the stick originally came from an emperor who gave it to the top boss of the beggars as a symbol of control. Therefore the staff is wrapped in yellow cotton, yellow being the imperial color. The pole can also become an instrument of punishment when necessary.[27]

Being the boss of the beggars is a powerful position. A boss oversees a core of street people who transfer to him the obedience usually given to a parent. This is called "flowers worship the staff." A child entering a group becomes an apprentice. He will be addressed as "little brother" until he grows up to take his own place on the street. After becoming an adult, the beggar moves through the ranks of the hierarchy.

The boss of the beggars assigns posts in his area. If there is a dispute between members of the guild, the boss acts as arbiter, settling the question. His decisions are taken as decrees and strictly obeyed. The position is lucrative. Guild members turn their daily take over to the boss. He then redistributes the money to each member as a daily allowance.

The beggar chief will exact a kind of informal tax—Gotō adds a question mark after the word "tax"—on the well-to-do of the city. During important life events—a birthday, for instance—the beggar chief will show up to the house where celebrations will take place. He offers congratulations as a representative of all the beggars, for which he receives a donation for his good wishes. In return he pastes a paper on the door. "May all gathered here on this happy occasion enjoy themselves with no disturbances." Should the householder be stingy with his gifts, no paper appears, and many filthy beggars will show up to the event begging for alms from the guests. Gotō presents this as a Harbin practice; in fact, this kind of social extortion could be found throughout China.[28]

Gotō notes that there are two types of beggars in Harbin. The professional beggars belong to the guild. Then there are those who have come from outside. These are migrants fallen on hard times who turn to begging in desperation. Gotō never met a single professional beggar in the Garden of Grand Vision. Even professional beggars found the place too dreary.

Successful beggars had a way to catch attention as they worked the streets. Each man or woman created some method that could be flamboyant, grotesque, or pathetic to attract public sympathy, necessary to draw in money. Gotō gives the routines names as he introduces us to some of the beggars in Harbin. He asks his readers to watch closely the next time they hurry through the streets. As we follow Gotō, we will notice beggars among us.

On Second Street, for instance, in front of Thunder Asia Market, we see a crazy-looking lout begging for coins. Around the corner, a woman with three children holds a sign reading, "We came to Harbin looking for our father." On Sixth Street, in the dirt in the middle of a busy tram stop, a woman calls out, "Pity me, pity me, pity me." A beggar sits by the road with puss-seeping sores on his outstretched legs. A beggar in the sun picks at lice and pops them in his mouth.

The theme of migration and loss plays well in Harbin, where most people have come from someplace else. On another street we meet an old woman with crooked teeth. She holds a sign reading, "I came here three years ago looking for my husband. He has died. Please help me." Each beggar has a distinctive cry. They roam around spots near tobacco kiosks and bus or trolley depots, where they hold out empty cans hoping to attract spare change.

Gotō calls the most common begging routine "backpacking." Beggars carrying burlap bags wander neighborhoods, going from house to house, asking for food or used clothes. Men like fifty-year-old Fifth Little Wang work in a group with other backpackers. They address each other like family members.

Some beggars develop routines that verge on street performance. One sort of begging, called "riches come in number," involves accosting potential donors on the street. A beggar carries a simple musical instrument, usually bamboo clappers, both large and small, to beat out a rhythm. He wanders the market streets, stopping when he finds a crowd. He pushes his face in front of a likely donor, spitting out a song: "Sir, you are so white. In the future you will grow rich," or "Sir, you are so robust, your butt must weigh half a pound." Those who pass him by without making a contribution hear a different tune:

"Sir, your heart is black. You will soon go broke."
"Sir, you are too cruel. You will be fucked by a chicken."
"Don't give money. I don't care. Save it to buy your coffin."
"You don't give? I won't beg! See how fast your children die!"
"Hey! Sir! Don't get mad. The sooner you give the sooner I leave!"[29]

Some go even beyond the patter of flattery and insult. Those who can sing opera arias or play instruments for people passing by.

Gotō lists three kinds of instruments used by beggars. Some are made of bone. Poor Mouth Liu uses this kind of tool. Gotō describes him as thin and short with a greenish color to his face. He carries a cow's thighbone with a bell and streamers attached to it. He sits outside the Great New Department Store on the main street of Fujiadian. His begging song, accompanied by the bells, includes a plug for the store's goods. Liu plays the bones in front of the Garden, singing his own dark praise to the building and its women.[30]

Some, like Big Belly Wang, carry bamboo clappers. Wang, as his name implies, is a hefty fellow with a dark red face. In his right hand he carries two bamboo slats tied together on one end. In the other hand he has a smaller version of the first. He can make a variety of sounds and rhythms, with which he sings along.[31]

Then there are the beggars who accompany themselves with bowls. Pesky Mao is this kind of beggar. He is only sixteen or seventeen years old. He is dark in complexion, moderate of height, and full of active eccentricity. His hair cascades over his face. He paints his cheeks white with flour. He bangs together two bowls to make music to accompany his songs.[32]

Gimpy Sun accompanies himself with an improvised drum made of a bamboo bucket covered with leather. The contraption is fairly large, three feet wide by six feet tall. He pushes it through the streets as he sings. He neither thanks those who give money nor curses those who do not.[33]

Zhang the Idiot carries two rusty swords. He uses them to strike at his arms and torso in a grand display of macho bravado. Zhang works the gambling stands in the neighborhood.[34]

Zhao the Barbarian, who is blind and bald with a drippy nose, beats himself all over his body with pieces of brick. He kneels in the road surrounded by waves of people. He puts a tattered bamboo basket in front of him to catch any donations that might come his way. He sings in a nerve-shattering voice, "Ladies and Gentlemen! Boys and Girls! Please give this blind man some money! Spare this man a penny!"[35]

Blind Wang wanders the streets like a sick horse. He carries a bamboo cane, holding out a straw hat for money. He sings, "Come all you good-looking and wealthy people. Pity the blind man."

Some play on the religious sentiments of the crowd. Ma the Old Beggar is twisted in body. His deformed hands and feet become his selling point. He drags himself through the dirt all day, crying out, "Do good!" or "Accumulate virtue!" and promising merit for a happy rebirth. In the same league, we meet Old Woman Huang. She has rheumy eyes. Her body is so contorted that her hands look like fighting chickens. She walks about with a stick and a tin can for money, crying out, "Pity me! Pity me!"

Paralyzed Wu can barely walk. He uses blocks of wood to help him drag his body through the streets. Gotō describes him as looking like a dog scratching in the street surrounded by waves of people.[36]

Having a catchy routine is clearly necessary for beggars the world over. George Orwell, like Gotō, spent time investigating life in the London slums. Unlike Gotō, he lived in a flophouse. He described people much like Zhao the Barbarian, calling them street performers, sidewalk artists, or screevers. One of Orwell's informants, Bozo, told him how a beggar had to cut the money out of passers by. "You know," he said, "you don't take a bob if you just sit and look at them." At best Bozo expected half a penny, but without some kind of "backchat," nothing would be forthcoming. Begging is a performance. As such it is hard, dirty work.[37]

Gotō paints a vivid picture of song and humor amid the noise, poverty, and physical deformity. Any one of these beggars looks absolutely pathetic. Still, Gotō tells us not to feel sorry for them. They enjoy themselves. Businesses in the area cater to them. As we came to the neighborhood, Gotō pointed out a flophouse called the Flower Shop. He reminds us of that as he tells us that in Manchuria "flower" is slang for "beggar." The Flower Shop is a flophouse for the beggars. Moreover Gotō finds these street people to be the most humane and virtuous of the residents in the area. Their organization provides them with the kinds of social connections that provide the security that is the basis of a good life.[38]

Yet Harbin developed a reputation for beggars. Journalists who reported on the new nation for an audience back home did not help the situation. One travel writer commented on the increase in beggars he experienced over years of travel to Harbin. He noticed Russian beggars in areas that their countrymen might frequent. The entrance to the Autumn Forest Department Store was one location favored by Russians down on their luck. On his way to Harbin for a third visit, he added, someone stole his luggage from the train. This made him sad. Harbin would be such a lovely town if only it could be swept clean of the beggars, he said.[39]

Those newcomers who came to Manchuria looking for a better life were among the throngs of men and women who did not make out so well. Manchuria, after all, was a frontier, where a person should find opportunity, make a living, and be able to send some money back home. But when opportunities proved elusive, many migrants fell on hard times. They then looked to the streets as their only recourse for survival in a harsh world. Unfortunately they found that even as a beggar or thief, having connections was an important ingredient of success.

Righteous Sun Street (1938 postcard from the collection of the author).

Jingyu Street today (photograph taken by the author).

Pingkangli, or the Circle (from the collection of Olga Bakich).

Chinese baroque (photograph taken by the author).

Chinese baroque neighborhood restoration (photograph taken by the author).

5

oↄↄ

Contested Land

After my return to Harbin as Zhang Zuolin's agent, outlaws of all sorts, racketeers, smugglers, white-slave traders and the underworld gentry declared war against me as openly as I had done against them.

—Amieto Vespa[1]

If the Russians conquer Manchuria, [I will] submit to the Russians. The highest goal of the people is to live.

—Zou Xisan, owner of the Garden of Grand Vision[2]

Everyone in Manchuria came from someplace else—or their parents did. There were notable exceptions of course. The descendants of the Juren tribe, whose ancestors had penetrated the Great Wall in 1644 to establish the last Chinese dynasty, could claim rightful possession of the land, had they wished. Their numbers were far too few to make such a claim. Gotō Reiji, Satō Shin'ichirō, and Katō Toyotaka were all migrants. They crossed the strait from Japan to stake their future careers in a new world. The same holds true for Zou Xisan, the slumlord, and for Feng Dengdiao, a gentleman beggar who became both a police informant and Gotō's friend. Han Chinese people made up the majority of those who would be called Manchukuoans after the nation was formally established in 1932. In the early 1900s, Chinese sovereignty in the Northeast was anything but clear.

Japanese military victory over Russia, a European power, in 1905 demonstrated once again the growing weakness of the Chinese Qing Dynasty. Its futile attempts at modern reform could not stem the tide of revolution.

The mounting failures of the moribund imperial house were not lost on Chinese people. By 1911, one in a series of spontaneous anti-Qing uprisings tipped the balance against the dying regime. Action began accidentally. As often happens with homemade devices, bomb-making Chinese revolutionaries fouled up the explosive recipe. The bomb went off, giving away their location. Instead of arresting them, the local army garrison, fed up with Qing corruption, joined in the uprising.

Within a month, the poorly planned action became a revolutionary movement. Sun Yat-sen, known as the father of the Chinese Revolution, was in Denver, Colorado. News of the revolt came to him as a surprise. Yet change was in the air; in fact, it was long overdue. By 1912 a republic of sorts had replaced the Qing Dynasty.

Sun Yat-sen was recognized as the head of the Revolutionary Alliance. This group, dedicated to ousting the Manchus, became the Nationalist Party (Guomindang) after 1912. Although Sun spent the revolutionary years far from China, he was a dynamic speaker with name recognition. He traveled widely, raising money and support for the cause wherever overseas Chinese settled. Sun spent much of his exile in Japan. There he joined a large community of Chinese students seeking to learn the secrets of Japanese modern success. In fact, Chinese people generally refer to Sun as Sun Zhongshan, the given name being the Chinese pronunciation of his Japanese alias, Nakayama. Every Chinese city, Harbin included, has a Zhongshan Avenue, Square, or Boulevard. His portrait graces Taiwan's currency. His face glared down at me from the Taiwan classroom wall where I studiously failed to master Chinese poetry.

Sun was quite clear about the need for a republican Chinese nation, one that would be democratic, economically viable, and a source of national pride for its people. Although he admired Western institutions, he wanted to free China from Western interference in national affairs. He did not like the excesses of pure capitalism; nor did he care for the violence inherent in Marxism. He called his philosophy the Three People's Principles—democracy, nationalism, and people's livelihood. He remained unclear about the way Manchuria would fit into his new China. In 1894, while organizing in Honolulu, he spoke of Manchuria as an alien place, saying, "The Manchus must be driven out. We will establish a republic. Our goal is to drive the Manchus back beyond the wall, then China will flourish."[3]

Satō Shin'ichirō, the scholar among the three police investigators, wrote about Sun Yat-sen after the war. He pointed out that the hero of the Chinese revolution, had he lived, would most likely have tolerated Japan's actions in Manchuria. In 1900, for instance, as Sun was seeking Japanese help with yet another uprising, he told a friend that after the revolution, Manchuria should be given to the Japanese. Six years later Sun admitted to a Russian fellow revolutionary that he did not have a clear idea as to what should become of Manchuria. By 1911, the year of the final uprising and the end of China's dynastic history, Sun had to concede that public opinion had annexed the Northeast. In the year of the revolution he apologized to a Japanese friend that, although he considered Japan a second home, many of his country's young heroes were suspicious of Japan in Manchuria.[4]

No one could question that Sun Yat-sen was anything but a true Chinese patriot; yet, when in Japan, he traveled in political circles that included ultranationalist activists. Many of these men became soldiers of fortune—the so-called China *ronin*—whose activities would later help separate Manchuria from China. In 1913, on a fund-raising tour in southern Japan, Sun witnessed a judo exhibition. Satomi Hajime, the young man who won the tournament, would go on to become a Chinese linguist, a newspaper reporter, and a supplier of illicit, and therefore untraceable, funds to those scheming to create a new Manchurian nation.[5]

Why would Japanese nationalists help someone like Sun Yat-sen? The easy answer is that they were spies. Although true, this explanation does not convey the complexities of the long-term relationships involved. In the early years of Sun's career, China *ronin* helped him out of the belief that guiding China along the path taken by Japan would cement Japanese influence in Asia. The vision shared by Sun and his Japanese activist friends was one of pan-Asianism. After 1912, as the Chinese republic failed, Japanese nationalists grew cynical. As Japanese adventurers advised warlord groups, they became convinced that guidance would require a sterner hand.[6]

After 1913 the heartland of China fell into a patchwork of violence instead of the orderly republic for which Sun hoped. The Chinese republic proved fragile and as disorganized as the revolt that led to its creation. By 1916 the republican fabric had disintegrated into civil war. Regional warlords dominated the first period of chaos. They fought one another over pieces of territory from which they gouged all the revenues they could. In the Northeast, Zhang Zuolin (1873–1928), a bandit turned army officer, held power in Manchuria. His government operated outside the Japanese railroad zone, away from the Liaodong Peninsula and its important port city, Dalian. However as Zhang consolidated control from his capital in Mukden, he became a threat to Japanese interests. His days were numbered.

Zhang came to prominence in Manchuria by helping the Japanese army with information about Russia during the Russo-Japanese War. Thereafter Zhang kept an uneasy peace with the Japanese Kantō Army, accepting Japanese advisors while remaining very much his own man. This allowed him to assert his authority in Manchuria after the 1911 revolution. From bandit he became military governor of the province. In the 1920s he created a semi-independent state in Manchuria. He would have flourished there had he not been lured into the civil wars south of the Wall. Tempted by the prospect of ruling North China, he extended his armies into Beijing.

Zhang Zuolin could be written off as just another warlord in a brutal ballet of civil anarchy that lasted from 1916 to 1927. Yet his territory occupied such a strategic location that his ambitions and his brutal death formed a tragic prelude to the events that led to the Second World War in Asia. The man's character is hard to qualify. Japanese military officers in the 1920s considered him corrupt and incompetent. More to the point, they could not trust his loyalty. They used his mismanagement of Manchuria as justification for extreme actions they would take in 1931. Colonel Kōmoto Daisaku, who engineered Zhang's death in 1928, wrote with pride about his role in the assassination in the magazine *Bungei Shunjū* for an admiring Japanese audience. Zhang Zuolin had picked up the habit of power, he wrote. His ambition grew; he moved into Beijing and gave himself the title field marshal. He forgot his obligations to Japan. Kōmoto himself witnessed insults to Japanese women and increasing anti-Japanese activity as he traveled incognito through Manchuria.[7]

Amieto Vespa (1888–1940), an Italian soldier of fortune, paints an entirely different picture of Zhang Zuolin. We will meet Vespa again, as he played a role in solving a dramatic murder in his adopted hometown, Harbin. Vespa came to Manchuria during the First World War as a spy for the Allied Intelligence Service. He traveled through Manchuria, Mongolia, and Siberia, searching for gunrunners and white-slave traffickers. At the end of the war, he found it dangerous to return to Italy. He remained in China, fell in love, and married a Chinese woman. Finding himself stateless, he hired on with Zhang Zuolin in 1920, continuing his work as a spy. In 1924 Vespa became a Chinese citizen.

Vespa and Kōmoto, both familiar with underground operations, could have been writing about two different people. Vespa found Zhang Zuolin the warlord to be a competent reformer. Zhang, he admits in his autobiography, was autocratic and could be vicious in dealings with his subordinates. But, Vespa assures us, life in Manchuria improved under his direction. Zhang was good at military organization and concerned with social reform in the Northeast. Vespa called him a "man of honor and courage" and "the best of all chiefs."[8]

The truth about the warlord Zhang Zuolin rests somewhere between Kōmoto's and Vespa's conflicting descriptions. In the early 1920s, the warlord had the foresight to hire an extremely competent financial officer who created reforms that enhanced the local economy. Using the Bank of Manchuria, the man set up a good tax base that brought in revenues and put the economy on a sound financial footing. Unfortunately the warlord Zhang Zuolin could not remain contentedly outside the Wall. He expanded his territory toward Beijing, only to be pushed back into Manchuria in 1922. Two years later, he tried again. By 1926 he had once again been repulsed. As surpluses in his treasury dwindled, his government printed money. He boosted revenues with an opium monopoly. Toward the end of his life, and by his own doing, Zhang Zuolin's well-run economy began to spin out of control.[9]

Opium was a natural place to turn for extra cash. Part of the Manchurian tax base came from agriculture. Especially lucrative was the opium harvest. In the south of the territory, the rich, fertile soil produced many crops. The open-frontier nature of the land attracted peasants who found that after three years' hard work they could have a productive farming homestead. As peasants considered what crops to plant, opium poppies became the natural choice. Opium brought in six times the profit of corn and eight times that of soy.

So many purple and white poppies appeared in the fields each spring that in some rural areas the population doubled during the late spring harvest time, when the flowers bloomed, dropped their petals, and produced the valuable sap. Impromptu shantytowns appeared as hired hands came to the villages to join in the labor-intensive business of making delicate incisions in the poppy pods to let the sap run free for collecting. Platoons of business folk followed the migrant farmhands: gamblers, prostitutes, actors, and puppeteers. For a month rural communities became like carnivals. Some likened the settlements in the countryside during the season to "Little Harbins."

Chinese often refer to opium simply as "smoke." Locals came to call the harvest season "the smoke season." Migrant workers became "smoke cutters." The newcomers chased the smoke season and lived together in drifter's smoke towns. Of course they referred to opium as black gold. Technically opium was outlawed, but there was so little concern for the law that signs openly read,

> Clear water; fragrant smoke
> Light a lamp with ease
> Beautiful women will wait upon you.[10]

Opium crops would later become a source of both revenue and headache for the Japanese-sponsored government that employed Gotō Reiji.[11]

Zou Xisan, owner of the Garden of Grand Vision, was a migrant with remarkably good luck. He prospered in Zhang Zuolin's Manchuria. It was during the warlord's reign that Zou moved to Harbin, found a position in the land office, purchased the land in Fujiadian, and built the Garden of Grand Vision. During these years he saw the Chinese population in his city grow. In the early 1920s, he most likely donated to the building funds that ensured that a Confucian temple and the Buddhist Temple of Extreme Joy took their place among the Russian church domes that dominated the Harbin skyline.

Even in the early years of Zou's sojourn to the Northeast, he would have run into Russian influence in Harbin. The earliest Russian migrants prospered working for the railway or as merchants. Russian émigrés built schools, luxurious city homes, and suitable country dachas. Tearooms catered to their tastes; department stores supplied them with the latest European fashions. Russians figured among the wealthiest and most influential in the city's early history. They built the exotic European backdrop that enchanted Japanese visitors in the 1930s.

Russian émigrés built not only churches but synagogues as well, for many of these pioneers were Jews. They found comfort in the familiar surroundings Harbin offered at a safe distance from the antisemitism back home. In Harbin Jews prospered. They contributed to the business community, the arts, sports, and entertainment. Harbin supported a strong Zionist movement, the first organization founded in 1912. This friendship was commemorated when, in 2004, then Israeli vice premier Emud Olmert visited the Harbin grave of his grandfather. Later he visited the Main Synagogue, which, like St. Sophia Cathedral, is now a museum.[12]

Suddenly, in 1917 the world turned upside down for the Russian émigrés. The October Revolution left them stateless. Most of the original Russian residents favored the old regime. Over the next several years, streams of refugees poured over the Siberian border fleeing conflict. Over a few months Harbin's population swelled with poverty-stricken Russian outcasts. The men found jobs as bodyguards or chauffeurs, like the men who drove Yanagida Momotarō and his imaginary guests on a tour of Harbin. The women turned to prostitution or danced in the cabarets, or both. Among these refugees, Amieto Vespa heard tales of white slavers trafficking women to points all around the world.

George Prujan's biography presents a snapshot of the riches-to-rags Russian experience in Harbin. Prujan grew up along with the city of Harbin. He arrived as a boy in 1903 when his father took an executive position with the Chinese Eastern Railway. At that time his family lived in a large house with stables, carriage, and staff. He attended the Harbin Engineering School, housed in an art nouveau building that is now the Harbin College of Architecture. He quit to train as a Russian cavalry officer. He claims that Japanese owned all the laundries at the time, from which they spied on Russians in preparation for the coming Russo-Japanese War. As we know from Captain Ishimitsu Makiyo's tale of espionage, Prujan was right. He just missed the spying photographer's studio.

At the Harbin Engineering School, Prujan followed a liberal academic curriculum, despite the school's name. He learned Chinese language and became an accomplished gymnast and horseman. These skills served him well, not only during the First World War—he served as an officer during the war's last year—but in the desperate years of the 1920s. When Prujan returned to Harbin in 1918, he found the city unchanged by the European conflict. His job prospects, however, were not as bright as they might have been before the war.

Through a friend's introduction, George Prujan got a job as a military advisor working for none other than the warlord Zhang Zuolin. Prujan did not stay long in the warlord's employ; nor did he give an opinion about the man's character. Prujan left the next year to fight against the Bolsheviks in Siberia, an ill-fated attempt to restore the Russian monarchy.

When Prujan returned to Harbin for a second time in 1921, the city had changed drastically. White Russian refugees flooded the town. Prujan could only find jobs as a guard for the Chinese Eastern Railway and a swimming instructor. With prospects bleak in the city of his youth, Prujan emigrated to the United States as soon as he could. His description of a city teeming with poor White Russian refugees depicts the general decline of his countrymen in Harbin of the 1920s.[13]

Population statistics reflect Prujan's life experiences writ large. In 1912, 43,091 Russians lived in Harbin, where they enjoyed relative ease. The number dropped to 34,118 in 1916 as many, like Prujan, left to join the war on the eastern front. Shortly after the October revolution, Harbin newspapers described the situation. The *Far Eastern Press* announced on March 31, 1918, "In recent days many refugees have come from Blagoveshchensk on the Siberian border. Because they have nowhere to stay, masses of them are in the streets. The Railroad Governing Board held a meeting to find a place for them." By September, the same paper would proclaim, "An extraordinary number of Russians fleeing from danger [are] passing through Vladivostok and Blagoveshchensk, into Harbin." That year the Russian population rose to 60,200. But the floodgates would not open until the failure of the counterrevolution in Siberia, which Prujan himself had joined. By 1923, the Russian population topped 200,000 as both refugees and remnants of the White Army poured into Harbin. These newcomers included Yul Brynner's family and Natalie Wood's mother.[14]

Harbin was a city rich in schools for such a remote location. There were the Russian schools, the engineering school, and a rabbinical school. Not to be outdone, in the 1920s the Japanese government established a girl's school, a high school, and the Harbin University. More importantly,

Japanese officials and military personnel, including Katō, Gotō's young assistant, attended the Harbin school to specialize in Russian language and literature.

Japanese living in the city counted Russians as their friends and neighbors. If they learned any foreign language at all, it was Russian, not Chinese. Visitors to the city liked to describe visits with Russian families. The experience of taking tea from a samovar reappears in the many memoirs of the city. Russian poverty brought a different kind of spectacle. Japanese visitors marveled at the sight—rare for someone living in Asia at the time—of Caucasians doing menial tasks usually reserved for Chinese coolies.

Japanese who moved to Harbin in the 1920s found they could live in a European style unimaginable back home. Yanagida Momotarō, the expatriate who penned such a vivid tour of Harbin, arrived in Manchuria as a young man to take up a position as a clerk for a Japanese trading company. In Japan, his salary had been rather small. Yet in Harbin he lived in a large European-style house, furnished with sofas, cabinets, large beds, and bookcases. Thanks to Russians like George Prujan, forced by circumstances to leave, all sorts of luxury items went on sale. Lavish homes, with carriages and stables, demanded the expense of a staff; nor could such items be transported abroad. Russians had to sell off houses, jewels, and furnishings just to survive. Yanagida benefited to his own personal comfort.[15]

Like Yanagida, Satō Shin'ichirō made Manchuria his home in the 1920s. Satō was born in northern Japan's Aomori Prefecture. His childhood was hard. His father, a man of talent, graduated from a private school. He spent ten years studying abroad in America. With those credentials he should have been successful in the last years of the 1800s, a period that saw rapid economic modernization and adaptation of ideas from the West. Instead he returned to his hometown in the North to work for local improvements. As a result, the family was poor. To make matters worse, when Satō's father died, a cousin cheated the family out of land.[16]

Satō's childhood must have been harsh. He mentions only that he experienced the old teaching style. As soon as he graduated from high school, he left home. For the next year he stayed with friends and, he tells us quite frankly, finally stopped wetting his bed at night. By the time he was nineteen years old, he had the credentials to teach at the elementary level. When he showed up for his first position, he went to see the headmaster, as good manners required. But when he got to the office, the man who would be his boss merely said, "Oh. You have arrived." The two stared at each other in stunned silence.

Later Satō learned the cause of the social awkwardness of his first day on the job. On one warm afternoon, he found the senior teacher sitting in the sunlight picking lice from his clothes. The man told Satō that the head-master wanted to hire a new teacher, but Satō was not his choice—not by a long shot. What could Satō do? He was working for a man who wished he would go away. Little more than a child himself, Satō liked teaching his students. He transferred to a different school, where he was put on night duty. He played with his charges, trying to make learning fun. In our day he would have been considered quite progressive, but this was the old school system. Teachers were meant to be strict. In no time his new headmaster told him that he was not suited to be a teacher.

In 1925, at the age of twenty, Satō transferred again, this time to the Japanese naval base in Lushun (he would have pronounced it "Ryushun"), at the southern tip of Manchuria. There he got a job teaching fifth graders in a Chinese elementary school. Again he liked his students. Whatever he said, they would all reply, "Yes, Teacher, we understand." It did not take him long to realize that, in fact, not one of them understood a thing he said. They just knew that when they said they understood, he rewarded them with a happy smile. As this dawned on him, he also felt that, with their 4,000-year heritage of history and culture, he should be learning from his students rather than the other way around. The experience drove him to study Chinese language. By the mid-1920s he was living in Beijing, gaining the skills that would bring him to the Garden of Grand Vision.[17]

In the same years that Satō immersed himself in Chinese language studies, his fellow Japanese residents in Manchuria saw their problems escalate. Those doing business endured an absolutely chaotic currency situation. All Japanese felt the sting of periodic anti-Japanese boycotts, which seemed to be especially strong in China's Northeast. Blame for these hardships fell squarely on the shoulders of Zhang Zuolin, who was neither a patriot nor a man of vision. He was a warlord with ambitions above his abilities. He milked what money he could from his people to fight useless battles in pursuit of the vain dream to extend his power into North China. That Manchuria experienced a robust economic develop-ment—as it did in the early 1920s—was due to the efforts of a capable civil governor who served at Zhang's pleasure. When this advisor died, Zhang fell victim to his own political ambition. He reversed his territory's fortunes by moving his army into Beijing, appointing himself marshal of the Republic of China, and spreading his resources too thin.

Zhang was a self-serving, brutal man not gifted with enough foresight to save himself. This became clear after 1927 when the Chinese civil war changed in nature from a free-for-all among warlords to a struggle be-tween Chiang Kai-shek's Nationalist Party and the Chinese Communist Party, soon to be led by Mao Zedong. Both organizations represented a shift from the superficial reform of the Qing Dynasty and the civil chaos left behind after the 1911 revolution produced warlords like Zhang

Zuolin. The Nationalist Party of Sun Yat-sen reorganized itself under Chiang Kai-shek in China's southern Guandong Province. From this stronghold, a new group of officers trained at the Whampoa Military Academy in modern warfare under Soviet advisors. From 1926 its graduates directed the Northern Expedition, a series of military operations to defeat one warlord after another or bring them into the Nationalist camp. By 1927, with the South secure, Chiang Kai-shek declared the southern city of Nanjing the capital of China. Beijing became Beiping. By 1928 Chiang's forces had closed in on the North.[18]

Zhang needed more money. His government began reading Chinese treaty obligations in the narrowest way possible. The patchwork of jurisdictions made this possible. Japanese businesses operating outside the railway concession zone became targets for tax increases. But the major problem vexing the entire multinational business community was the absence of a single Manchurian currency. Different banks issued their own share of specie. The Bank of Harbin was one such issuer. Its currency was worthless despite attempts to prop it up. Its value fluctuated wildly, often based on the doings of Zhang Zuolin in his North China adventures. As a result foreign businesses preferred to use stable currencies, especially US dollars and Japanese yen. To counter this, Harbin City officials issued laws demanding that all transactions be made in Harbin dollars. The laws were ignored. Even the local police commissioner, when he bought himself two new American cars, paid for them in gold-backed US dollars.[19]

George C. Hanson watched the drama unfolding around him from the American consulate in Harbin. Like Satō Shin'ichirō, Hanson found in Manchuria a place where he could thrive. And, like Satō, he had trouble with his superiors back home. Hanson was the kind of person well suited to the Manchurian landscape. Therefore his activities went beyond gathering the local news and issuing visas. This taste for adventure often got him into trouble with the US State Department.

George Hanson was not a typical diplomat of the day. He was a tall, stocky, "bear of a man" who fit into the frontier atmosphere of Manchuria. He was a hunter, a marksman, and a friend of the spy Amieto Vespa, among others in the expat community. Eventually he would be called the "mayor of Harbin" or "Mr. Manchuria." One American called Hanson the "king of Manchuria," a "man whose heart fills the whole of him, which is large."[20] Born in 1883 to a solidly middle-class family from Bridgeport, Connecticut, Hanson earned an engineering degree from Cornell University. He was adventurous. In 1909, after graduation, instead of seeking posts requiring technical skills, he entered the Foreign Service to train as a linguist. Hanson had a flair for languages. Soon he was fluent in standard Mandarin Chinese and could hold his own in several regional dialects as well. He later added Russian to his resume.

Hanson made it into the diplomatic corps through talent rather than connections. With language skills that many consuls lacked, he may have assumed he would thrive in the China service. He was wrong. Hanson had joined an elite club. In the early twentieth century, most American diplomats had private means. His colleagues had all gone to the most exclusive prep schools, then on to Harvard or Yale. They knew each other from these old school ties. It was often called a pretty good club.[21]

Salaries were low. Most of his colleagues could cover extra expenses from family trust funds. Hanson could not. His private correspondence with the State Department bubbled with constant pleas for money. When his post changed from the coastal city of Xiantou (Swatow) to inland Chongqing (Chungking) in 1919, for instance, he found the climate unhealthy and living expenses high. He pleaded for a raise, pointing out that he had been forced to sell his furniture from the old post rather than cover the cost of moving everything inland. He paid his own travel expenses.[22]

Diplomats entertain—it is part of their job. Many a deal can be struck over cocktails and dinner. As a consul, George Hanson was expected to host local business and government dignitaries, both Chinese and European. In Chungking, the British and French consulates held grand parties for the local communities on notable holidays. Hanson knew that both local government officials and Americans living in the area would expect the same of their consulate on the Fourth of July. Hanson pointed out that his yearly stipend of US$2,500 barely covered his living expenses, let alone grand entertainments.[23]

After two years in Chongqing, Hanson transferred back to coastal Fuzhou (Foochow). His entertainment expenses increased dramatically in the port city. He made contact with local Chinese officials, which, he pointed out, brought lucrative jobs for American companies. He described his successes in detail in his letters to his bosses in Washington, DC. He wanted a promotion to consul class four, with its annul salary of $4,500. This would put him at the same level as his predecessors. "You have not distinguished yourself for activity or efficiency," was the reply.[24]

George Hanson got along with his local Chinese colleagues markedly better than with his own government. Local officials liked working with an American consul who spoke their language. Who would not? He was tirelessly curious. He ventured into the countryside wherever he was posted. As he traveled he made acquaintances and picked up useful local knowledge. His trips outside his post city met with sharp criticism from the State Department, but the information he gathered proved useful on more than one occasion.

In 1921, just before Hanson left Fuzhou for Harbin, the military governor of the province called on him to solve a problem. Local bandits had stolen US$8,000 from the United Methodist Episcopal Mission in Xiamen

(Amoy), a large city to the south. Xiamen had its own American consulate, but the military governor turned to Hanson in Fuzhou to handle the problem—which he did, winning the thanks of the local Chinese government. But when Hanson asked his own department to reimburse the US$36 he paid out in travel expenses, he received a reprimand for his troubles. The department did not appreciate the way he had upstaged his colleague in Xiamian. Nevertheless, handling problems with bandits would become one of Hanson's strong suits once he reached outlaw-infested Manchuria.[25]

Hanson transferred to Harbin just before Christmas 1922. The consul could not have found the deep cold of the Siberian winter welcoming. Yet Harbin would be his home for the next ten years. He would find in its rugged wilderness a place that matched his personality. Yet he went with no pay raise and no stipend. His Chinese clerk began seeking other employment. Hanson immediately sent a letter requesting both promotion and a raise. Food in Harbin was more expensive than in China proper. He had no place to entertain. He had to travel by rented horse cart while his Japanese and British counterparts afforded chauffeured cars.[26]

Perhaps George Hanson did not possess the kind of personality that would thrive at diplomatic parties. He was outspoken, a trait that would prove his undoing. But in the frozen North, he hit his stride. He was an avid outdoorsman. As soon as he took up the new position, he began entertaining American visitors to Manchuria, escorting them on hunting expeditions into the northern wilds. Dealing with bandits was one of Hanson's talents. He was renowned for, among other things, securing the release of "pigheaded missionaries" kidnapped by bandits by sitting down for a drink with their captors and telling them dirty jokes in Chinese.[27]

On one hunting trip Hanson demonstrated this talent. He and his party of several prominent American businessmen traveled north by train, which derailed en route. While the Chinese crew complained about faulty Russian workmanship, a band of Mongolian freebooters attacked. Hanson managed to talk his party's way out of danger, but in the process he and his guests spent some time at the local police office. The decrepit building lacked decoration except for a display of severed ears strung up with wire in the courtyard.[28]

Yet Hanson received consistently lukewarm performance reviews. Often chastised for traveling away from his post, he was branded a maverick. "The Department has had trouble over Mr. Hanson for years," read his 1930 review. This was because "he had a penchant for doing what he wanted without regard to rules or regulations."[29] Raises and promotions came slowly, often requiring open prodding on Hanson's part, despite letter after letter of support and praise arriving at the US State Department from American businessmen who concluded lucrative deals or made valuable business connections because of him. In one of many, a manager from a New York City bank wrote to Henry Stimson, then secretary of state, testifying to Hanson's value in his own business ventures in Harbin: "He gets on with whites and reds [exiles and Soviets]. He speaks Russian with both."[30]

As part of his job, Hanson sent in monthly reports to the US State Department. His description of conditions in Harbin verifies many of the complaints voiced by the local Japanese community in the Northeast. His list could have come from the Japanese consul himself, although it lacked the later man's rancor.

Point: Japanese doing business along the rail lines outside the city were taxed heavily with the claim that they operated outside the concession and so were outside the treaty's reach.
Point: There was an attempt to drive out the yen. The warlord's government demanded all transactions be made in the hated Harbin currency. Most businesses, including the Chinese Eastern Railway, which kept its accounts in yen at the Soviet Delbank, preferred to use the safer yen or dollar.
Point: The warlord's government set up telegraph and rail lines in competition with Japanese lines and in violation of treaties.
Point: The local official promoted anti-Japanese activities.
Point: Chinese authorities cancelled Japanese leases held on the racetrack.

The last point distressed Hanson, who remarked, "It is the end of racing. The Russians have some fine horses."[31]

In 1928 Zhang Zuolin felt the pressure of change. With his Manchurian economy weakening and the new Nationalist Army pushing in from the south, he opted to join the Nationalists rather than losing everything. He retreated home from Beijing to Mukden, his capital. On June 4, 1928, as his train approached his native city, it crossed beneath the South Manchuria Railway. At the precise moment that Zhang's car passed under the Japanese-owned tracks, a well-placed bomb exploded, ending Zhang Zuolin's life in a ball of fire. American consul George C. Hanson reported to the American State Department from his post in Harbin. "The month passed quietly," he wrote, "in spite of temporary unrest caused by the death of Zhang Zuolin."[32] The assassination drama in Mukden notwithstanding, currency problems dominated conversations in the clubs and offices in Harbin.

George Hanson, fluent in both Chinese and Russian, was a good source for what was happening in Manchuria. During the month of June, he spoke to a government official who had been accompanying the ill-fated warlord on his way home from Beijing. The official described the fiery attack that destroyed three rail cars. He claimed that the bombs fell from above as Zhang's train, traveling on Chinese-owned track, passed under a bridge owned by the Japanese South Manchuria Railway. Both men noticed an increasing number of Japanese tourists strolling along the Songhua riverbank. Hanson suspected these sightseers were really Japanese spies.[33] As usual, George Hanson's instinct was right on the money.

6

⚭

Conflict

Recently Chinese people from Shandong Province have been coming in waves as migrants to the eastern three provinces. Shouldn't our fellow countrymen in Manchuria take precautions against this?

—Amakasu Masahiko[1]

I want to say a word to my colleagues. I hope that you will live up to my principles. Do not speak, do not get excited, and do not be conspicuous. You must be quiet and simply stab, stick, cut, and shoot. . . . Just sacrifice your life.

—Asahi Heigo, ultranationalist[2]

Kōmoto Daisaku thought that killing the warlord whom Japanese officers in the Kantō Army no longer trusted would bring the Northeast under control. He was wrong. Zhang Xueliang (1901–2001), the warlord's eldest son, lived the life of a playboy in Shanghai, where he patronized cabarets and nurtured a healthy opium addiction. To the Japanese plotters, friends of Kōmoto Daisaku, he must have seemed an easy man to manipulate. Not so. The brutal murder of Zhang Zuolin, an admittedly brutal father, sobered his son up overnight. Zhang Xueliang relinquished his playboy life, returned to Manchuria, and actively worked against the Japanese living in his homeland.[3]

US Consul George C. Hanson reported an unexpected quiet after the death of the warlord Zhang Zuolin in 1928. Within a year, uneasy calm gave way to explosive anti-Japanese boycotts. On May 3, 1929, for instance, 3,000 students in Harbin held anti-Japanese demonstrations.

Crowds gathered in Fujiadian. Marchers made speeches as they snaked their way from Daowai, winding through the Nangang district, before turning north into Daoli. They stopped at crowded street corners along the way, giving more speeches, setting off firecrackers, and proudly carrying pictures of Sun Yat-sen. They agitated to have the flag of the Nationalist government in Nanjing fly in Manchuria as well. The Japanese consul protested. He demanded that the local authorities contain anti-Japanese agitation—to no avail. Three weeks later 5,000 students staged a larger demonstration. The intensity of the anti-Japanese activity provided an excuse for the coming preemptive strike.[4]

When Gotō Reiji talks about Chinese disorganization, he is reflecting on the failure of the 1911 revolution. He, like many, saw the hopelessly unending civil war and the cruelty, veniality, and petty mindedness of the warlords. He compared this to the progress of Japan, ranked third in world power by the 1920s. He ignored, underneath the political chaos, a growing grassroots Chinese nationalism, albeit one without strong leadership. In the 1920s that force gave rise to loud and vocal anti-Japanese boycotts, especially among students in China's modern universities.

For people like Gotō—and, more importantly, for his superior officers in the Japanese Kantō Army in Manchuria—anti-Japanese boycotts proved the growing need for decisive action to protect Japanese interests in Asia. Could they trust the Nationalist Party, now under the control of Chiang Kai-shek? They certainly did not trust the Chinese Communist Party, especially with Soviet Russia threatening from the north. When Kōmoto Daisaku bragged about his role in planning the assassination of the warlord Zhang Zuolin, he cited Chinese actions against Japanese interests as his motive.[5]

Kōmoto Daisaku orchestrated Zhang Zuolin's fiery death. For his trouble, he was recalled to Tokyo in response to international protests. Within a year, a ship docked at Dalian carrying a passenger who would play a pivotal role in China's Northeast. In the Japanese romance of Manchuria, no name stands out like that of Amakasu Masahiko (1891–1945). Born in northeastern Japan, he was the eldest of nine children. His policeman father and his mother both came from samurai families with ancient lineages. Both parents, strict and hardworking, would pass this trait on to their son. At his court-martial, after his fate changed for the worse, his lawyer adduced his illustrious ancestors as a point in his favor.

Amakasu was fourteen years old at the height of the Russo-Japanese War. Tales told by his teachers of heroic soldiers in the field caught the boy's fancy. He chose a military career and thrived in the harsh barracks life of the military academy. From his first year at the school, Amakasu gained a reputation as a sharp student, dedicated to the emperor. At school he met Tōjō Hideki (1884–1948). As a general, Tōjō would become the wartime prime minister of Japan (1941–1944). With his sharp face and round glasses, he supplied the face of the enemy caricatured in American propaganda posters. At the time, however, a young Tōjō, focused on an army career rather than political ambitions, taught at the military academy. As he came to know Amakasu, he took an interest in the younger man's career, beginning an uneasy relationship between the two.

Amakasu graduated with honor and with good connections. He moved quickly through the ranks, beginning in the infantry before securing a coveted transfer into the Kempeitai, or military police. The Kempeitai, like the German SS, acquired a most fearsome reputation among the Japanese government's critics at home and opponents abroad. Yet, for a young officer, a posting in the Kempeitai was a sure road to success. In 1923, however, events took a course that would bring Amakasu fame of a sort, while ending his military career.

On September 1, 1923, a massive earthquake rocked the eastern plain of Japan. The initial shock leveled entire neighborhoods of Tokyo and Yokohama. The quake came as women tended fires for the noonday meal. The resulting firestorms turned swaths of urban landscape to ash. In the panic that followed, suspicions of Korean duplicity swept through the city. Thousands of Koreans had migrated to Japan seeking employment opportunities closed to them at home. They came as colonial subjects, taking the worst jobs and enduring a prejudice that lingers against Korean residents in Japan to this day. After the quake rumors that Korean subjects had poisoned the drinking water circulated among the hysterical population of cities reduced to rubble. Between 3,000 and 6,000 Korean scapegoats lost their lives as victims of fear-induced violence (although the estimates vary radically, the ugly ferocity remains the same).[6]

In the midst of destruction, panic, and random slaughter, Amakasu Masahiko led local police in rounding up labor union activists. The group captured one popular leader, Ōsugi Sakae (1885–1923), along with Itō Noe, his lover, and Ōsugi's six-year-old nephew, who lived with the couple at the time. All three were savagely beaten and strangled, their corpses disposed of without ceremony. Ōsugi had been an outspoken political figure and advocate of free love throughout the 1910s and into the early 1920s. Itō was a famous feminist and author. The murders, especially of the young boy, created a public scandal. The publicity set in motion a military investigation.

Amakasu was court-martialed, found guilty, and sent to military prison. He is referred to as "Captain Amakasu of the Ōsugi Murder Case" in both Japanese and Chinese sources.[7] Throughout the rest of his eventful life, he never escaped the notoriety of this one episode. His younger brother felt that the stigma made him a lonely person, despite his magnetic personality. Everywhere Amakasu went, the story followed. Upon meeting him for the first time, acquaintances all remember the thought "Oh! This is the murderer of Ōsugi!" jumping into their minds—and often out of their mouths in greeting.[8] The scene is repeated in the many memoirs featuring the man.

One of Amakasu's many friends recalled a meal the two shared in a Japanese restaurant in Dalian. After eating, Amakasu lounged in his seat, sipping whiskey, his drink of choice. He brooded with a sad, faraway look in his eyes. The friend, perhaps uncomfortable in the silence, ventured to ask, "Is it the ghost of Ōsugi's nephew?" Amakasu bolted up in his seat. "Even you think of me this way?" he asked. The friend apologized for his insensitivity. But the episode shows the depth of the stigma Amakasu carried with him. He is remembered for the murder to this day.[9]

Amakasu spent four years in prison for his crime, only to be pardoned by imperial decree. After his release he fled Japan, spending two years as an exile in France. There he enjoyed the bohemian life, living in Paris with expatriate Japanese artists. In 1930 he returned home, crossing immediately to Manchuria, where his former army colleagues welcomed him as a kindred spirit, if no longer a brother officer.

Amakasu went to Manchuria harboring the same ideals as Kōmoto Daisaku, who had plotted and carried out the murder of Zhang Zuolin two years earlier. Like Kōmoto and most Japanese living in Manchuria, Amakasu considered the situation to the south, in China proper, threatening. The poison of Chinese chaos seemed to be pouring into Manchuria along with a rise in Chinese migrants escaping hard times at home. Anti-Japanese demonstrations increased, as did boycotts of Japanese goods. Japanese civilians feared for their lives. Japanese merchants felt the pinch in their bottom lines.

When Amakasu, his fellow officers, and the Japanese expat community looked to their home government for support, they despaired of the liberal, antimilitary atmosphere prevailing in Tokyo. They saw a government staffed with corrupt politicians whom they considered soft and compliant. Indeed, the 1920s in Japan, as in America, brought a new, modern culture—at least for those living in urban areas. While Japanese society did not exactly roar, it did hold out a promise of a deepening democracy that would bring more of the benefits of consumer culture to more people, including some young women who seemed ready to break free of tradition. The modern girl (*moga*) became an icon of the new age, much like the flapper in America. Politicians and people were more willing to join international arms-limitations treaties. Military budget cuts threatened.

The post–First World War atmosphere of the early decade saw the rise of labor organizations, calls for extended suffrage, and politicians who were not shy about cutting the army's budget. Ōsugi actively participated in this climate. His writings made him a public figure, so his untimely death drew public notice. Thus in 1930, Amakasu left a Japan that was not welcoming of the kind of social rigor a military state might demand. In Manchuria he met like-minded activist army officers worried about more than Japanese weakness in China. In Manchuria the man estranged from his native land found purpose in a new home.

Officers like Amakasu hated soft-seeming politicians. These included venal cabinet ministers from political parties; earlier ministers had wielded bureaucratic or clan-affiliated credentials. One example of this softness came in the years immediately following the First World War, when the government, led by the Seiyukai (Friends of Government) party, reduced the army by four divisions, cutting expenses as it did so. Moreover party governments participated in international arms-limitation conferences. Especially galling were the terms of the Washington Arms Limitation Treaty of 1921–1922 and the London Naval Conference of 1930. These international conferences limited the size of navies by a ratio of 5:5:3 and later 10:10:7. Japan was allotted the lower ratio each time. The willingness of Japanese civilian officials to weaken military defenses rankled in the minds of younger officers like Kōmoto and Amakasu.[10]

Yet the decade of the 1920s, which began in a progressive mood, ended with the rise of populist ultranationalist agitation. Party-led governments gave themselves a bad reputation with their antics. The fluctuations in the global economy did not support a liberalizing agenda. The era began with rapid postwar inflation, followed by a recession that brought panics and bankruptcies. In 1927 a major bank failure led to a run on banks and subsequent bank failures. The era ended with the Stock Market Crash of 1929. The Japanese economy felt its severe consequences.[11]

Throughout the decade, politicians in the Japanese cabinet and diet worked harder to feather their own political nests than to establish a solid base with the electorate. Factions in the political arena split their membership to form new parties, reorganize old parties, or merge groups together, often coming to blows on the diet floor. Following the political quadrille of the 1920s is dizzying to any dedicated reader of history. How much more confusing it must have seemed to the population of the day. In the midst of financial crisis, elected representatives kept the government in gridlock. Corruption practiced by those in office seemed the one political constant.

By the early 1930s social upheaval had reached a high mark. Bands of right-wing extremists—the ultranationalists—plotted against the Japanese government. Like young officers in the army, they condemned the Meiji constitutional system, with its cabinet, diet, and corporate economic system. They rallied against modern Japanese society corrupted by Western immorality and softened by imported pleasures. Ultranationalists formed into small groups with wonderful names: the Patriotic Society, the League of Blood, the Cherry Blossom Society, the back-to-nature Love of Country School.

Underscoring the point, the 1920s opened and closed with assassinations by ultranationalists of sitting prime ministers: Hara Takashi (1858–1921) in 1921 and Hamaguchi Osachi (1870–1931) in 1930 (he died of his wounds the next year); both men were attacked in Tokyo Station. In 1932 a third prime minister, Inukai Kii (Tsuyoshi, 1855–1932), fell to assassins. The decade that began with labor union activity ended with ultranationalist declarations of pure patriotism.[12]

International treaties, especially those limiting naval buildup, became proof that misguided politicians in Tokyo, following a misplaced idealization of the West, would lead the home government to certain weakness. As a result, throughout the 1920s Japanese subjects living in China felt increasingly threatened as they faced a groundswell of Chinese nationalism through periodic boycotts. Could they trust politicians to back them up with necessary force? At the same time, they were acutely aware of a strong Soviet presence directly to their north. In such a precarious situation, Japanese living in Manchuria, like Gotō, easily understood the creation of the newly independent state of Manchukuo as a triumph of spirit in which Japanese soldiers defied a foreign treaty system built to benefit Western nations. Kantō Army officers acted even when their own government would not. Thus Manchukuo became a noble experiment in pan-Asian government. For Gotō, it represented triumph over international danger, Chinese ineptitude, and political weakness at home. This was a tall order.

Gotō Reiji, his colleagues, and their friends in the Japanese army lived on the ground in Manchuria through the 1920s. They watched growing Chinese civil instability. They concluded, as did their own officers, that problems in northeastern Asia could only be—in fact had to be—solved by Japanese leadership for the safety of Japan and the benefit of China. Otherwise the ongoing chaos would create a dangerous situation, inviting interference from other foreign powers. Left in chaos, the Chinese people might succumb to radical beliefs. In other words, if Japan did not solve the China problem, would the Soviet Union step in? Would European powers and America expand their influence in the territory? Would Chinese communism spread? International treaties and organizations seemed to ignore Japan's need for regional security.

In such a climate, the goal of the military men whom Amakasu met in Manchuria went beyond establishing a safe environment for Japanese businesses in Manchuria. The young officers with whom Amakasu worked envisioned the creation of a new East Asian state. It would take the lead in China, while it became a beacon for needed reform in Japan.

Amakasu was the perfect coconspirator in the plot to bring this state into being. His sympathies lay squarely with the young officers in both desire for action in Manchuria and disdain for the politicians in Japan. The soft government officials and their liberal policies led Amakasu to remark that the ideals of the French Revolution—liberty, equality, and fraternity—had no place in the Japanese political system.[13]

Amakasu worked with military activists ready to force events from Manchuria. The two men given credit for the plot—Ishiwara Kanji (1889–1949) and Itagaki Seishirō (1885–1948)—became heroes, the authors of Manchukuo. Amakasu, no longer an officer but a colleague and friend, enjoyed complete deniability. He worked underground to help finance the plot that brought Manchukuo into existence.

Amakasu became the perfect ally for officers in the military who wanted to take the bold actions that their government would not. Who better to help with covert operations? Unauthorized military action required supplies. Supplies required money, but money could not come from official coffers. Amakasu, no longer in the military but friendly with his former fellow officers, could be trusted—he was a known entity. He also enjoyed the advantage of living outside official circles. In 1930–1931 he moved back and forth between Mukden, Dalian, and Tokyo under the radar of official scrutiny.

Ultranationalists' goals included a return to a simpler, agrarian Japanese society, free of imported institutions, with the emperor directly in contact with his people. The tactics they advocated were violent. Between 1929 and 1932, not only did two prime ministers die at the hands of assassins, but a former politician and the head of Mitsui Corporation also fell to ultranationalist plots. Other coup d'état plots were foiled before their execution. Ultranationalists were not military men, but many in the Japanese army sympathized with their ideas. And they could be useful. Amakasu knew this well.

Amakasu Masahiko moved among ultranationalists groups like a fish through water. In 1929 after Amakasu returned to Tokyo from France, he traveled through the city meeting old friends. That July he took a short trip through Manchuria, in part to attend the wedding of his younger brother. There he found his calling. For the next year and a half, he traveled back and forth between Manchuria and Japan. He was a connection between radical elements—military and paramilitary, at home and on the continent—who wanted change in Japan's governing system and a stronger foreign policy.

The people Amakasu visited during his forays formed a veritable who's who of the ultranationalist movement in Japan. His contacts included Ōkawa Shūmei (1886–1957), an intellectual proponent of pan-Asianism who wrote with passion about Asia's clash with the West.

He knew Chō Isamu (1895–1945), prominent in both the military action to create Manchukuo and in covert activities in Tokyo. Amakasu also became close friends with Colonel Hashimoto Kingorō (1890–1957). Hashimoto was actively involved in bringing together like-minded political activists, including Ōkawa and Chō, to form the Cherry Blossom Society. In March 1931 and again in October 1931, the Cherry Blossom Society planned coups d'état, both unsuccessful. In the midst of his coup activities Hashimoto also helped raise money for Manchurian activities. Hashimoto recalls that Amakasu was so dedicated to the Manchukuo project that he sold a poem in the hand of the Meiji emperor and donated the proceeds to the cause.

Amakasu also visited Takahata Jun at his home in Kamakura. Not as well known as Ōkawa, Chō, or Hashimoto, Takahata was himself steeped in ultranationalist activities, and he had ties to both Tōjō Hideki and Hashimoto. Takahata's father oversaw the planting of poppies on Hainan Island in southern China. As such he was friendly with Satomi Hajime, the judo expert who so impressed Sun Yat-sen. Satomi ran an illicit opium and heroin operation, the proceeds of which fueled undercover operations for the Japanese military. Amakasu, as a friend of Hashimoto and a confidant of the officers in Manchuria, became the perfect conduit for illicit funds to grease the cogs of adventure. Satomi Hajime proved generous with contributions to the cause. Amakasu ferried money between Tokyo and Mukden to supply arms and ammunition for an operation that had no official sanction, one kept secret from the staff officers back home.

The names of two men stand out in the history of Manchukuo: Itagaki Seishirō and Ishiwara Kanji. Both men transferred to Manchuria late in 1928. They arrived in the wake of the Zhang Zuolin assassination. On their arrival they found the Kantō Army in disarray. The murder of the warlord produced no results. Their own colleague, Kōmoto Daisaku, author of the plot, received an unfavorable transfer to a backwater posting as his reward for decisive action. Meanwhile Chinese anti-Japanese hostility increased. Zhang Xueliang, the warlord's son, began building programs in direct competition with Japanese businesses. Tensions reached new highs during the summer of 1931 when Chinese snipers murdered Captain Nakamura Shintarō of the Kantō Army while he traveled on assignment through the Manchurian countryside. That same summer, Chinese farmers attacked Korean migrants putting in irrigation ditches in Manchuria's western territory. Situations in both Japan and Manchuria were heating up.[14]

Colonels Itagaki and Ishiwara hatched plans for the attack on Zhang Xueliang well in advance of September 1931. They understood that lack of a follow-up plan of action had been a weakness in the assassination of Zhang Zuolin, the father. Moreover, the Japanese military situation in Manchuria represented a police presence, not a full-service army. The Kantō command involved one division stationed in Port Arthur at the tip of the Liaodong Peninsula. Japanese garrisons guarded the major cities along the South Manchuria Railway. With little more than 10,000 troops in Manchuria, protecting Japanese interests in the area proved difficult in times of uncertain peace. How much more daunting would an invasion be against Zhang Xueliang's army of 200,000 soldiers, especially one with no official sanction?[15]

The two officers' personalities complimented each other. Itagaki Seishirō was a man of action. Well liked by fellow officers, he thrived in the Manchurian frontier atmosphere. He was a good horseman, gregarious, and adventurous. During the Second World War, Itagaki went on to become commander in chief of Chinese expeditionary forces and head of Japan's army in Korea. After Japan surrendered in 1945, Itagaki faced the International Military Tribunal as a Class A war criminal. He was hanged December 1948.

Ishiwara Kanji's life followed a different course. An idea man, he viewed the course of the world's history as a military drama careening toward a grand conflict that would usher in an age of peace. Japan, of course, was to play a decisive role in what he called the "final war" to be fought, he predicted, against the United States in the air. As such, Manchurian resources became a vital part of Japan's preparation. Ishiwara also firmly believed that Manchukuo should fulfill its destiny as an independent nation.

Ishiwara returned from Manchuria a hero. He received promotions and postings appropriate to his career until 1937, when war expanded into China proper. In an about-face, Ishiwara vigorously argued against expanding Japan's military operations into an exhausting Chinese theater. He predicted, correctly, that the Japanese army would get bogged down in a wasteful situation with no end. Ishiwara had an acerbic personality in the best of times. While arguing his point, he ran afoul of his fellow military officers anxious for glory on the battlefield. By 1941 Ishiwara's career was over. He survived the war in retirement. He even made an appearance in his friend's behalf at the International Military Tribunal.[16]

Amakasu admired and assisted Ishiwara Kanji's bold vision and decisive action. After 1937, however, when Ishiwara warned against moving into China, Amakasu's opinion changed. One of Amakasu's colleagues remembers working with him on a propaganda poster. The men wanted to use a photo commemorating Japanese victories in China. The image showed Japanese soldiers on a Chinese city wall with Chinese crowds cheering them from the ground. Because of the skewed camera angle, the Japanese soldiers' boots might seem to be treading on the heads of the Chinese crowd. Should they use the picture or not? In the midst of the discussion, Ishiwara himself entered the room. "Keep the photo," said Ishiwara. "That is exactly what is happening in China." After Ishiwara left the room, Amakasu commented with a sigh, "I am afraid that Ishiwara has grown soft in Tokyo."[17]

The hardships these men would face in the tragic future could not be predicted in 1929 as Itagaki and Ishiwara began to plan the capture of Manchuria with likeminded conspirators. They gained official permission to update a strategic survey of the Manchurian terrain. They organized sightseeing trips of Manchuria outside the railway zone for officers of the Kantō Army. Far from being lively jaunts, these tours were reconnaissance missions, carefully planned, the results duly noted for future action. This was the kind of "tourist" activity George Hanson found suspicious.

Japanese conspirators faced two considerable opponents. In Manchuria Zhang Xueliang inherited his father's military. In Mukden alone, Japanese troops would be outmanned two to one. More importantly, the conspirators knew their own government at home would not support their cause. Indeed rumors that the army in Manchuria was up to something reached the Japanese consul in Mukden, who reported to his superiors in the Foreign Office. The government in Tokyo dispatched General Tatakawa Yoshisugu to Manchuria to bring any such plot under control. The general arrived in Mukden on September 18; however, he was the wrong man for the mission. Sympathetic to the goals of the conspirators, he drank the night away while Japanese army engineers placed and detonated a bomb on the tracks of the South Manchuria Railway.

The area of tracks picked for the explosion was unremarkable in itself, but it was close to a Chinese barracks. A colonel in the sappers had arranged for explosives to leave his charge. Just after 10:20 on the evening of September 18, 1931, they went off. Soldiers shot six unlucky Chinese civilians found near the tracks. Their bodies became makeshift evidence that the explosion had been more anti-Japanese treachery. Years after the war's end, Satō Shin'ichirō and several of his friends from Manchukuo days would drink a commemorative toast to these hapless Chinese who became the first casualties of the northeastern occupation.[18]

Thus young officers of the Japanese Kantō Army showed the world just how fragile the international treaty system really was, even as their superior officer drank with colleagues. A careful follow-up plan went into effect immediately. Japanese soldiers surrounded the Chinese garrison in Mukden. Soldiers fanned out to capture the Manchurian heartland. The overt invasion of China had begun. The incident initiated a new era, one that would end in 1949 with the victory of the People's Liberation Army.

Contrary to expectation, Zhang Xueliang, the warlord's son, did little to thwart the Japanese invasion. In a show of national pride, he strengthened his alliance with the Nationalist government based in Nanjing hoping to fight Japan. Instead he received orders from Chiang Kai-shek not to resist. Through the early 1930s, acquiescence to Japanese territorial expansion would remain Chiang's policy, despite growing Chinese anger. Using the slogan "Unity first; resistance second," Chiang was determined to finish the civil war with his Chinese Communist nemesis before taking on a foreign adversary.

Indeed, Chiang would not resolve to take up arms against Japan until December 1936. At that time Zhang Xueliang, disgusted, like many in China, with continued submission to Japanese encroachment into North China, kidnapped the generalissimo. Over two weeks in December, Zhang held Chiang Kai-shek at gunpoint until the general agreed to resist Japan. After the drama, dubbed the Xi'an Incident, with Chiang Kai-shek again in control of the Nationalist government, Zhang Xueliang became Chiang's prisoner, living under house arrest until 1985.[19]

The Mukden Incident, a daring move on the part of the young officers, came as an unwelcome surprise to the politicians in Tokyo. The sitting prime minister and his foreign minister, both of whom represented the soft, diplomatic approach to world affairs so despised by the army, had to scramble in the days following the explosion in September 1931. International criticism poured in from all quarters. The Japanese Foreign Ministry assured foreign critics that the fighting in China represented a local skirmish and would not spread beyond Mukden. Yet it did spread, first to the south, then northward. When pressed, the Japanese government promised that military action would be contained. It was not. Such promises rang false as Itagaki's army moved from Mukden into the south, taking Jinzhou in October. The American public interpreted the disconnect between words and actions as innate Japanese duplicity, especially when it looked back on the affair after the attack on Pearl Harbor. In fact, the disconnect stemmed from a systematic power struggle between army activists and civil politicians.

On September 21, 1931, three days after the incident, China, represented by the Nationalist government, protested Japan's aggression to the League of Nations, citing Article Eleven of the Covenant of the League. In response the international body created a study group, headed by Lord V. A. G. R. Bulwer-Lytton (1876–1947), to investigate conditions in Manchuria. Dr. V. K. Wellington Koo (1887–1985), Chinese representative to the league in Geneva, sent volumes of memoranda briefing the investigators as to the Chinese position. In a long report he chronicled the progress of the Japanese action. He pointed out that the magnitude of the Japanese attack demonstrated the action had been planned well in advance. He mentioned that the blast had done so little damage to the track that the 11:30 p.m. train to Qiqihar (a city to the northeast of Harbin) passed over the track, arriving at the station on time. Prophetically, he asked, "Where will Japan stop? When will that unquenchable thirst for conquest be satis-fied?"[20]

The Lytton board of inquiry traveled through China, arriving in Muk-den in September and leaving from Harbin in November 1932. Agents watched the board members' every move throughout their travels. At each stop on their journey, they met with "Manchukuoans" whose views about recent events had been clearly rehearsed. Japanese guards kept close watch over their movements. Hotel staff also included careful watchers. In Harbin, Chinese tried to hand over letters of protest. Their efforts were in vain; police hauled them off to prison. At the end of the trip, the board of inquiry produced a report. Although it suggested that Japanese residents in Manchuria had legitimate grievances against the Chinese administration in Manchuria, it concluded that Manchukuo "cannot be considered to have been called into existence by a genuine and spontaneous independent movement."[21]

Europeans and Americans debated the appropriate action to take in response. Economic boycott of Japan seemed a good way to proceed. Yet in 1932 the world was in the grip of the deepest economic depression to date. The idea of cutting off trade could only be toyed with, not carried out. In the end no boycott was implemented. In America, Secretary of State Henry Stimsen sent a note refusing to recognize the state of Man-chukuo. Other Western nations followed suit. Will Rogers, the political wit and, as it happened, a friend of Consul George Hanson, summarized the debate succinctly: "What's a few thousand dead Chinamen compared to Japan as a cash customer?"[22]

Dr. V. K. Wellington Koo thanked the Lytton Commission for its careful work and praised its efforts in China's behalf. "The time has come now for prompt and effective action by the League," he added. Mao Zedong, from his rebel base camp in the hills of Jiangxi Province, called the Lytton Commission and the League of Nations a "band of lying and murderous thieves."[23]

Even as their politicians scrambled to answer international criticism, the Japanese public and press had a positive impression of the army ac-tion in Manchuria. In the fall of 1931, Japanese people could look back on a decade of relatively liberal governments and general economic prosperity, at least in the cities. Unfortunately, the era of the 1920s also included the kind of political theatrics that give politicians a bad name. Open corruption and endless wrangling on the diet floor, often ending in fistfights, marred the business of running the Japanese government. Then came the American stock market collapse in 1929. The prosperity of the 1920s ended in Japan as it did in the rest of the world.

In this atmosphere, bold action in China by a handful of warrior ideal-ists became a welcome diversion from economic uncertainty and political corruption. By December 1931, the Japanese prime minister dissolved the government. Assassins disposed of his successor in February 1932. The Japanese cabinets that followed provided a governing body compatible with military adventure. Then, on February 26, 1936, a snowy day, ultra-nationalist army officers staged a coup. They held the center of Tokyo for three days, assassinating three government ministers. The prime minister survived only because of a case of mistaken identity. His brother-in-law was murdered in his place.

The solders belonged to the Imperial Way faction. They advocated a Showa Restoration, demanding a revision of the government that would bring the emperor and people into a vaguely conceived populist harmony. Yet, within three days, the army itself had brought the situation under control. Those officers who instigated the coup were court-martialed and executed. Those in the military who sympathized with them found themselves sidelined. The army was disciplining its own. Yet, in the atmosphere engendered by corrupt politicians, ultranationalist assassinations, and economic uncertainty, decisive action by any political group gave the military a measure of prestige. That the group of officers who took charge of affairs after the February 26 incident was known as the Control Faction should have been a warning. They advocated a national-defense state, one that could best utilize resources from Manchukuo for war. The militarist Japan that would go to war with the United States was born.

The Manchukuo envisioned by Ishiwara Kanji and people like Gotō's scholarly assistant, Satō Shin'ichirō, was meant to be a multinational independent nation, albeit one with close ties to Japan. This ideal began to unravel from the start. Many of the actors in the Manchukuo drama had different kinds of plans. Amakasu Masahiko was one of these men. The moment the young officers' plot of September 18, 1931, bore fruit, one of his friends commented, "So that's where Amakasu has been these past two years."[24] As a reward for his activities, Amakasu may have received a Manchurian gold mine—or he may not have.[25] The story about the gold mine forms one of the many layers of conflicting myth that make up the saga of Amakasu. It is one of many riddles surrounding the man.

Harbin Station (postcard from the collection of the author).

Harbin Station with waiting carriages (postcard from the collection of the author).

Tower of Loyal Souls (postcard from the collection of the author).

The Harbin Shinto shrine (postcard from the collection of the author).

Postcard view of St. Nicholas (Central) Cathedral showing the Harbin Museum (postcard from the collection of the author).

Central Square today (photograph taken by the author).

St. Sophia Cathedral. It has taken the place of St. Nicholas Cathedral as an icon of the city (photograph taken by the author).

Postcard view of the Japanese consulate. Katō Toyotaka, along with other police colleagues, was held prisoner in the building's basement before being transferred to a Soviet labor camp (postcard from the collection of the author).

The Modern Hotel (photograph taken by the author).

The Harbin Yamato Hotel (postcard from the collection of the author).

The Harbin Yamato Hotel, today the Longmen Hotel (photograph taken by the author).

7

❧

Manchukuo

Manchukuo was established on the principle of creating in the Manchurian and Mongolian area a paradise based on the Kingly Way of racial harmony, of Japanese and Manchukuoans sharing one virtue, one heart. One difficulty is the difference between Japanese language, customs and practices and those of the Manchukuoans.

—Satō Shin'ichirō[1]

Among Chinese with whom I talked [I] found not one even among those in Manchukuo service who was favorable [to] Manchukuo and who did not detest the Japanese.

—George C. Hanson[2]

Harbin's Chinese slums are "a sneering slur on the triumph of Manchukuo."[3] These words open *Autopsy of the Garden of Grand Vision*. With one sentence Gotō Reiji and his two colleagues, Satō Shin'ichirō and Katō Toyotaka, remind their readers of the idealism that accompanied the birth of the new nation. Yet their assignment—to study the traditions and conditions of the Chinese living in the northeasternmost three provinces—took them into dark places that most Japanese in Manchukuo would never enter. Their adventure, they hoped, would contribute to the well-being of a new nation created as an experiment in racial harmony and Confucian modernity. This conviction—that Manchukuo was a triumph—runs counter to memories shared by the rest of the world.

The creation of Manchukuo, the name meaning literally "the nation of Manchuria," in 1931 was, strictly speaking, the opening salvo of the

Second World War, Pacific Theater. As Americans, we learn about Manchukuo only briefly, if at all. The events of September 18, 1931, show up in history texts as prelude to the longer Asian conflict. The existence of the country is adduced as proof that the League of Nations did not work. The international treaty system built in the 1920s by people worldwide who still remembered with horror the trenches, poison gas, and general carnage of the Great War had failed. This interwar system included the Washington, DC, and London naval disarmament agreements (1921 and 1930) limiting the size of battleships, as well as the much-ridiculed 1928 Kellogg-Briand Pact—the International Kiss—that ended warfare on paper, if not in fact. The agreements, despised by the Japanese officers in Manchukuo, were well intentioned. Nonetheless, while the 1920s roared, the decade turned out to be only a pause in a long period of conflict.

In China to this day Manchukuo is not forgotten. Memories are strong, bitter, and harsh. First of all, the name Manchuria is not used. "Manchu" refers to the original inhabitants of the area, people who ruled in the last Chinese dynasty. The area itself is called Dongbei, the Northeast, or by the names of the three provinces outside the Wall: Liaoning, Jilin, and Heilongjiang. In Chinese history books, the state of Manchukuo, the time it existed, its government, and the officials who worked there are all designated as *wei*, meaning bogus, phony, or counterfeit. We read about phony Manchukuo (*Wei Man*) and the phony Manchukuo government (*wei zhengfu*); Gotō worked for the phony police force (*wei jingcha bu*).

Chinese people have good reasons for hostility. Go to Shenyang, the city known in American history books as Mukden. Visit the September 18 History Museum filled with exhibits about the Japanese occupation. Today's guidebooks mention the museum but warn, "Not for the faint of heart" and "rather gruesome."[4] The museum speaks volumes to remembered bitterness. The simple date 9/18—the month and day the bomb blew a small bit from the Japanese tracks outside Mukden—appears with the same force in Chinese memoirs and modern-day blogs as does 9/11 in contemporary American media. The date draws a sharp line between the China in which treaty terms pecked away at state sovereignty and a nation invaded. Even in our new century, September 18 brings the appearance of signs like the one in a restaurant in Yunnan Province: "No Dogs or Japanese."[5]

Two decades after the 1911 revolution, violent civil war left a power vacuum in North China, inviting Japanese adventure. The formal establishment of Manchukuo carved out a new nation in an area of Chinese strategic vulnerability. Yet Manchukuo's borders remained dangerously fluid. The area became a corridor as Japanese control expanded south of the Wall into China. First came the addition of Rehe in 1933. More land was seized in 1935. By 1937, Japanese armies easily moved from Manchukuo, capturing Beijing in July; Shanghai and Nanjing fell by the end of the year. The Second World War had begun in earnest.

Gotō and his companions began their Harbin survey three years into the war with China. For these men the China situation complicated a noble experiment in the North. They believed in a heroic Manchukuo created by dedicated Japanese army officers with the courage to lead a preemptive strike in a land riddled with conflict and corruption. In doing so these young officers stabilized an area of insecurity for the safety of Japan as it faced a hostile world.

Harbin resisted the grasp of Manchukuo. The Japanese military moved into the city on January 26, 1932. This northern conquest was not smooth or easy. Chinese troops, with no help from the Chinese government inside the Wall, resisted Japanese invasion for over a month—the last northeastern holdout. Early in January 1932, the Japanese Kantō Army began a northern thrust toward Harbin. As the Japanese soldiers advanced north, life in Harbin came to an uncertain disquiet. Chinese attacks on Japanese and Koreans increased. This only created further justification for invasion. Members of the Japanese Residents' Association, already active, requested protection from their home government. For two weeks, all commerce in Harbin came to a halt. The streets emptied in anticipation of the coming battle. Then, on January 26, cannon and machine-gun fire replaced the unnatural stillness in the air. Japanese troops entered the city. Harbin capitulated to Japanese forces on February 5, 1932.

Chinese soldiers put up a measure of resistance until one local leader changed allegiance and joined the Japanese side. The fighters scattered, some retreating into China proper, others joining resistance groups in the wilderness border areas. From their border hideouts, armed groups of Chinese men harassed Manchukuo institutions throughout the nation's brief history. Calling these fighters "bandits" in official documents, the Manchukuo police maintained units to patrol outside the city. Eventually there would be a River Constabulary, a Forest Constabulary, and a Border Protection Constabulary. Their duties involved soldiering more than crime prevention, despite the choice of words.[6]

What resistance Japan faced came from independent Chinese forces in northern Manchuria. But these efforts lacked coordinated national assistance from Nanjing. Chiang Kai-shek, leader of the Nationalist government, refused to fight Japan while he concentrated on eliminating the Chinese Communist Party. By March 1932, Manchuria was in the hands of the Japanese military. A Japanese intelligence officer smuggled the surviving Qing emperor, Henry Puyi, from his home in Tianjin to Changchun, renamed Shinkyō, the new capital of Manchukuo. When the man destined to become the last emperor yet again arrived in port in his new kingdom, Amakasu Masahiko was there to greet him. The new nation officially opened for business.

Official government pronouncements promoted Manchukuo as a model of racial equality in which Japanese leaders would do what they did best—rule—while Chinese and other ethnic groups would enjoy the benefits of an Asian modernism. One Japanese expatriate was so hopeful for the new nation that he named his son after the two officers who had carried the plot to completion. Taking the "sei" from Itagaki Seishirō and the "ji" from Ishiwara Kanji, Ozawa Seiji's father gave the man who would become a musician and conductor of international stature a name to honor decisive action on the battlefield. This hopeful component of the project was captured in Gotō's opening to *Autopsy of the Garden of Grand Vision*.

It is hard for us living in a different century and cognizant of the horrors of the Second World War to grasp just how hopeful the dream of Manchukuo was for Japanese in the 1930s. It offered a fresh start, a third alternative in global modern development. Advocating neither communism nor capitalism, Manchukuo officials talked about the "Kingly Way," a combination of modern technology and Asian Confucian ideals boiled down into an ideology. Manchukuo official publications described the Kingly Way as a desire of the Chinese people to turn back to tradition after the failure of the republic. Manchukuoans would find models of morality in the sage kings of old, cultivate themselves, bring peace to others, and create a moral world. The promise of a paradise of five races living the Kingly Way had attracted Satō Shin'ichirō to the Northeast. "I left everything behind from my native village. I found a home in Manchukuo."[7] Satō was not alone in his idealism. Ishiwara Kanji, instrumental in founding the new nation, believed in a utopian future for the country. Muto Nobuyoshi (1868–1933) came to Manchukuo as both commander in chief of Japanese forces and as ambassador extraordinary, hoping to help establish a vigorous new nation. He died a year later under mysterious circumstances. Both Amieto Vespa the spy and Edgar Snow the journalist claimed that he committed ritual suicide to protest the brutality and corruption he discovered.[8]

Over the thirteen years of the country's existence, media in both Japan and Manchukuo talked of racial harmony, cooperation among the many ethnic groups living in the new nation, and unity among peoples from all corners of the world. Yet the propaganda always assumed that the prosperity of Manchukuo would come under the leadership of the Japanese military's own derring-do. To this end, the new government formed the Concordia Society to increase harmony between Chinese and Japanese peoples and to enhance the moral vision of the Kingly Way. Leaders deemed the spiritual training of Manchukuo youth especially important.

In reality, the Concordia Society did not have such a rosy reputation. Members became leaders of local organizations to keep track of their neighbor's activities. Some engaged in police activities. Chinese people living in Manchukuo, who suddenly found themselves classified as Manchukuoan, referred to their compatriots who supported the new regime as "Kingly Way types."[9]

The international press referred to Manchukuo as a puppet state. The designation persists in modern textbooks. In Manchukuo, officers of the Kantō Army tasked with fashioning a new state hoped their creation would become a model for reform in Japan as well as in Asia. They put aside the cabinet system of their home island, setting up instead a bureaucracy attached to a legislative council made up of representatives from the many Manchurian ethnic groups. A Chinese (now Manchukuoan) aristocrat and poet, Zheng Xiaoxu (1860–1938), became the first prime minister of the new nation. Yet this was all for show. The entire political apparatus ran through the direction of the General Affairs Office, where Japanese army officers held key positions. Here the puppet masters could be found. For every Chinese bureaucrat who headed a department, there was a Japanese vice department head who called the shots. In Manchukuo this arrangement was called the internal guidance policy.[10]

A graphic picture of internal guidance and border policing in the new state came from American consul general George C. Hanson. His superiors in Washington, DC, repeatedly accused him of traveling away from his post for pleasure. Indeed he enjoyed his adventures into the Manchurian countryside. But he kept his eyes and ears wide open during these trips. In 1932, after Manchukuo began its short history, George Hanson traveled north several times. He described a multiethnic border situation of shifting alliances, naked power grabs, and unspeakable violence. His memos provide an early prediction of the bloodshed to come. After one trip in July 1932, he described scenes of Japanese Kempeitai making trouble on the Soviet border, effectively shutting down trade. A certain Mr. Saynjoth, a Norwegian who had been working for Chinese customs, learned about the Kempeitai the hard way. Kempeitai officers pulled Saynjoth from a train, held him prisoner, and questioned him for hours. The man came away from the ordeal a physical and mental wreck. He lost his job and his home and feared for his life. The wife of one of Saynjoth's colleagues reported that her husband had been held in a Japanese prison for three days, sleeping on a cement floor with no food or water.

A second jaunt into the countryside came after Hanson met the new head of the local Japanese military mission, who spoke some English, and the new Japanese chief of police, who spoke excellent Russian. After learning that they all shared a love of shooting, all three took off in the general's Buick for a day in the country. Hanson got along with these newfound friends. This did not alter his pessimistic view of Manchukuo. He sent a full report to the state department describing waning Russian influence in North Manchuria. "Russians see their businesses fall into Japanese hands," he reported, "and they are right."

Hanson described local Mongol tribesmen pretending to like the Chinese when it suited their interests but favoring Japan in their actions. He reported Japanese claims that where there were no Chinese soldiers, there were no bandits. Hanson, however, reported that one local Chinese resistance leader, described by his Japanese friends as a vicious bandit, in fact acted like a gentleman for the short time he was able to fight his enemy. Hanson's Japanese shooting partner, charming as he may have been, was charged with eliminating local resistance even as he moved his own family into a lovely, confiscated Russian house.[11]

After his third and last trip, Hanson related a story he learned from Chinese he met on the way. His sources described a Japanese drive against Chinese fighting in the forest area of the North. These were the Forest Police, soldiers in all but name, who came upon a group of Chinese woodsmen from a local lumber camp. The soldiers asked if there were any brigands in the area. Not really understanding the question, the lumbermen replied no. Further along the road, the Japanese solders came under fire. As they retreated past the lumber camp, they took their revenge. They killed everyone. Hanson commented that such tragedies would surely increase. The Japanese soldiers knew some Russian but lacked even basic Chinese-language skills.[12]

New Capital became the political center of Manchukuo, moving politics north, away from the Zhang family's power base in Mukden. The Central Police Bureau, an integral part of the General Affairs Office, oversaw the management of police through the new state. Japanese officers recruited from the military, joined by a number of carpetbaggers, became directors of local police forces staffed with personnel on the job from the days of the warlords. The first national police commissioner was none other than Amakasu Masahiko. He commanded the creation of the organization for which Gotō and his colleagues would work at a lower level.

Amakasu organized the police even as the League of Nations investigated the events surrounding the creation of Manchukuo. Lord Lytton led his international team through China to Mukden amid rumors that Amakasu would arrange to sabotage the train on which they traveled. In fact, Amakasu made sure nothing untoward that might threaten the future of Manchukuo befell the delegates. Nonetheless, knowing that Amakasu acted as the guardian of the league delegates, is it any wonder that spies, agents, and obstreperous bodyguards dogged the representatives' journey?

Amakasu wore many different hats in the Manchukuo enterprise. He organized the police. Later he became the head of the Concordia Society. It was his job to make propaganda work. Officials promoted the Concordia Society as a civic organization to instill national pride in Manchukuo. Chinese suspected that the society was in fact a spy operation. They were not far from wrong. The society maintained contacts with the Manchukuo bureaucracy. Mutō Tomio was a young man working in the legal department in the Manchukuo government. In 1934 his boss pulled him aside to tell him that he had been assigned to make connections between his office and the Concordia Society, a job that would bring him into contact with Amakasu.

As with everyone who had dealings with Amakasu, Mutō's first reaction was fear. Amakasu, the murderer of Ōsugi? How could they put a murderer in charge of the Concordia Society? Yet, when Mutō went to his first meeting with the man, a genial fellow, fair of face and smiling, stood before him. Only two deep creases between his brows hinted at his difficult past. Amakasu greeted by name all those who came to this general-affairs meeting of the Concordia Society. He smiled warmly and joked with people as he shook their hands one by one. Could this be a murderer? Mutō wondered.

Amakasu asked Mutō for help with an essay he had penned. Mutō found the writing sincere but utterly garbled. Subjects did not match predicates. Ideas refused to come through the grammar clearly. Mutō spent two days editing the messy words. After he passed it back to Amakasu, the grateful spy asked him to join him for dinner. The two went to a restaurant. Mutō, a Christian, did not drink. When a geisha appeared to serve Amakasu, it became clear he was a familiar guest. Amakasu teased the woman about the low quality of the geisha in the house. The woman retorted, telling Mutō that the old man was too cheap to part with his money. The two men spent the evening talking about history and art. In the end Mutō began to doubt the facts of the Ōsugi murder case he had heard as a boy. Like many others charmed by the man, Mutō came to suspect that Amakasu had been scapegoated.[13]

Amakasu Masahiko held many posts in Manchukuo, but he lived in the shadows. He made a fortune as a spy, spending money as quickly as he made it. His family lived in a mansion in Dalian, while Amakasu stayed at the Yamato Hotel in New Capital or at the better hotels as he traveled. Wherever he went, he enjoyed the company of geisha. Chinese who knew of his darker side characterized him as a womanizer who spent little time with his wife; those closer to Amakasu, however, recall that he often expressed a deep affection for his family. One night, for example, when he was asked to make some after-dinner comments, he mentioned that the warriors of old, in times of war, refused to marry. "Those warriors must have been terribly lonely."[14]

Amakasu specialized in dirty tricks. He stayed in Manchukuo even as his military friends rotated in and out of the country, rising in rank as they followed their career paths. Throughout the short history of Manchukuo, Amakasu appears wherever intrigue would benefit the new state. He created spy agencies and propaganda organizations. At his bidding the admittedly shy Mutō Tomio became propaganda minister. A saying in Manchukuo, repeated often, held that during the day the Kantō Army ran Manchukuo, but Amakasu ran the country by night.

As befits a spy, personal accounts of Amakasu offer radically different profiles. Some depict a man of darkly evil character; others remember an artistic sensibility; many are certain he was a totally misunderstood scapegoat for the crimes of others. Memoirs from police who worked with him lay all problems with corruption at his door. According to his Japanese biographer, Amakasu was not entirely comfortable with the undercover role that brought him wealth. He presented a sharp, emotionless face to the world, but he craved the public acknowledgment that might have been his had his military career not been interrupted. This may explain why, in 1939, he became head of Man'ei, the Manchukuo film studio. In addition to spying, he produced films promoting Manchukuo and the military values supported by the venture. He enjoyed entertaining officials of the Manchukuo government with private screenings of Hollywood films he acquired on the black market.

Was the career shift a psychological search for status? Amakasu's Chinese biographer tells a different story. In the Chinese version, Amakasu was such an arrogant bastard that even Japanese army officers got sick of him. They gave him the film studio and the mansion in Dalian to get him out of their offices, out of their lives, and out of their business.[15]

Whether Amakasu craved legitimacy or faced a kind of exile, the Man'ei film studio became his pet project. Running a film studio brought out his hidden creative talents. Zhang Yi (no relation to the warlord Zhang Zuolin) directed films for the company. He described Amakasu as a cultured man with a strict military bearing and remembered clearly the day that Amakasu took his post as head of the company. Amakasu called all the employees to a general assembly. In a brief speech he told the assembled that they worked for a great enterprise. He made it clear that though there were differences between the Japanese staff and their Manchukuoan counterparts, as director he would tolerate no arguments or conflicts. If such problems arose, he continued, he would discipline the Japanese staff first.

Amakasu had strategic reasons for this policy. The Man'ei company, founded in 1937, had become the home for Japanese migrants with no film experience. Yet these expats demanded high salaries. More to the point, the military authorities in Manchukuo considered them "agents of disorder"—in other words, leftists escaping from militarist Japan. Within two weeks of taking over the studio, Amakasu began to censor closely the contents of all films made at the studio. Yet he gained the admiration of the Manchukuoan staff, including Zhang Yi.

Amakasu's first move got their attention. He raised everyone's pay. All but the actresses with top billing earned a mere M$18 per month. Amakasu raised all of their salaries to M$45 a month. The beautiful Japanese actress Li Xianglan,[16] who charmed audiences in both Chinese and Japanese, commanded a respectable M$250 each month, thanks to Amakasu. He began hiring talent from Beijing. Before Amakasu arrived on the scene, Man'ei had produced dull propaganda films few wanted to see. Amakasu urged his directors to make the kind of films Manchukuo-ans would enjoy, films based on Beijing opera plots or historical adventures. In an act of generosity, one that contained an irony that must have amused Amakasu, he invited his staff to banquets. His Chinese employees went to the Yamato Hotel, where they enjoyed top-flight Western cuisine. His Japanese staff joined him in the company dining hall, where they ate Chinese food.

Amakasu spent a lot of time at the film company. He always appeared dressed in the military uniform of an army cadet, always clean shaven with hair neatly trimmed, clad in a highly polished pair of boots. He threw himself into the business of film with enthusiasm. The film industry became one of his passions, along with drinking, smoking, and fishing.[17]

Amakasu had influence that reached well beyond the studio. Zhang remembers one October day in 1943. He had just finished shooting the film *Swallow Green and Li Shishi*, a heroic swashbuckling adventure from an old Chinese novel. He was having lunch with a friend when his wife called him home. A Japanese man, wearing thick-rimmed glasses—Zhang remembers the glasses with a cold shiver we can feel in his memoir—told him that he was wanted at the studio club. But when he got to the waiting car, two men grabbed him from behind, covered his head with a blanket, and wrestled him into the car's back seat. Instead of being taken to the club, Zhang found himself in a windowless room in the basement of a building, he knew not where. There the man with the thick-rimmed glasses joined several interrogators in army uniforms who began to question him.

"Are you responsible for these?" One man shoved a series of comics at poor Zhang.

"Not at all."

The comics were anti-Japanese. One showed arrows piercing a dog with a Japanese flag on its stomach. Captions read, "Fight Japanese imperialism" and "We will resist Japanese aggression forever."

"Did you graduate from Jilin High School of the Arts?"

"I did."

"Did you know that there is a strong anti-Japanese element in that school? We have closed the school and arrested the teachers."

"I have nothing to do with them."

The guards beat Zhang Yi senseless and locked him in a cell over night. The questioning and beatings continued the next day, and the next. Then, suddenly, he was released, but not without the warning that he would be watched and his case continued. As he left the building, this time without the blanket over his head, he was shocked to see he had been in the headquarters of the Kempeitai. He remembered that it was common knowledge that "of the people who go in there, nine will die and only one will live."

When he returned to work, his Japanese section boss commiserated with him. "It is not just Chinese, we Japanese also fear the Kempeitai. Take a few days off to recover."[18]

Zhang Yi later learned that when he did not return home in the evening, his wife went to the studio to find out what was wrong. During her enquiries, Amakasu learned of Zhang's detention. It was Amakasu who had rescued Zhang from what would surely have been a terrible death.[19]

The Chinese creative staff liked Amakasu. The regular staff—janitors, cooks, drivers—had a different impression of the man. Amakasu insisted on military order. As the head of the agency, he appeared every day at 9 a.m. sharp, despite his bouts of nocturnal drinking. He insisted that offices, studios, and hallways all be pristine. One day at a competition, Amakasu ran a race with a clearly injured foot. Everyone praised his manly warrior spirit. But those in the know revealed that he had sprained his ankle kicking a poor orderly who did not clean a latrine to his satisfaction.[20]

Amakasu was a complex person. He loved art and music. He lectured his fellow officers for hours about European painting. They found him pedantic. For a conservative military man, his choice of friends was wide reaching. He befriended people he found interesting, no matter their politics. Many leftists stayed out of jail through Amakasu's intervention. On the other hand, he could not tolerate boors or phonies. When he first returned to Japan from France, he went to visit a certain Katō Kanji (1884–1967), an ultranationalist who ran a back-to-the-soil farm to instill virtue in young men. Katō sported a big, bushy beard. The young men who lived in his community farmed all day and practiced martial arts at night. Amakasu had nothing but bad things to say about Katō. He hated the beard and the pretense; he despised what the man was doing to ruin the lives of young people. Amakasu felt that youth should have fun, play games, and go to museums to learn about beauty. Such inconsistencies thread through all descriptions of Amakasu's character. Those who remember him often use the word "enigma."[21]

Manchukuo authorities knew that even as the Japanese government invested in the state, Chinese capital remained untapped. Amakasu got the job of finding ways to gain access to Chinese investments. Mutō Tomio saw how he worked in a case involving Man'ei. The studio needed money. Amakasu wanted to expand film distribution and improve the quality of the studios. He invited wealthy Chinese in New Capital to a banquet given by Man'ei. He asked them why they did not invest in the studio. They replied that except for the theaters in the center of town, nothing to do with Man'ei was profitable. Amakasu responded, "All right then, if it is not profitable, I will close down all theaters." That proposal upset the Chinese. He managed to convince them to invest in the theater system. With the new money, he created traveling film shows. Portable projectors using sixteen-millimeter film traveled into the small towns of Manchukuo to be set up in government offices for a showing of films to entertain. The Chinese who invested found they profited handsomely from their contribution.

Amakasu Masahiko made a similar contribution to the Manchukuo economic system. He created the Dadong Labor Company, at the behest of the military, to bring Chinese workers to the Northeast. Supplying jobs would not seem the sort of enterprise to require a specialist in espionage. But that is just what was needed. After 1931 the waves of migration from North China to Manchuria came to a sudden halt. Nevertheless growing Japanese-run economic-growth industries and military installations required more and more coolie labor. The state needed ways to attract it while making sure that no spies infiltrated work crews. Dadong scouted for contract labor in the North China area. At the same time the names of any men hired could be checked through Japanese intelligence records as much as possible. Despite ill will toward Japan, many desperate laborers left home to toil in Manchukuo. One such person was Feng Dengdiao, police informant and Gotō Reiji's friend.

The life of Feng Dengdiao presents an altogether different snapshot of life in Manchukuo. Gotō met Feng while walking through Fujiadian on a cold February morning. Or rather, Feng latched onto Gotō from his perch by the busy roadside. A thin man, thirty-eight years old, Feng had a frozen icicle of snot hanging from his nose. An empty soy sauce can dangled from his thin, chilblained hand. A sign written in an educated style hung from the can. "I have caught cold. Have pity on me. Please spare me the cost of a night's lodging."[22]

Feng was what might be called a "dignified beggar," a category in the Chinese profession of panhandling comprising those who had fallen from comfortable homes through cruel twists of fate. Having been educated, they could produce beautiful calligraphy, paintings, or poems to display as proof of their earlier, happier life. These sorts of beggars could gain a special kind of sympathy from people passing on the street. After all, only a cruel fate could drive an educated man or woman so far from home. This ploy certainly worked with Gotō, who found in Feng, with his upper-class diction, a kindred spirit as well as an informant.[23]

Gotō led Feng to the Spring Forest Lodge in the Garden of Grand Vision. He shelled out M$0.60 to pay for one week's lodging on a bunk in a dorm room under the eaves of the lodge. For Gotō, who probably earned M$300 per month, the amount was a pittance; yet through this act of kindness, the officer befriended Feng, who willingly told him his own story as well as tales of others living in the Garden.

Feng was the eldest son of a landowning family from the south of Hebei Province, close to Shandong. Located along the Yellow River about 150 miles south of Beijing, it was a fertile land of farms, steeped in Chinese antiquity. In today's China, it is an active industrial area. Feng's family owned more than forty *mou* of farmland, a sizable plot for a northern Chinese family (6.6 *mou* equals one acre as a rule of thumb). The land produced the sorghum, millet, wheat, and vegetables common to agriculture in the area. Feng grew up in a spacious nine-room house, where he received a classical Chinese education. The one luxury from his past he brought to the frozen street corner was his stately calligraphy.

In the early decades of the twentieth century, the North China area where Feng grew up fell into anarchy. The years following the overthrow of the Qing Dynasty in 1911 brought the ruthless rule of autocratic warlords who battled each other for petty pieces of territory, plunging the nation into a fifty-year civil war. From 1927 to 1949 the power vacuum worsened. Even the Chinese capital was moved from Beijing to Nanjing in the South, and the Nationalist government led by Chiang Kai-shek all but abandoned the northern area. This situation had invited the Japanese invasion.

Feng needed work. The northern soil, fertile during good years, was unforgiving in years of flood or drought. The early 1900s brought both to eastern China. Warlord activities wreaked havoc on any transportation systems that would have helped peasants market their harvests. Feng had to support fifteen people in the nine-room house: a wife, four children, a brother's family, and several elderly aunts and uncles. For a time he worked in the office of a company making military uniforms for a warlord army, but the instability of the economy in North China forced the company to close. Therefore in April 1938 Feng left his family behind and headed north to Beijing, where he lived with a relative. While taking in the sights of the erstwhile capital, Feng visited a cheap amusement center called the Heavenly Bridge. There he heard the street-side harangue of a hawker promising good jobs for high pay in Tianjin, the industrial city an hour east of Beijing.

The next day a hopeful Feng took off for Tianjin, where his nightmare began. He signed on with the Beijing Labor Company, which gave him a few coins and a ragged sleeping mat. He did not become aware until too late that he was entering into contract slavery. Korean middlemen sold him and others like him as coolies to the Continental Labor Company for M$35 per person. The company Feng signed on with was a Japanese-owned operation using Korean middlemen to supply cheap labor for the expanding Japanese industrial and military projects in Manchukuo. Labor in Manchuria presented a double-edged problem in the 1930s. Japanese authorities needed labor to supply an insatiable war effort. Yet could they trust Chinese migrating to the area? Were Chinese workers like Feng seeking jobs or plotting attack? Labor companies provided a solution to the dilemma. The Continental Labor Company, like Amakasu's Dadong Labor Company, supplied needed labor while filtering out potential troublemakers.[24]

Feng Dengdiao worked on a construction crew outside New Capital, moving dirt and mud all day. At night he slept in an impromptu tent city with other migrant laborers, eating not much more than sorghum gruel. He stuck it out for five months. Hearing about the wonders and opportunities in Harbin, where beer flowed freely and Russian chorus girls danced in the many nightclubs, he escaped one night, fleeing north. Instead of finding fortune in the business center of the city, however, he ended up begging in the streets outside the Garden of Grand Vision.

Katō Toyotaka came to Manchukuo in 1938 seeking a future. He found a happier environment in Harbin than Feng, one that provided the young man with needed companionship and role models. Katō came from a samurai family, which the abrupt shift to the modern world had left in genteel poverty, as it had many others. Still, the samurai ethic drove his father to seek education, even though he had to walk miles to go to school. Katō never knew his father. The man fell victim to the 1918 flu pandemic only months before Katō Toyotaka's birth. Katō's mother remarried, but a doting grandmother raised the boy. In 1938, when Katō joined the Harbin police, he found a place where he belonged, an organization that provided the young man with the father figures he had lacked in his youth.

When Gotō Reiji wrote about the triumph of Manchukuo, he was thinking of the hopeful experiment that had attracted people like his younger assistants Satō and Katō to the open land. He could see the new nation as the logical solution to the unsolved problems of a violent Asian century. Chinese language, literature, and culture might be eloquent, but their very age kept the Chinese people trapped in tradition. For Gotō, Manchukuo would be the place where successful Japan could withstand Western assaults and lead Asia to a new age. But first it had to be brought under control.

8

Control

The wind blows over the sorghum fields
Deep in the dewy night
In a far off village a dog barks
The police on the beat protect against crime
When the police are awake
The people sleep in safety

—Manchukuo police anthem[1]

We could say that the years 1937 to 1940 were the golden age of the Manchukuo police. Policing and the work of enforcing public order moved ahead relatively smoothly.

—Katō Toyotaka[2]

Gotō Reiji and his colleagues, like most of the people they were apt to meet, came to Manchuria to make a future in a new world. Being fortunate in their contacts, they did not have to spend their nights collecting rat corpses for a living. They found their calling in the newly organized Manchukuo police. Like many Japanese in Manchuria, they sought more than a job. They wanted to build a model society out of anarchy. Their contribution to the new nation would be a modern, efficient police bureau, one that would ensure social stability and public order. As policemen they would work for the nation by serving at the local level.

In this goal they were successful. Katō Toyotaka congratulates himself and his colleagues for it. In 1932, when the Japanese military took over Harbin, its arrival added to the chaos and corruption. Disorder seeped to the basics of daily life. One travel writer commented, after a 1932 visit to Harbin, that the city was a symbol of dirt. An early government survey found that of 392 restaurants, only 11 met the most basic of safety standards. The same survey reported low standards in barbershops, food suppliers, and apartments.[3] By 1938, when the Hinkō (Harbin) County police commissioner authorized Gotō's study, the force had settled into an efficient operation that rewarded professionalism. Unfortunately, the resulting efficiencies only made a harsh occupation even more brutal.

Creating a model police force was not an easy task. Early in 1932, just before the official establishment of Manchukuo as a nation, the new government faced the daunting task of stabilizing the region that its own actions had thrown into further turmoil. A police system became a top priority. Who better to do the job than Amakasu Masahiko? Called away from his dirty tricks in Harbin, Amakasu arrived in New Capital—formerly and now Changchun—to create a new police structure. His task proceeded under the official title "Public Order and Enforcement Operation." Nishimura Tadataka joined his ad hoc group in a Japanese-style inn in New Capital. Nishimura remembers working feverishly for days creating a new police structure centered in the General Affairs Office. They had no guidance and only a mimeographed copy of a sketchy legal code. They paid for the material out of pocket.[4]

The first police structure, by necessity, incorporated local personnel into the new system. Newly labeled as "Manchukuoan," these Chinese policemen had hired on under Zhang Zuolin, the warlord who met his fiery death at the hands of the Japanese military. Now they began taking orders from Japanese officers recruited quickly from the Kempeitai or brought in from older Japanese colonies. Within a year the American consul in Harbin reported in confidence to his ambassador that the Manchukuoan police were unhappy with the new situation. This statement explains the number of men labeled as "former police" who owned flophouse franchises in the Garden of Grand Vision.[5]

Japanese authorities did not find the police system they inherited or its personnel at all up to their standards. Neither did many of their Chinese employees. One former Chinese police officer remembers that in his jurisdiction, just outside Harbin, 80 percent of the police could not read. Many were addicts.[6]

When Japanese troops first took over Harbin, the sitting police chief, appointed by Zhang Xueliang, the warlord's son, was already considered an ineffective disappointment. At the time of his appointment foreign residents hoped the new man, who had a military background, would bring much needed discipline to the force. Instead he proved a lackadaisical administrator. Nor did he display a sense of loyalty. After the Mukden Incident in September 1931, the man actively sided against Japan. Still, when Harbin fell, he agreed to continue in his job. He was, however, expected to salute his three Japanese handlers, one of whom was a former smuggler named Nikolai Nikolaievich Yagi.[7]

Initially, controlling Harbin, as well as Manchukuo, was not easy. The central government in New Capital constantly fiddled with the system to make it work. Authorities established new police academies throughout Manchukuo to address the low quality of precinct-level police. By 1937, after a thorough overhaul, the police organization included 163 county public offices, 37 banner offices, and 1,067 police bureaus with 3,612 precincts; 77,736 police worked in these offices, 7,480 of them Japanese and 5,000 Russian. The authorities arranged communities, urban and rural, in the traditional *baojia* system, making representatives responsible for collections of families in an ever-widening pyramid of mutual responsibility. Health police responded to the need for public sanitation. An additional Forest Constabulary of 100,000 men patrolled for bandits in the countryside.[8]

The later reform included a sinister addition: the Peace Preservation Bureau, perhaps better translated as the "Internal Security Bureau." Created in 1938, it became an underground organization dedicated to spying on prominent Manchukuoans, ferreting out foreign agents and enemies of the state, and—despite a truce—spying on the Soviet Union to the north. It included its own training center where future agents learned foreign languages, the arts of coding and decoding, wire tapping, and dirty tricks. One section of special police, referred to simply as the Branch Office, carried out secret investigations and committed the worst of the human rights crimes. Its agents were located in the major cities and along the Soviet border. The Peace Preservation Bureau excelled at planting listening devices in places where unsuspecting Manchukuoans might gather and gossip. Much of China's Northeast was bugged.[9] But these reforms, with their institutional horrors, would come later. In 1932 quickly bringing northern Manchukuo under control was the top priority.[10]

Harbin was the last area in China's Northeast to join the new nation. After Chiang Kai-shek gave his fateful military orders for officers not to resist Japan, China's Northeast fell easily to the occupying army. Not so Harbin. In late November 1931, the Japanese Kantō Army sent a force of Chinese sympathizers to control the North. Instead this newly minted Manchukuoan military faced stiff resistance from a hastily organized Harbin Self-Defense Army. Irregular Chinese troops, with little help from the Chinese government inside the Wall, resisted Japanese invasion for over a month. The situation required a northern thrust led by General Tamon Jirō. His brigade inched north along the frozen Chinese Eastern Railway, then still in Soviet hands. At one point his men were surprised by a dawn attack, barely pulling through the encounter. They did not approach Harbin until late January 1932.[11]

Harbin capitulated to Japanese forces on February 5, 1932. As the city returned to normal, Manchukuo authorities planned celebrations to rally popular support for their action. White Russians living in the city greeted the Japanese troops waving flags in hopes the change in government would work in their favor and against their Soviet rivals.[12] Propaganda films capture the scene of throngs of Chinese, White Russians, and local ethnic groups crowding the streets, all holding Japanese flags, to welcome a parade of tanks and smartly uniformed Japanese troops as they passed.[13]

George Hanson, the American consul in Harbin, was a perceptive observer of the celebrations. On the surface, he said, the crowds seemed festive. The new city government declared March 10, 11, and 12 holidays. Arches of lights glowed with the message "Light of East Asia" along the main streets. Banners reading "Universal Harmony" decorated walls. A popular subscription raised money for the festivities. The days were filled with dragon dances and parades.

In fact, Hanson noted, police squeezed subscription money from Chinese bankers to pay for the event. Chinese shops were pressed to send representatives to join the crowds. One artful protester took a paintbrush and with one stroke changed the characters for "universal harmony" (大同) to "dog harmony" (犬同). It portended how difficult controlling Harbin and North Manchukuo would be.[14]

Many among the Chinese-majority population, now labeled "Manchukuoan," did not share in the excitement. People showed up to victory celebrations out of curiosity, or coercion, or for the bribes that came with attendance, or all three. The Manchukuo films portrayed the event as a great moment in history. Some Chinese kept up the pretense of cooperation; others went about their business, hoping Japanese rule would bring stability; still others continued the battle against Japan from the mountainous border regions. They joined bandit groups, which had already given northern Manchuria a wild frontier reputation. Securing this northern city was essential to pacifying the border region. Harbin became a center for Border Pacification Constabulary. At the same time bringing Harbin's multinational civic organization under Japanese control was no easy task; nor did it go smoothly in the first few years.[15]

The first crisis Harbin faced was flood. In early August 1932, torrential rains pelted North Manchuria. On August 5, the Songhua River breeched its banks. The river periodically threatened to flood, but the 1932 rains came in sheets, overtaxing all drainage systems. By August 7, river water surged into the Daowai streets. The next morning even the prosperous Daoli section felt the fury of the water. People fled their homes, groggy with sleep, able to take nothing with them but their lives. They sought refuge in the Temple of Extreme Joy or in Nangang, where makeshift camps lined up in open spaces like scales on a fish.[16]

Photos from the summer of the flood show Kitaiskaia Street under water. Fashionable ladies wade through knee-deep sludge as they pass the stylish shop windows. A Japanese officer on a horse pushes through water up to the horse's shoulder. Well-dressed businessmen row down the avenue in boats. One clever—or desperate—man has turned a wooden tub into a rowboat. Families in Fujiadian, the area hardest hit, sit on roofs for temporary safety.[17]

Harbin's new government did little to prevent the situation. When the waters first threatened, the government made no effort to shore up the levees with sandbags. As the crisis intensified, Zhang Jinghui, the city's unhappy puppet mayor, led a group of monks from the Temple of Extreme Joy through the streets to the center of Daoli. The procession chanted prayers and made offerings of paper charms and incense in hopes of calming the angry Dragon King.

One modern commentator calls the parade a "muddleheaded bit of theater." Theater it was, a kind of ancient ceremony, older than Buddhism despite the monks' role in the procession, older than Confucianism, and much older than any military presence. Anyone who has lived in a Chinese city can picture the scene: horns and cymbals beating out a rhythmic cacophony, a paper goat or pig carried on a bier to be burned at the water's edge, perhaps even a shaman going into a trance. We can forgive the mayor for reverting to a cultural tradition springing from an early landscape prone to flooding, especially given the lack of civic direction from the new Japanese handlers.[18]

The floodwater retreated more slowly than it came. It left in its wake thousands of refugees and numerous outbreaks of cholera. The population declined as people either died or left the destruction, never to return. By September the military had slowly regained control of the city. It proceeded to carry on with building schemes.[19]

The flood provided a tremendous opportunity for the young Yanagida Momotarō, who gave us such a cheerful tour of the city. He had come to Manchukuo to work for the International Shipping Company, but when the flood began, he left his job to volunteer to help with relief efforts. As the waters receded, he remained with the Harbin municipal planning office, taking a cut in pay. He and several colleagues oversaw the reworking of the riverfront, building levees, the park, and drainage systems. When heavy rains threatened again two summers later, the city was spared a second flooding. For Yanagida, working for Manchukuo gave him a noble purpose. Today, in the square where the old Kitaiskaia Street meets the river, there is a monument to the heroes of victory over the floodwaters. A line on the base marks the water level of the 1932 flood. It is not, however, a monument to the Manchukuo government.

The 1932 flood was not an auspicious beginning for the new regime. In fact, things would get worse. Lawlessness took the place of water threatening the lives of the residents. And where were the police? The American consul for the city, George Hanson, sent reports to the US State Department describing a situation altogether different from the rosy self-congratulations found in Japanese propaganda. In April 1932 he described a legal system in disarray as qualified Chinese judges left their posts. Political hacks filled the vacuum. Japanese agents took over banks, rail and steamship companies, and the electric system. There seemed to be an ongoing internal battle between military and civilian interests. In the city itself, no one was safe from crime.[20]

Hanson, like other American and European residents of Harbin, felt the sting of sudden change not in insult to national pride so much as danger to him personally. Hanson himself related a troubling experience. In 1932, after driving him home from a social event, Hanson's Russian chauffeur was beaten by a drunk Kempeitai officer of the Manchukuo government. The intoxicated officer had mistaken the consul's car for a cab. Hanson came down from his apartment to help his employee, later getting a direct apology from the Japanese authorities. The unpleasant incident was charged with the tension felt by residents of the city. It also indicates that even after ten years of service, Hanson still camped out in an apartment above the consulate. His Japanese colleague, meanwhile, enjoyed a lovely new residence.[21]

The founders of Manchukuo believed in pan-Asianism—Asia for the Asians. Thus Japanese authorities undoubtedly were not overly upset when lawlessness targeted Europeans and Americans. The comfortable life of the foreign community disappeared, especially in Harbin. Perhaps for the first time in expat memory, elite clubs did not provide a barrier from the hardships of life in Asia—a reality brought home when bandits attacked a party of British sportsmen as they finished a round of golf. They just barely escaped from the green with their lives. The murder of a British woman, the young Mrs. Woodruff, a bride who had only just come to Harbin to join her husband, followed the golfing tragedy. Many Europeans sent their wives home.[22]

Life was hardly safer for Japanese living in Manchukuo. Attacks on Japanese skyrocketed as ordinary banditry became guerrilla warfare. Trains on the rail lines running north had to be fortified. Night travel ceased. Pillboxes and patrol cars protected rail lines. Bunkers appeared at the bridges on the main trunk line between New Capital and Harbin. Rumor had it that there was a bounty on the heads of Japanese soldiers, including M$2,000 for an officer and M$30,000 for a general. Japanese bombing raids flew into the mountainous North to crush bandit strongholds, often destroying the homes and lives of civilians along with their intended targets. Police and military missions blurred under the heading "bandit-suppression operations."[23]

Hanson's monthly dispatches described unfettered corruption in the early years of the Harbin police system. Quality of policing had not improved, he noted, with the influx of Japanese advisors. Typical of the newcomers was one officer with the improbable name Nikolai Nikolaievich Yagi. Hanson concluded that Yagi's interests centered more on gambling, opium, and thuggery than on the business of sound police work. Hanson himself carried a pistol everywhere he went.

Nikolai Yagi was a Japanese adventurer who had lived in Harbin for some time. He had a good knowledge of Russian and had ostensibly converted to the Eastern Orthodox Church, thus his odd combination of names. Yagi was more opportunist than pious religious seeker. He and a group of his Russian cronies earned a good living in the Harbin narcotics racket in the 1920s. In 1932 he easily gained a high-ranking post in the city police bureau. He was one of the advisors whom Hanson found lacking. His presence boded ill for his fellow Harbiners, especially the Russians who had welcomed the Japanese troops into Harbin at first.

Yagi entered the police service as one of several Japanese who would oversee a force of Russians, Chinese, and Koreans. The service itself fit into the larger government of Manchukuo through the centralized General Affairs Office, which ran the entire enterprise. On paper Manchukuo strived for multiethnic harmony through an inclusive personnel roster. The structure of the government included a constitution, a consultative assembly, and a judiciary, all under the reign of the last Qing emperor, the unlucky Henry Puyi. In fact a policy of "internal guidance" guaranteed the Japanese military retained control.

In practice, the instruments of government had as little real authority as the puppet emperor they served. A flow chart of Japanese political organization shows the General Affairs Office under the control of the Consultative Assembly. In fact, Japanese military personnel in the General Affairs Office held the reigns of power. For every Chinese minister in a position of authority, a Japanese vice minister called the shots. This was the case everywhere from the central authority in New Capital to the police bureau in Harbin. Over time, the number of Chinese and other ethnic groups serving in official posts decreased. Their authority was never genuine. This "internal guidance" was meant to serve as an Asian model to replace the cabinet system imported from the West. Its unofficial support agency was the Concordia Society, and its program was the Kingly Way.[24]

In the early days of Manchukuo's development, police organizations throughout the length and breadth of the land remained pretty much intact. Men who served Zhang Zuolin remained in place. The new government needed police with local knowledge. They merely added Japanese advisors to the top of the old warlord system. Yagi represented the sort of carpetbagger who crawled out of the woodwork to grab a sudden opportunity for enrichment. At the head of the new national police organization was the adventurer and spy Amakasu Masahiko. As we have seen, Amakasu left Harbin for New Capital immediately after completing his dirty work. He became the first director of the Manchukuo Police Bureau. To fill the top jobs, he turned to his old organization, the notorious Kempeitai. A Chinese police chief took office in New Capital, giving the police institution a multiethnic look of independence. In fact, Amakasu or his successors ran the show.

Given the large Russian population of the greater Harbin area, the police needed Russian-speaking officers for the service. Thus Yagi found his early opportunity for enrichment. Later authorities would send promising officers like the young Katō Toyotaka to the Harbin Russian Academy to study the language. Elsewhere police colleagues included Mongolian and Korean staff wherever their fellow countrymen lived in sufficient numbers to warrant them.

By 1940 the Harbin City Police Central Administration consisted of seven divisions: Police Affairs, Special Branch, Foreign Affairs, Judicial, Internal Security, Economic Order, and Public Health. These offices oversaw five districts: Daoli, Daowai, Fragrant Mill, Nangang, and supervised towns and villages adjacent to the city itself. Each district was further divided into local precinct and subprecinct police stations. Gotō worked out of the Police Affairs Division.[25]

The majority of the police serving at the local level were Chinese. Gotō indicated his contempt for the local Chinese police. They took bribes. They colluded in narcotics trafficking. They were not to be trusted. Outside Manchukuo, the view of these men was much worse. Chinese patriots south of the Wall called all government officials who stayed in Manchukuo traitors. Having worked for the murdered Zhang Zuolin, how could they refuse to follow his son out of Manchuria to continue the battle for China.

Chinese police in Manchukuo were more than just corrupt. Stories of the vicious behavior of local police toward the people they were meant to protect are ghastly. For instance, Li Runzhi—people called him Sticky Skin Li—was a village police chief who excelled at extortion. Once he had gained a reputation for using brutal torture on his captives, he easily persuaded the families of his arrestees to buy their loved ones out of his clutches. He based his captures on the wealth of the family rather than any evidence of wrongdoing.[26]

Many among the ranks of local police had little option but to stay in their jobs. Some even used their positions to fight for China on a hidden front. Fan Chuanzhong was such a person. A Harbin man himself, he served as police chief in a town just outside his native city. While in this post he remained in contact with anti-Japanese forces operating out of the border region and helped them procure needed supplies and information. His status as an informer came to an end in 1939 when a colleague ratted him out to the Japanese Kempeitai. Fan was arrested with ten others. His captor, who followed him in the post, ordered his lackeys to tie him up in a burlap bag, hang him in a tree, and beat him to within an inch of his life.[27]

If Chinese police were corrupt, the early Japanese organization they served was little better. Arrests of Russians, White and Red alike, began soon after the capture of Harbin. The victims found themselves in police custody on trumped up accusations of Marxist activity. Police proved such charges conveniently by planting Soviet propaganda pamphlets in their victim's homes. Unless a relative paid for early release, a gruesome interrogation would follow arrest. One eyewitness account of the procedures reported the following water torture: "The hands and feet of the prisoner are securely bound and his mouth is sealed with adhesive plaster. He is placed in an approximately horizontal position with his head at a lower level than his feet. An instrument shaped somewhat like a funnel, having two outlets which are placed tightly in his nostrils, is used for pouring water mixed with turpentine or benzine [*sic*] into the nasal passages. This treatment causes the prisoner to experience a sensation similar to that of drowning and he eventually loses consciousness."[28] Other witnesses described beatings targeting sensitive lymph gland areas to maximize pain. The situation was such that a group of Russian taxi drivers, who could barely eke out a living driving twelve hours a day, returned to the Soviet Union they had earlier escaped. To save face, the Manchukuo government listed them as deportees. The situation for Russians improved only after the Soviet government promised equally brutal treatment for Japanese prisoners and turned over their section of the rail trunk line to Japanese control in 1935.[29]

Cruelty within the Japanese agencies of wartime control comes as no surprise to any of us after a lifetime's exposure to Second World War memoirs, novels, and movies. Yagi fits the stereotype to a tee. Yet, by 1939, Gotō Reiji and his colleagues strived for professionalism in their work. Nor did they work with the disreputable Mr. Yagi. Serving next to the corrupt police were equally ardent reformers striving for an international standard in their investigations. When police reform came to Harbin, it included a clean sweep of upper-level officers. Changes came due equally to the central government's vision of consolidation and to a local Harbin scandal that garnered international attention. The Simon Kaspe murder case publicly tarnished the Harbin police department's reputation. The case demonstrated the viciousness, barely hidden beneath the

veneer of reform, of the Manchukuo project. It involved collusion between White Russian and Japanese officers.

From the early Manchukuo years, the Harbin police gained a well-
deserved reputation for collusion with kidnappers and brutal treatment
of any wretch unlucky enough to fall into their custody. Anyone, Chinese
or foreign, who appeared wealthy risked kidnapping. Gangs of Russian
thugs abducted family members, asking huge ransoms for their victims'
safe return. The proceeds they shared with Japanese authorities. The
Kempeitai especially benefited from the epidemic of kidnapping. The
situation was desperate enough in the early years that Consul George
Hanson traveled about the town with a revolver at his side and in the
company of bodyguards. Edgar Snow (1905–1972), the journalist who
would later chronical the rise of the Chinese Communist Party in his book
Red Star over China, visited Harbin during this time of uncertainty. He visited Hanson at a shack by the Songhua River, where he found the consul
equipped with a "small arsenal of rifles and automatics." Hanson clearly
had the personality to thrive in what Snow called the "Wild East."[30]

In the middle of the kidnapping epidemic, Simon Kaspe, the son of
a wealthy Russian Jewish Harbin family, came home to visit his family. His father, Abraham, had grown in wealth and status with the city
itself. Abraham Kaspe came to Harbin in 1903, making his fortune selling
jewelry and real estate. He owned the Modern Hotel, providing luxury
accommodations on Kitaiskaia Street. He also owned a movie theater. The
Modern Hotel, still in business, is a pink confection with an art nouveau
lobby (a visit is more than worth the price of a cocktail in its overpriced
bar). Abraham was known to be a wealthy patron of the arts. He sent his
children to France for schooling in order to obtain French citizenship for
the entire family. He displayed the French flag prominently in both his
hotel and theater. As it turned out, this was a smart move on his part.[31]

The young Simon, a man in his mid-twenties, was a talented pianist,
establishing a reputation on the concert circuits in Europe. He lived in
Paris and enjoyed French citizenship. In the summer of 1933, he returned
to his Harbin hometown for a family visit. Being a handsome young man
in a city of clubs, Simon the playboy escorted lovely young women to the
bars and cabarets that made Harbin famous.

Late one August night, while he was seeing a lady home from a night
on the town, thugs abducted Simon. Abraham received demands for
M$300,000 in ransom. Stubbornly, the father refused to pay, hoping the
Harbin police would track down the culprits. Young Simon was held cap-
tive for months. His father received the boy's severed ears as a warning.
Still the old man would offer only a tenth of the demanded ransom. He refused to pay anything until after his son's release. Simon's captors proved
equally stubborn. They tortured him. They fed him little and allowed him

to freeze as the weather turned cold. Those in the know assumed that Simon would never return alive. He knew too much, specifically about the complicity of the Japanese Kempeitai in his ordeal.[32]

Late in November police discovered Simon's battered corpse in a shallow grave outside Harbin. His murder remained a mystery, which, the Harbin police claimed, they could not solve. The police continued to drag their feet, claiming the case baffled them. Unfortunately for the Harbin authorities, the French consulate considered Simon one of their own. The French vice consul raised the alarm, bringing formal complaints against the Japanese-run Harbin police. Both the consul and the Jewish community of Harbin kept the case in the public eye.

The French consul hired Amieto Vespa to do what the Harbin police would not. Vespa, we will remember, liked and admired the warlord Zhang Zuolin, the best of all bosses. Now a Chinese citizen with a wife and family, Vespa joined the ranks of the bureaucratic holdovers from the warlord era. Like many precinct police, he found his employer had changed but not his duties. Vespa was not happy with the new situation. He had planned to leave with his family at the creation of Manchukuo. Instead a Japanese intelligence officer, whose name Vespa never learned—he called him "the Chief"—summoned him to army headquarters and told him quite frankly, "We have your file containing a record of all your activities from the moment you set foot in China in 1912." He added that "many Japanese officers . . . entertain a very high opinion of you." For that reason the Japanese authorities assumed that Vespa would willingly work for them. If not, the chief made it clear that Vespa's family would be in danger.[33]

The Chief then spelled out for Vespa, in excellent English, a plan to organize White Russians, harass Red Russians and Russian Jews, and create a system to bring money into the Manchukuo coffers. Vespa admitted that he had once thought of the Japanese soldiers as chivalrous. He had ignored rumors about the mistreatment of Koreans and Chinese as groundless. After his first visit with the Chief, Vespa realized the true nightmare in Manchukuo was only beginning. He knew that if he did not play by the Japanese rules, his wife, two children, and mother-in-law would be in danger.

An unhappy Vespa spied on Russians in Manchukuo. Vespa hated the Japanese for whom he worked. In the process, however, he gained valuable contacts that would help him solve the Simon Kaspe murder case. Vespa used his underworld contacts to uncover and make public the truth about the young man's kidnapping and death. He learned that White Russian thugs with both fascist leanings and close ties to the Harbin police operation had kidnapped Simon. The gang specialized in kidnapping prominent Harbin citizens to raise money, its members claimed, to work against Bolsheviks at home.[34]

Vespa discovered that one of the kidnappers was a Russian Harbin police officer, a Mr. Martinoff. And Martinoff's Japanese superior was none other than Nikolai Nikolaievich Yagi, then serving as head of the foreign section in the Harbin police. During Vespa's investigation into the death of Simon Kaspe, it became clear that Yagi had worked closely with Martinoff to keep the case unsolved. This was not the best example of scientific police work.

The Harbin police made statements to excuse their own lax investigations. They accused the French vice consul of interfering with the case. When the names of the criminals became public, despite Yagi's remarkable lack of effort or interest in investigating the case, an official police statement announced that the kidnappers' motives had been patriotic. For this reason, they said, the culprits should be treated leniently. French diplomatic pressure continued nonetheless, leading to the arrest of the kidnappers.

In June 1936, six White Russians went on trial for the murder of Simon Kaspe. Two judges—one Chinese and the other Japanese (and really the man in charge)—sentenced four of the culprits to death. Two more received prison terms of life in hard labor camps. The next year in February, however, all six received pardons. They left police custody having served little time in jail for their gruesome crime.

Abraham Kaspe never got over the death of his son. He sold the Modern Hotel and left Harbin in 1939. Yet his spirit is very much in the building. Portraits of Abraham, his wife Anna, and Simon standing by a grand piano welcome visitors in the hallway between the ornate coffee shop and the even more ornate bar. Photographs of the many opera singers, ballet dancers, and actors who came to Harbin sponsored by Abraham or who stayed in the hotel surround the likenesses of the owner and his family. The waitstaff will tell a curious person that Abraham's ghost haunts the halls. If it does, one has to wonder what that opera-loving spirit thinks of the Russian rock singer performing for nighttime crowds on Center Street, surrounded by neon splendor on the second-floor balcony of the Modern Hotel.

The publicity of the case left a well-deserved impression of corruption at the top of the Harbin police structure and a stain on the service. In 1937, during nationwide reforms, authorities in New Capital cleaned out the top brass of the Harbin police. Yagi rotated out of Harbin. By the time Gotō began his study of the Harbin slums, his supervising officers were all different men from the days of Yagi. A notable presence was Shibuya Saburō, whose professionalism would impress his Chinese colleagues when he became police inspector in the central government.[35]

In its early days, the Manchukuo Police Bureau recruited from an influx of Japanese carpetbaggers, soldiers of fortune living in Manchukuo, and power brokers whose scams set back any reform agenda. In 1937 the entire national force underwent a streamlining reorganization. More Japanese officers rotated into the service, allowing tighter control over the rank-and-file police. The service began to take on the appearance of a modern force. Reforms included the addition of police academies, a center for fingerprint analysis, entrance examinations, and even the addition of a Manchukuo policeman's anthem. Instead of coming from questionable backgrounds like Yagi, new hires came out of police academies.

By the end of the decade, recruiting had been standardized, requiring candidates to have a police background or academy training. Police academies fed trained officers to precincts through the country. By 1945 the fingerprint bureau had over four million prints on file. Most of these prints came from Chinese and Korean laborers—potentially dangerous men like Gotō's informant Feng Dengdiao. The local newspaper hailed fingerprinting as a "first step in scientific investigation."[36]

As a young man Yue Ruheng tested into the Harbin police academy in 1940. There he was taught by a staff of fifteen Japanese, twenty or so Chinese, and four White Russians. He and his classmates were classified by test results. Those with the lowest scores trained for ordinary police work. Yue tested into the top rank of his class. This slotted him to become a police lieutenant. For six months he studied police procedures, criminal law, and Japanese language. He also trained in swords and firearms. After graduating, he was assigned to a police precinct in his hometown.[37]

From 1932 to the fall of Manchukuo in 1945, a string of assistant police commissioners and other high-ranking police officials filled the post first occupied by Amakasu Masahiko, who left the public position for the shadows of espionage after less than a year. Knowing what we do of the savage treatment prisoners received at the hands of the Japanese military, of the relationship between policing and intelligence, and of the character of Amakasu, we might expect these officers to be grisly characters of ill repute. In fact, except for one brief period when Amakasu's own brother-in-law used the office to enrich himself, each police commissioner and his immediate assistants brought hard work, dedication, and the desire to make the system work to the job. Testimonials to the character of these commissioners come from Chinese sources. They describe ambitious men desperately—and futilely—laboring to create a professional service against staggering odds. Their obstacle: powerful people in their own organization.

One example is Nagao Yoshigorō. Born in 1882, Nagao came to the post from the Kempeitai. Yet he is described as a modest and polite man of few words who impressed people as a scholar rather than a soldier. Nagao was assisted by Satō Tarō, also from the Kempeitai. Satō (no relation to Satō of the Garden report) was a forceful man who did much to centralize the police service and bring it up to professional standards. A law school graduate and a Buddhist scholar also held central leadership posts. Chinese officials who worked for these men praised them for their dedication to reform and justice. They were fighting a losing battle.[38]

The most interesting person to hold the post of police commissioner was Shibuya Saburō, who graduated with honors from the Japanese military academy. He rose to the rank of brigade commander, serving in Tokyo in 1936. On February 26 of that fateful year, radical army officers attempted a coup d'état. The action failed, but before the end, several politicians died. The center of Tokyo came under martial law before the rebellious officers were captured and peace restored. Though not part of the rebellion, Shibuya was suspected as a sympathizer. His career in jeopardy, he retired to Manchukuo, where he found work as the new commissioner of the Harbin City Police. He brought honesty to the job, restoring a measure of integrity to the force after international scandal had revealed it to be a nest of corruption.

Shibuya thrived in Manchukuo. He was fluent in Russian and had an inborn flair for adventure. He liked to tell the story of the time when, early in his career, he was posted to the Japanese embassy in Germany. On his own initiative, he took a trip into the newly formed Soviet Union. There he was arrested and detained for several days. He described jails filled with bedbugs that kept him awake all night long. At the end of his career he returned to Harbin as dean of the Harbin Russian Academy. His colleagues remember Shibuya as a cheerful man, calling him Happy Saburō.

Of course, although the Japanese officers ran the show, their title always implied that they were second in command. One Manchukuoan who headed the Police Affairs Division around the same time that Katō served in Harbin was Yu Zhishan (1882–1951), a toad of a man. In his youth, Yu attended the military academy in Mukden. He then joined the military working for the warlord Zhang Zuolin. After Zhang senior's murder and the defeat of the younger Zhang, Yu Zhishan moved straight into the service of the new Manchukuo government, where he held several posts in the central government. His photograph shows a smiling man with chipmunk cheeks, wearing a fur hat and jodhpurs, standing in front of the police bureau office building. Next to and behind him are two assistants—his Japanese handlers. The photograph is a visual testament to the way internal guidance worked in real life. After 1949, Yu was labeled as a traitor. He died in prison.

Police reforms brought results. Kidnapping for ransom abated under foreign protests and local scandal. Bandits continued to disrupt the countryside, pursuing an anti-Japanese agenda. Yet urban policing became efficient. Street crime, out of control at the beginning of the Manchukuo period, dropped noticeably. Traffic control made driving more orderly. One consul noted that the Japanese "inclination for detail and thoroughness, while at times a nuisance, is evident in the working of the Manchukuo police system." The officers looked brighter and smarter, showing a high level of morale.[39] Like the need for flood control, initial civil chaos led to a search for professionalism.

Public order had its darker side. The central reforms added the inward-looking Peace Preservation Bureau to police administrations throughout Manchukuo. At the same time that they brought modern professionalism to the nation, they became instruments of tighter control. Recruits to the Peace Protection Bureau came from the police academy. Once chosen, a person studied for an additional year. That recruit could specialize in the dark arts needed for spying, such as surveillance. Or, like Gotō, he could focus on language and sociology.

The Peace Preservation Bureau worked to prevent crimes against the Manchukuo state. Its agents picked up political prisoners, most of whom disappeared into an unpleasant oblivion. Among police it was simply known as the Branch Office. The organization had a fearsome reputation. Suspects disappeared into the so-called special asylums of the Branch Office with no recourse to the law. Harsh interrogation was the rule. Yue, who trained at the police academy, described the kind of fearsome treatment prisoners faced. They might have hot pepper water forced into their bodies. Torturers flogged their victims with a cowhide whip, two inches thick and about a meter long, which could make a person beg for death after only one stroke. Even crueler was "the telephone." The torturer disentangled wires from a field telephone, separating the ground and hot wires. By connecting the wires to a battery at one end and clamping the ground wire to the victim's thumb, the tormentor could cause serious pain by using the hot wire to run an electric current through the victim's body each time the phone was dialed (or cranked). This torture caused damage to the heart and nervous system. This was something our police cadet found impossible to watch.[40]

Many prisoners who came into the hands of the Branch Office died miserable deaths in Pingfang in the suburbs of Harbin. There they became unfortunate victims of gruesome biological experiments. The village of Pingfang lay about twenty-five miles southwest of Harbin. Guidebooks of the day never recommended a visit to this town. In fact, the area was off-limits. Even today, when urban sprawl has gobbled the village into the city itself, tourists seldom seek the place out. Yet it leaves its own macabre legacy. One brown building, surrounded by parkland, survives. It is now a museum documenting the horrors that occurred at the place. This is the site of Unit 731 run by Dr. Ishii Shirō.

In 1938 the Japanese military established the Biological Research and Water Purification Bureau in the Harbin area. The facility was a medical experimentation laboratory headed by Dr. Ishii. Attached to the army as Unit 731, it was both laboratory and prison. Pity the poor souls, political prisoners mostly, who ended up in this institution. They were healthy as they entered, one criterion for selection. In the research facility they became guinea pigs. After they were injected with plague, subjected to freezing and frostbite, or scalded with hot water, doctors recorded the precise stages of their resultant deaths.

The records kept by the medical personnel working for the brigade were so precise that they were confiscated by the Americans after the Second World War. The information disappeared into the US Centers for Disease Control until a Japanese reporter in the 1980s began to unearth and publicize the story.

The Biological Research and Water Purification Bureau, or Unit 731, fit into the realm of activities at which the Japanese army excelled: detailed research gathering and dirty tricks. Unit 731 not only collected information about disease but bred rats, lice, and fleas. These disease vectors were wanted for planned operations involving the controlled release of plague in enemy territory, a crude sort of germ warfare.[41] Healthy arrestees became experimental subjects in Pingfang.

Thus the Harbin police blotter reads, "July, 1941—Two Soviets arrested by the Harbin Police Justice Bureau. The Foreign Division arrested six Soviet men. Based on the evidence given by Matsumoto Hideo of the said police bureau all eight are Soviet spies. All eight are certified for transfer to the Ishii Brigade."[42] Gotō knew about the research facility. Like many others at the time, he soothed any qualms he may have had by telling himself that the research done there was in the interest of science—a service to the greater good. He worked for the Peace Preservation Bureau himself, but as a linguist and culture expert, not as a spy. Gotō focused on the crime he saw everyday in the Garden of Grand Vision. He saved his empathy for the women who worked as prostitutes to pay for drugs for themselves, their clients, and their pimps.

Amakasu Masahiko.

A sex worker and her client. We are asked to notice the sexual lust in the client's expression (Hara Shobō).

A sex worker and her client. The caption asks us to notice the way life has drained out of the woman's body. The makeshift wall decorations show pictures of happy families rather than the kind of decor that one might expect to find at the brothel down the street (Hara Shobō).

Consul George C. Hanson. This picture appeared in the *New York Times* on June 25, 1935, as Hanson left for Ethiopia. The journey would be his last (permission granted by Times World Wide Prints/The New York Times/Redux).

Feng Dengdiao, the policeman's friend and informant (Hara Shobō).

Shibuya Saburō. Every memoir mentions Shibuya as a cheerful and honorable man (from Manchukuo Police History, published in Manchukuo in 1942).

Chief of Police Yu Zhishan. This picture says it all about the running of Manchukuo. Yu is the man smiling on the left. The two scowling assistants are the real power behind his office (Seki Hiroshige, Seki Paper Company, Matsuyama, Japan).

Simon Kaspe. The photograph hangs alongside one of his mother and father in the lobby of the Modern Hotel (photograph taken by the author).

9

✑

Working Girls

Remove prostitutes from human affairs and you will destroy everything with lust.

—St. Augustine[1]

In Fujiadian the ratio between men and women is frightfully imbalanced. The population is swollen by tramps acting under the compulsion of unnatural instincts. The women become commodities, acting as a safety valve for those who are unsatisfied. They cannot hope for love, for love in their limited understanding is an illusion.

—Gotō Reiji[2]

All of the women in the Garden of Grand Vision worked. They sold their bodies to support husbands, lovers, and children. Their working conditions were harsh, but in the Garden, they were hardly more desperate than their men.[3]

East Asian society in general tolerated prostitution. High-class courtesans could be glamorous, talented women. Men of means and status gathered openly in expensive luxurious brothels where fashionable women entertained them in style. Such women could earn a reputation for beauty and singing skills, making them as famous as actresses or singers are in today's world. A few such courtesans became poets of note. These women were the Chinese sing-song girls or the Japanese geisha. Their lives have been captured in movies such as *Rouge, Flowers of Shanghai,* and *Memoirs of a Geisha.*[4] Yet the profession still carried a stigma. Traditional Chinese law included prostitutes, along with actors and litigators, in the category of "mean people." As they were legal, they could be taxed; still, they were distained and relegated to specific urban neighborhoods.[5]

Tolerance did not equal status or safety. Even women working in high-class brothels could not be certain of a life of ease. Entrance into the world of the courtesan brought a woman education, culture, and beautiful clothes. It gave her contact with some of the wealthiest men in her community. Clever women turned this to their advantage. If they saved enough money, they could some day own a brothel themselves. Most, however, enjoyed a few brief seasons before their beauty faded. As they aged, their procurers passed them on to progressively lower-class brothels. They ended their lives at the very bottom of the profession, as streetwalkers—"wild pheasants" in Chinese slang. Or they ended their days in places like the Garden of Grand Vision.[6]

Braying Mule Wang's woman had followed just such a career path. She brought knowledge of erotic drug-taking techniques with her from the upper-class houses. Braying Mule Wang found her intoxicating.[7]

Harbin teemed with brothels, ranging from expensive and ornate to cheap and practical. Establishments catered to any client's preference in terms of price, gender, and nationality. They also catered to the multiethnic population of the city. Japanese, Korean, and Russian brothels offered services to both the affluent and the not so well-heeled of each community.

The earliest red-light district in the Daowai Chinese section of town, Peach Blossom Alley, catered to the wealthy Chinese of Harbin. Lush Flowers Lane attracted a more eclectic clientele. The many houses had elegant names—Welcoming Spring Hall, Spring Swan Hall, Rich Spring Pavilion—"spring" being a euphemism for prostitution. These districts of flowers and willows, as they were known, attracted talented beauties who served wealthy customers. An ad in the paper from 1919 announced that a "beautiful flower named Gao Xiaojin" had just arrived, having made her name in Shanghai, Tianjin, and Wuhan. Gao brought two companions with her. The article praised the girl's singing.[8]

Just down the street from the Garden of Grand Vision was the Pingkangli brothel quadrant. A circular wooden structure sat in the middle of the area, with alleys where the girls worked radiating from its center. Most people did not refer to the area by its official name: Peace and Health Alley. Instead they named their preferred brothel or simply called the entire area "the Circle" for the signature building. There were more than forty brothels in the quadrant. In the local slang, the character for "cave" was used for brothels. The madams who ran the establishments were called "bustards," whereas the pimps were called "pronged poles."[9]

Most brothels were not high tone or expensive. In all the houses, whether glamorous or plain, the women lived lives of hardship. They worked under the strict control of brothel owners, often women themselves. They came to the profession through traffickers who bought girls in the countryside from parents in economic distress. Everything a woman used, from beautiful clothing to jewels, belonged to the brothel.

One woman working in the Noble Treasure Hall had been raised there since childhood. At sixteen she began receiving guests. At the age of eighteen, she fell in love with a client and thought of running away with him. The brothel owner learned of her plans, stripped off her clothes, and threw her out into the snow. She survived a suicide attempt, only to contract syphilis. When the procuress brought her a folk remedy, the young woman died of the cure.[10]

If the singsong girls of Peach Blossom Alley represented the elite of Chinese prostitution and the working girls in the Circle catered to regular folk, the women in the Garden occupied the absolute lowest rung of desirability and fashion. They were lower in status than even women in the poorest of brothels. In the Garden, a prostitute's workday began early in the afternoon. Gotō Reiji describes men swarming around the south entrance to the Garden as the women took up posts along the hallways, on the stairs, and in front of the flophouse doors. They would call out to the customers, "Shall we go inside and talk?" or "Fifty cents and let's do it." Our investigator described them as thin, with sagging skin and half-transparent eyes. Their expressionless faces contrasted sharply with their tempting words. Men eating melon seeds bantered and made obscene jokes with the women.[11]

Gotō sympathized with these women. He saw how their working conditions damaged their bodies and health. He deplored their shriveled features and sagging skin. Overwork, poor diet, and the stifling atmosphere of the Garden destroyed them. They appeared in the hallways and along the stairwells of the building like apparitions "wrapped in the shadow of death."[12] Corruption warped their bodies; passion burnt them up like candles. Gotō described how their bodies became commodities, sacrificing the gentler feelings of love to carnal gratification.[13]

Gotō met working girls ranging in age from thirteen to sixty. The youngest was the daughter of Ning Changhai. Ning, along with his wife and two daughters—thirteen and seventeen years old—had been occupying a room in the Spring Forest Lodge for over a year when Gotō first ran into them. Ning himself escaped into the pleasures of morphine each day while his wife and two daughters worked.

At the other end of the age scale was the woman of the Wang family, sixty years old, who haunted the darkness of the stairs, expressionless as a stone on the road. White flour coated her face, caking in the deep tracks of her wrinkles. She used hair oil to hide her age. She told people that she was forty-seven.[14]

In our Western world, prostitution carries the permanent stain of sin. In the media, a woman's choice to follow the profession is explained as a result of personal trauma, family violence, drug use, or male exploitation. It is given as a symptom of family breakdown. Gotō was not blind to the role of trauma, violence, and addiction in the lives of the women he met. He came from a culture in which a prostitute could be seen as tragically heroic. A woman could earn money with her body. She became an asset for a family in distress. Families facing hard times sold daughters to brothels, reluctantly in most cases. Such girls were filial daughters. Their sacrifice held families together rather than breaking them apart. Zou the landlord reminded Gotō of the Confucian virtue of these women while trying to convince him that the slum served a social purpose in a harsh world.

"But if a mother makes a daughter sell her body so the mother can smoke morphine, is this filial behavior?" Gotō asked.

"It is. The life of the parent is important," answered the landlord.

"But the daughters calmly have sex in front of the parents and even other children."

"What are they to do? There is no space available."[15]

Gotō had his qualms about propriety in the Garden.

The stigma of prostitution lasted only as long as these women worked. Unlike their Western counterparts, should they find a sponsor to buy out their contract or if they could do so themselves, they could return home, or marry, or carry on a business without enduring shame. This would be true as long as their flirtatious behavior changed when they were reintroduced to family life. A prostitute's dream was to have a rich client fall in love with her, pay her bondage debt, and take her as a concubine. Gotō himself, despite his reservations about family life in the Garden, considered buying out the contract of a particularly pretty woman working there. When his offer failed, he consoled himself by commenting that she really enjoyed the life.[16]

As Gotō points out, many of the women in Fujiadian worked within their immediate family units. Others worked as pawns to help their families manage through a crisis. If prostitution was considered a symptom of social breakdown, and Gotō certainly thought as much, it was as a sign of the destruction of traditional village life and the extended families that held the countryside together. Nuclear families made do as best they could once their sources of livelihood in the villages changed. But from the Asian standpoint, a family of two parents raising their children alone—something we would consider normal—already represented a broken home and community. Gotō's understanding of this is reflected in the stories he tells us as he introduces us to women working in the Garden.

In number four of the Spring Forest Lodge, we meet the Zhang woman who has followed her mother-in-law into the career. In room number seven of the same lodge, the Ning women work together to support their patriarch's morphine habit. In room number nine, eighteen-year-old Wang Xianzhou lives with his wife and mother. The young man has mental problems. His wife works alongside the young man's mother, earning money to care for her helpless spouse.

Gotō tells us that each day mother Wang brings customers for the young prostitute wife. The sad husband stands by the door as she entertains a client. Filled with jealousy and desire, the young husband seems to Gotō to be possessed by a demon. When the client finally leaves, young Wang runs into the room to embrace his wife himself. His mother, meanwhile, searches for new clients.[17]

A Russian woman lives in the Zhizhong Lodge. She is in her late teens, married to a Chinese man, and raising a young child. At one point she tried to refuse to sell herself because she was pregnant. In response, her husband kicked her so badly that she miscarried. The neighbors call her "Old Hairy." She must have stood out in the Garden of Grand Vision. Russian women rarely appeared in the Chinese section of town, although not because they were wealthy. After the 1917 revolution, White Russian women entered the business out of desperation, but they rarely worked in the Chinese slums. Their presence as showgirls and entertainers in the cabarets of Daoli gave Harbin the exotic European flavor that Japanese tourists loved. They excelled in the art of getting shy Japanese men to join them in the latest American dance steps. Despite their being European, poverty made Russians subject to racial slurs.[18]

Madam Li heads a family of women all working together. They came into the business following a series of tragedies in their North China countryside village. Madam Li was a widow with three daughters aged eight to seventeen. The eldest daughter joined the profession first. A neighbor kidnapped her, selling her to a brothel in the Circle for M$1,000. When Madam Li learned of her daughter's whereabouts, she followed, bringing the two other girls with her. In doing so she escaped harsh conditions at home caused by a year of flooding. She moved into the Garden to be near her eldest daughter. In this way she managed to keep the family together

Some of the women's stories reflect the social uncertainties that came with Manchukuo's creation. The woman Wang, forty-five years old and living in Peace Lodge, is one example. Her husband had been a colonel under the old regime. As a crony of the Manchurian warlord's son, Zhang Xueliang,[19] the husband Wang had been powerful and rich. He once enjoyed the company of four concubines in his family circle. After the Mukden Incident of September 1931, Wang's fortune declined. He worked briefly for the Manchukuo police but soon quit. He opened a hotel, which did poorly. Wang tried his hand at running a brothel. He lost a lawsuit and went bankrupt. His concubines deserted him. Only his long-suffering wife joined him in the Garden of Grand Vision. Yet remembering a happier past, the woman Wang puts on airs as she stands in the hallway waiting for customers.[20]

One woman works voluntarily. Old Mrs. Cheng in room two of Spring Forest Lodge left her family after a fight with her mother-in-law. She worked as a maid for a while, then turned to prostitution when she moved into the Garden of Grand Vision. She seems genuinely happy with her solitary life.[21]

Gotō Reiji worried about the young girls growing up in the Garden of Grand Vision. They had no way to learn a moral code that was not debased. They could only follow their mothers into prostitution. Take fourteen-year-old Sun Jinzi. Her father had been a jailer in a town outside Harbin. After he died, the child came with her mother to the Garden of Grand Vision. The little girl plays happily, running up and down the halls and staircase of the building wearing a coat made of cat skin. She flirts and pretends to sell herself to the would-be buyers surrounding her. She once bragged to Gotō that she worked as a shill standing outside the Garden's main gate. One of Gotō's informants, however, claimed that the young girl was not pretending or playing but had already entered the profession. It was the only business she would know—yet it was a business. Leave it to Gotō to keep track of the money.[22]

Prostitutes in the Garden offered three kinds of services based on time. The most common was called "close the door." This entitled the customer to one quick sex act and cost between M$0.20 and M$0.40. Gotō commented that both the poor and those who ejaculated too quickly preferred "close the door." "Pull out the futon" entitled the customer to an entire hour with the woman and cost between M$0.40 and M$0.60, although a pretty and self-confident woman could charge up to M$1.50. "Living style" cost between M$1.00 and M$1.50, and the client could stay the night. A customer would pay first, handing the money over to the husband, debt owner, or parent of the woman whose services he purchased. A woman would only receive up to 20 percent of her earnings. The rest went to a manager.[23]

The women had a poem to describe their life:

> Cry, die, be ransomed, escape (哭死徙良跑)
> Pinch, hit, twist, curse, bite (搯打擰罵咬).

The men had a poem to rate the women, or rather their vaginas, contrasting good with bad:

Fragrant, warm, dry, tight, shallow (香暖乾緊淺)
Smelly, cold, wet, broad, deep (臭冷濕寬深)

And then there were outer and inner techniques. The first involved turning (巔), slanting, (歪) shaking, (搖) curtaining (幌), and spreading (攞). Inner techniques involved inserting (夾) and welcoming (迎). We have to use our imaginations because Gotō's translations, Chinese into Japanese, have been censored.[24]

People in the Garden could not afford medicines, so folk remedies cured their ills. Indeed the cures were perhaps worse than the diseases. Residents of the Garden, both the working girls and their clients, had to confront bouts of syphilis. To combat the disease they turned to a remedy called "Great Poison Conqueror," a concoction claiming to be made from scorpions and spiders. It worked on the theory of using poison to cure poison. It could be taken two or three times a month, but the patient's urine would turn green. Our officer mentioned seeing evidence of this in the public latrines of the Garden.[25]

Garden residents also drank concoctions made with sulfur to keep warm in the winter. Liberal amounts of ground hot pepper kept hunger pangs at bay.

Peasants could ill afford petroleum products. Instead they used soybean oil. They used it to lubricate cart axles and in lamps. Rural people seldom bathed. On special occasions, such as weddings, when a good cleaning was needed, soy oil worked its magic. Caked-on dirt that would not give in to scrubbings with water could be easily lifted off with the application of soy oil. In the Garden of Grand Vision, soy oil was used in the lamps needed for smoking opium. The working women used it as a vaginal lubricant.[26]

Women came to the profession to leave abusive homes, to buy medicine for a sick family member, or to pay for their own or their husband's drug habit or gambling debts. An active group of kidnappers worked in and around the Garden stealing hapless girls to sell into the trade. Young girls followed their mothers into the life. And many of the women in the Garden took a less familiar route into the trade. They served as collateral on family loans. In room number eight of the Spring Forest Lodge, for instance, a young woman served as security on a loan and as such worked as a prostitute.

How can a woman serve as security on a loan like an item to be pawned? In Manchuria of the 1930s, this was a variation on the more common debt bondage that still plagues the rural poor in third-world countries. In the Spring Forest Lodge's room number eight, Old Woman Li, aged sixty, lives with a thirty-year-old woman. The two women addressed each other as "Mother" and "Daughter," but it was known that the younger woman is really the collateral on money the old woman loaned out. The woman living with Mr. Wang in room three is a pledge on a gambling debt.

People possessing a women as collateral—usually, but not always, these were men—were called *ling jia'r* in the local argot, which translates roughly to "collar on the house" or "receiving the house," or, to be blunt, a pimp. In essence, the women became pawned items. A woman could be used to secure a loan in amounts from M$20 up to M$300, depending on her looks and age. A collateral woman would turn over all of her earnings to the *ling jia'r* who advanced money to her family. When and if her family repaid the loan amount, she would be free to return home. There was no fee on such loans; the woman's services paid the interest.[27] *Ling jia'r* often controlled more than one woman or had more than one source of income. One female *ling jia'r* living in the Prosperity Lodge sent her charge into prostitution while she herself sold morphine

The women entertained guests all day without a break. While customers were present, the *ling jia'r* would act as host, bringing water and making tea. Once the paying guests left, vicious arguing usually broke out between a woman and her temporary boss. This was especially true of Wang Three the Villain, living in room three. Wang had a woman working for him as collateral on her husband's gambling debt. He yelled at her constantly, screaming, "I don't have to eat off of your cunt."[28] Gotō, ever the gentleman, gave the Chinese word but used the Japanese "butt" for his readers, explaining apologetically that the phrase was hard to translate.

Ling jia'r is not a common Chinese expression. After the war, Gotō's young assistant simply translated the word as "pimp." But "pimp" does not convey the complexity of relationships found in and around the Garden. Husbands and mothers-in-law played the role of procurer, as did the people who held women as pawns. Women often ran the brothels, serving as owner and procurer. Flophouse owners functioned as pimps on a regular basis.

An army of men worked to supply women for the sex industry. Gotō calls them villains. They specialized in how they obtained the girls. One group of men roamed the countryside locating families in distress and making contracts for their young daughters. They had a special name that can roughly be translated "running tents." Zhu Chengguang, who lived in the Prosperity Lodge in the Garden, did a job known on the street as "pulling the tow rope." He made deals between those who had kidnapped women and those who wanted to buy them. While the women remained in his custody, he would sweet-talk them in a charming way, but soon he would pass them on to a brothel, receiving a 20 to 30 percent commission for his trouble. With such variety, the word "pimp" hardly suffices.

Women in the Garden openly flirted with Gotō. As for prostitutes in all areas in the world, maintaining good relationships with local police could make the difference between success or failure on the job. Indeed, Gotō admits to helping the women in the Garden. He used his influence with the city government to keep their businesses up and running in 1940, when the Manchukuo government ordered all houses of prostitution closed during an official census.

Madam Li considered Gotō a possible asset. She came from Hebei in North China. She was thirty-six and lived in the Peace Lodge. She liked to dress in bright red. She regularly beckoned to Gotō, addressing him as "My Lord." She often invited him into her room saying, "Don't you want to investigate?" or "Relax and become a customer. I really know how to go along with police. Come on into your concubine's room."[29]

Gotō had an ambivalent relationship with one woman in particular. Chun Fang of the Zhizhong Lodge was a twenty-three-year-old girl who began her career when her father passed away. She provided the sole support for her mother and two young brothers. Gotō said of her, "She seems admirable, but just recently she has come to enjoy the taste of opium and the life of sensuality." Is Gotō telling us that the girl's sexuality negates her heroism?

Chun Fang flirted with Gotō, and she acted as an informant. At one point Gotō bought her a gift of opium—from the Harbin monopoly, he is quick to point out. She laughed happily and dropped her trousers to offer him her services as well. At that moment the precinct police appeared in her room brandishing swords, she calmly handed them a M$2 bribe, after which they left, making no comments at all.[30]

As we can see from the hints of intimacy related above, there was more to the story of Gotō and Chun Fang. Writing after the war, Gotō's young assistant added a romantic twist to the relationship between the policeman and the working girl. Katō Toyotaka, the young assistant, describes Chun Fang as a beautiful woman who grew up in the Japanese leased territory of the Guandong Peninsula. As a result she spoke Japanese and could carry on with Japanese manners. Chinese people in Harbin called such imposters "false devils" because they mimicked the Japanese "Eastern Ocean devils."

Lin Jitang of the Spring Forest Lodge found Chun Fang in the port city of Dalian. He brought her with him to Harbin. Yang, the proprietor of the Zhizhong Lodge, took over her contract for himself. Yang received 60 percent of her earnings, Lin took 20 percent for his commission, and the pretty Chun Fang kept the remaining 20 percent for herself.

Gotō was quite taken with the young lady. He began negotiations with Lin to ransom her. Such was the dream of prostitutes—to win the heart of a powerful man who would buy out her contract and bring her into his own family as a concubine. But Gotō found the asking price too high. Moreover, he already had a jealous mistress who wanted no rival, so he never completed the transaction.[31]

Gotō Reiji did not stigmatize the working girls he met. Precociously, he called the women "sex workers." This is a term adopted only recently in the West. As groups like COYOTE have started organizing prostitutes to achieve better conditions in the face of HIV/AIDS, Western scholars have started to treat sex work as a labor issue. Gotō described the women he met as victims of a social order that favored men, denying women access to education and effectively barring them from earning a livelihood outside the role of daughter, wife, mother, housemaid, or prostitute. Not one of these women could even write her name, he tells us. To suddenly find someone in the 1940s talking about sex workers brings a shock of unexpected recognition to a modern reader—at least at first.

Gotō Reiji happily blamed Chinese society—especially Chinese men— for the sorry state of the women in the Garden. Chinese men treated all women as imbeciles, he tells us, allowing them no economic role other than wife, mother, and, in times of distress, prostitute. He further charged Chinese men with an extraordinary interest in lascivious behavior.[32] Gotō was, after all, making his study to justify Japanese leadership in Asia. What better way to do so than to describe the men in the Garden of Grand Vision in the most damning light. We should not think of him as too precocious.

Gotō sympathizes with the women. He worries about the effects the life will have on their children; he condemns the men who use them. Yet there is something disingenuous about his concern, or, should we say, hypocritical. Writing after the war, Katō has Braying Mule Wang point out the obvious. Japanese men were no strangers to brothels. Gotō himself was involved with a geisha in training who worked at a Harbin restaurant, the Little Warrior's Storehouse. Perhaps intimacy with this woman gave him insight into the uglier side of the trade. More likely, though, his condemnation was his way of enhancing the moral imperative of the Manchukuo mission.

Gotō acknowledged the importance of the women living in the slums. He called them a safety valve in the desperate atmosphere of Fujiadian. He did not pull that idea out of thin air. From the beginning of Japan's transition away from feudalism, officials thought of modernity in terms of public health. The new government included a Central Sanitary Bureau (established 1873). The new conscript army induction process included testing for sexually transmitted disease. As Japanese soldiers moved into

China, worries about infection prompted the military to take action. During the First Sino-Japanese War (1894–1895), official documents warned about Chinese promiscuity. At home a prevailing idea that prostitution was necessary to control men's desire led to a system of registration and medical examination for working girls in Japan. Concern for health, especially for soldiers abroad, led to an unpleasant outcome: in the name of hygiene, army personnel kidnapped thousands of Asian women to serve the army as "military comfort women"—hardly the outcome envisioned by COYOTE.[33]

Even more than a safety valve, working girls in the Garden of Grand Vision provided a link to the security of family and village. The report gives a catalog of the vocabulary that the prostitutes and their clients used to address each other. The slang was not crude. It was remarkably family oriented. Women called their customers "big brother," "father," or "precious." Men, in turn called the women "sister," "sweetheart," or "wife." Photographs of the women at work paint a sad picture. In one shot, the caption asks us to notice the sagging, dried-out breasts of the prostitute. Looking deeper into the picture, however, we see that someone has cut pictures from magazine advertisements to brighten up the wall. Adding a touch of decoration to a drab interior, they feature family scenes of robust mothers holding chubby infants. They provide a stark contrast to the environment of the Garden and testify to a longing for a life half forgotten.

Gotō Reiji described most of the women as drained of vitality. Worn out by their endless entertainment of customers and plagued with syphilis and gonorrhea, most of the prostitutes turned to narcotics for solace. Our police investigator told of seeing women securing their M$0.50 packet of heroin and immediately—and without modesty—peeling off their clothes to rub the powder into their sore vaginas. For the ladies of the Garden, opiates provided self-medication and oblivion. For Gotō Reiji the trail of illicit drugs was a major point of investigation.

10

⌘

Harbin Vice

Drugs

Japanese people consider opium to be a moral issue. The Chinese consider opium a kind of food that completes life. People who taste the divine pleasure of opium afterward fall into depravity and the vulgar commands of pleasure. To this extent, the nature of opium is consistent with the character and thinking of the Chinese race.

—Gotō Reiji[1]

Opium smoke is a kind of poison that harms people's minds and health. It has a long history in Harbin. At times there were prohibitions, but without much effect.

—Lu Shouxin[2]

An amazing array of goods and services could be had for a pittance in the Garden of Grand Vision. Most of the residents spent their working days pilfering, gambling, or turning tricks to earn money for opium or heroin. Scores of hardy entrepreneurs supplied this market. The Manchukuo government itself ran Harbin Opium Dispensary Number Thirty-Four from the rear building of the complex.[3] In addition, forty unlicensed narcotics sellers openly conducted business from rooms in the Garden's flophouses and the immediate neighborhood. Technically illegal, such businesses were so numerous, and so generous with bribes to the right officials, that the government of Manchukuo treated them in a downright bipolar manner. It tolerated those dealers who paid off the right officials. Periodically well-publicized raids shut down the competition.

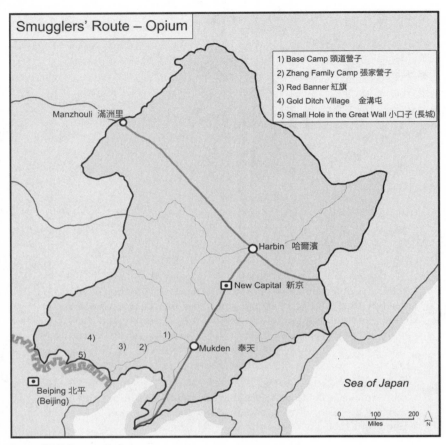

Smugglers' Route, Opium

The Japanese legal system strictly controlled narcotic drugs on the home islands. Yet Japan's Colonial Office approved the sale of opium under a government-licensed monopoly in all of its Asian territories. Government officials created the model for their monopoly policy in 1895 when Japan acquired Taiwan as its first overseas possession—the spoils of the First Sino-Japanese War. As the empire expanded into Korea and then into the Manchurian leased territory, the opium monopoly system grew. The idea was not a Japanese invention. Its author, Gotō Shimpei, copied the British system used in Hong Kong, Malaya, and Singapore, as well as a French monopoly in Indochina. Addiction, Japanese officials argued, was a peculiarly Chinese disease. Any major power with a large Chinese population in its colonies had to come to terms with opium.[4]

The opium monopoly aimed to gradually reduce the number of addicts. On Taiwan the system worked reasonably well. But as it moved onto the Asian mainland, problems with the system became clear. It leaked, especially in the Manchurian leased territory, close as it was to China and complicated by mixed jurisdictions. The train routes through the North became a smuggler's paradise. Japanese traffickers and their Korean surrogates competed with traffickers from around the globe. In the North China region of the 1920s, where a political vacuum set the stage for civil war and invasion, narcotics became a currency. Just as in Afghanistan today, drugs provided the economic foundation of military adventure. After the 1931 Mukden Incident, the new Manchukuo government began to bring narcotics under its control, or at least it tried.[5]

Lu Shouxin, who grew up in Harbin, remembered the many attempts to control opium in Harbin. All resulted in spotty results and unintended consequences. He recalled that as early as 1927, the warlord Zhang Zuolin had turned opium into a state monopoly. The program was stricter in central Jilin Province than in the northern Heilongjiang Province. For Harbin City the difference was crucial. The Songhua River formed the boundary between the two provinces. At the time Harbin, especially Fujiadian, situated south of the Songhua, faced stringent regulations. Not a problem. By simply crossing the river to an area known as the Ma Family Port, a person in search of opium could find 140 to 150 opium dens. In 1929 Zhang Xueliang, the warlord's son, strengthened the laws, bringing Heilongjiang under tighter regulation. The opium dens simply moved into villages. The regulations did little to curb opium use. Addicts will travel.[6]

Once the Japanese military occupied Manchuria, it brought its own model of opium control. The first Opium Control Regulation went into effect in September 1932. During this first period of opium control, Japanese-sponsored factories produced opium paste, selling it through approved, yet privately owned, retail shops. This opium monopoly ran out of New Capital. The monopoly opened an opium paste factory in Harbin. There the government produced brands of opium with names that sound ironic to our ears. Opium labels like "Wealth" or "Prosperity" are exquisite examples of false advertising. The drug was sold under names like "Plum," "Bamboo," "Pine," and, my favorite, "Long Life." For every ounce of opium sold, the city received M$0.10 in tax. Harbin had 120 private opium shops in this early period.[7]

Japanese authorities in Manchukuo, at least those serving in the public sector, sincerely wanted to control the problem. Drug indulgence was not part of the Kingly Way image. The Manchukuo government slowly whittled down the number of opium shops until by 1937 only seventy-seven were doing business in the city. In 1938, a new set of regulations tightened the monopoly system. Shops became government operations.

Only twenty large government-controlled opium dispensaries remained in Harbin—legally, at least. At the same time, healthy-living centers—we would call them detox centers—opened throughout the city. Healthy-Living Reporting Brigades operated in the city to keep an eye on recovering addicts. In our contemporary world, we call this kind of approach harm reduction.[8] It should have worked well. Gotō Reiji tells a different story, however.

Gotō begins the "Opium" chapter of *Autopsy of the Garden of Grand Vision* with a clear-sighted acknowledgement of failure. He tells his readers frankly, "Right now Harbin is the center of a fierce struggle taking place in Northern Manchuria between official and unlicensed opium."[9] He does not tell us outright, but we can surmise that his interest in unlicensed morphine and opium included their political potential. Just as the opium monopoly contributed to Manchukuo government operations, illegal drugs funded rebellion. In the years between 1932 and 1939, the new government faced anti-Japanese insurrections in the border regions. Narcotics control challenged the finances of Chinese bandits.

Bandits—groups of armed youth with nothing to do—had plagued the countryside even before the 1931 events that created Manchukuo. A Japanese estimate put the number of pre-Manchukuo bandits at 250,000 and boasted that Japanese guidance had helped bring the number down to merely 30,000 by 1936. But these numbers do not tell the entire story. As bandits decreased in number, new members from a different constituency joined their ranks, giving the bands new energy and political purpose.

During the early days of the puppet state, Japanese officers began to incorporate Manchukuoan—that is, Chinese—troops into a new national military. Reports came to Harbin that these soldiers did less than necessary to pacify the new country's border regions. Some of these Chinese soldiers reconsidered their loyalty to Japan. One such incident occurred on March 12, 1932, only days after the formal creation of the new state. Manchukuoan troops in a border garrison near Blagoveschensk, on the Soviet border, demonstrated against the new Manchukuo flag being raised over their barracks. Two days later soldiers in Manchuli, on the same sensitive border further to the west, went on a rampage, looting stores and killing three shopkeepers, two of them Chinese and the other Japanese. Three days later soldiers in groups of one hundred were said to be leaving the border garrison posts, making the local Japanese consul nervous.[10] These men gave new direction to the border region bandits. They put energy into disrupting the progress of the new state.

In their early years, Manchukuo bandits raided strongholds, disrupted train service, and kidnapped Chinese and foreigners alike with ever-greater derring-do. Japanese official reports might claim that the number of bandits had decreased, but the audacity and organization of the raids and the image bandits presented to the Chinese public all improved. Farmers, once the target of harassment, began to view the bandits as Robin Hood–type heroes. Their hero image increased as they attacked Korean settlers, brought in by Japanese officials, who competed with Chinese for the best farmland with Japanese backing. The bandits destroyed train tracks; they attacked trains. By the end of 1936, Japanese living in Manchukuo barricaded their residences. Commercial trains traveled behind armed pilot trains. Bridges and tunnels sported pillboxes.[11] This was not the way Manchukuo was meant to be.

American consuls living in Harbin acknowledged that banditry was nothing new. After the creation of Manchukuo, they saw—and duly reported home—an injection of purpose into old-fashioned larceny. Manchukuo officials experimented with ways to end the violence that made exploiting Manchurian resources difficult and dangerous. In their first attempt, they established the Border Pacification Constabulary. Japanese officers led bands of Manchukuoan Chinese soldiers into the rugged frontier. They offered amnesty to any bandit who would give up his activities and turn over his weapons. The organization fit with the official ideology of racial harmony, but the units proved next to useless.

One foreign Harbin resident, a certain Dr. Nielson, spent four months with the bandits as a kidnapping victim. He spoke good Chinese and got to know his captors, and so he was able to provide an intimate look into a bandit camp. He described well-armed fighters who could be cruel but who treated him well enough. According to Nielson, as he traveled with these men through the mountain landscapes in the northeastern borderlands, the Border Pacification Constabulary posed little danger. The bandits showed little respect for Chinese police units trained by the Japanese to stabilize the area. In fact, they saw them as comrades, referring to them as their twins. Any day any one of them might switch sides and rejoin them.

A second victim of kidnapping, Maryknoll priest Father Gerald Donavan, did not get rescued. His organization, by policy, would not pay ransom. As a result, he was passed from one bandit group to the next, as a kind of currency. With each trade his treatment grew harsher, and his health deteriorated. Japanese police brigades tried to track him, with no success. Finally, a captured member of the First Anti-Japanese Communist Army admitted that the priest had died of exposure.[12]

The bandits, as described by Dr. Nielson, were well armed and could be cruel. More to the point, they were political. Bandits had contacts with patriotic groups in China proper. They raised money from ransoms paid out by kidnap victims' families. But even more cash came from healthy underground opium-smuggling operations. Given a tense situation in which smuggled opium supported political banditry, controlling the traffic had more than the moral purpose that Gotō indicated in the opening lines of his "Opium" chapter. It had more to do with political legitimacy and control.

Opium could work for Japanese interests as well. One bandit, a man named Li Kuiwu known as Old Second Brother, was a rascal often compared to a wild wolf. Born in 1911, the year of Sun Yat-sen's revolution, Li menaced friends and family from his early childhood. He got into fights; he stole his friends' toys. By the time he was twenty, he had left life on the farm behind. Leading a band of twenty or so young thugs, he roamed the countryside, stealing, setting fires, and committing murder and rape.

After the Mukden Incident of September 1931, Li learned of the support anti-Japanese actions could gain from Chinese groups on the other side of the Wall. Sensing an opportunity, Li took up the fight. An innate cunning motivated the man much more than any sense of patriotism. He harassed Manchukuo government installations until he learned of the amnesty in 1936. Turning over his weapons to Japanese authorities, Li settled into a fairly comfortable life. He even gained the means to earn a living—an opium concession.[13]

Struggle for control of the countryside became part of the ugly legacy of fifteen years of war. Here the distinction between police and the Japanese Kantō Army blurred. Border constabulary began pacification patrols. Small units spread out through the countryside. They built roads to facilitate troop movement to the borderlands. More importantly, the Japanese army made conciliatory gestures, accompanied by money, to any bandit, like Li Kuiwu, who would put down his arms. Those who would not change sides received harsh treatment, as did their friends and family.

The Kantō Army moved farmers into protected villages—something on the order of the strategic hamlets of the Vietnam War. There, villagers lived surrounded by walls, moats, and barbed wire. Improved roadways may have made life easier, but the system also connected those in the remote countryside to Japanese military command centers. Each village had an appointed headman who lived in terror of the Japanese army. One Japanese lieutenant described the situation thus: "This county is truly an accursed place. We can't tell the bandits from the people. As positive means we summon the village headmen (a function of the *baojia* system) and threaten them with cruel punishment if they traffic with bandits."[14] By 1939, border banditry had lessened, at least for a time. Yet the unlicensed narcotics trade persisted. It had to be brought under control. As we shall see, by the 1940s, this concentrate-and-guard method had become something of a model for dealing with addiction and vagrancy as well.

With banditry in the background, Gotō Reiji and his colleagues began their catalog of the entire drug-trafficking network operating in the Fujiadian area. Gotō describes for us, and for his readers in the government,

three intersecting areas of the narcotics traffic—legal government operations, illicit heroin sales, and the trafficking systems that supplied both
operations. With his eye for the details of networking, he demonstrates
the sophisticated routes that narcotics traveled—into, out of, and through
Manchukuo—back and forth between the licit and illicit markets. We follow Gotō as he begins his tour of the narcotics markets. Where to begin?
The logical place to start is in the Garden of Grand Vision itself, with the
daily operations of Harbin Opium Dispensary Number Thirty-Four. Gotō
introduces us to the people who work there.

The licensed Dispensary Number Thirty-Four occupies a large section
of the first floor of theVillage of Grand Vision behind the main building.
The dispensary is open for business everyday from 9 a.m. to 4 p.m. Zhang
Zhensan manages the operation. He, like so many others we have met,
comes from Shandong Province. He has been running the shop for five
years and earns M$1.80 a day, with which he supports a wife and four
children. His assistant, Ge Chunfang, keeps the books. Ge supports ten
family members on M$1.80 a day.[15]

The dispensary hires a lamp chief and nine lamp boys. These employees bring out the opium paste and smoking equipment for the customers. Smoking opium is not a simple affair. Smokers enjoy their drug
while reclining, for it induces a dreamlike trance. Nor is opium smoked
like tobacco. Prepared paste is held over or rolled into the bowl of the
pipe with a pin. The bowl is then gently heated over a lamp, allowing
the smoke to be inhaled. The pipe, the lamp, and the pin can all be
treasured items made of jade, silver, or exotic wood. In the Manchukuo
dispensaries, they are of the cheapest sort—bamboo and tin. Lamp boys
are important to the operation as they have the skills required to prepare
the opium paste, set up the lamps, and handle the clients. Each earns
about M$1 per day.[16]

Addicts who register with government-run dispensaries receive daily
opium to smoke for a controlled price.[17] Clients have to be registered.
They can only purchase enough opium paste for one smoke at a time.
They are required to return the residue from their pipes to the counter
when done. The shop must return any residue, along with the used official paper wrappers, to the Harbin branch of the Mukden Opium Processing Plant, located at 16 Thread Street in Daoli. The residue still contains
morphia, which can be mixed into inferior opium gum and resold. Employees collect used wrappers to prevent unauthorized opium from being
sold as government product. The opium comes from the branch factory in
1.4 gram bundles. These are broken down into four or five portions and
sold to the addicts for M$0.50. Dispensary Number Thirty-Four inside the
Village serves 141 male and 64 female registered addicts, selling them 681
portions of opium a day.[18] At least, this is what official documents claim.

In 1934, while establishing the details of the Manchukuo state, Harbin city hall placed the licensed opium dispensary inside the rear building of the Garden complex as part of the official opium monopoly network. The Manchukuo occupation government also set up forty-six withdrawal centers for addicts to use, should they wish to take the cure. Most did not. Gotō's sometime informant, Feng Dengdiao, who claimed he was not an addict, turned himself over to a withdrawal center one winter when he was desperate for shelter. He received room and board for several weeks during the harsh winter months. He left with a warm coat.[19]

Gotō knew, of course, that there were problems with the system. Government opium was inferior. Smokers liked to boost the product quality by adding heroin. They called the result gold inside silver. The practice guaranteed a harsher habit. Government dispensaries provided the pills; one pill contained 0.10 gram of heroin and 0.10 gram of lactose. The pills could be dissolved in water and the contents injected. The price of a pill, like the price of a package of narcotics at the unlicensed, in other words, illicit, shops, cost M$0.50.[20]

As a young man, Gao Zuozhi worked in the retail opium trade in the Manchurian countryside. He described the licensed opium shops in much the same way as Gotō. Gao began his career as a young man working as a clerk in a variety shop. His third cousin ran a retail opium shop called the Cloud Fairy Pavilion. In the early Manchukuo period, retailers like Gao's cousin bought supplies from the Manchukuo opium monopoly factory in Mukden. The Cloud Fairy Pavilion was a two-story building. The opium shop occupied the first floor. As the owner, Gao's cousin lived in the east suite on the second floor. Two of the rooms served as smoking areas. Gao's cousin rented out the other rooms as he could. When the young Gao lost his job at the variety store, he went to work as a bookkeeper at the Cloud Fairy Pavilion, where he lived in a room on the first floor.

The shop was open from 8 a.m. to 11 p.m. Smokers could buy as much opium as they wanted, but they had to have an "opium addict smoking permit" approved by the local police. The shops bought their opium from the central opium factory in Mukden along with wrappers stamped with the characters for "to go" or "to smoke." Two-tenths of an ounce would cost M$0.25 to go or M$0.20 if smoked on the premises. There was a lot of competition among the retail shops. Most hired women to serve the customers. The opium came from the factory in fifty-ounce packets with labels like "Bamboo," "Pine," and "Orchid." This opium came from Jilin Province and was not considered to be of such good quality. Opium called "Wealth" and "Long Life" came from Rehe and was said to produce a much nicer, smoother smoke.

The Cloud Fairy Pavilion was not in a slum like the Garden of Grand Vision. Nonetheless, Gao did not like his job. He worried about the kind of trouble his clients attracted. One autumn night a local police lieutenant swaggered into the Cloud Fairy Pavilion carrying a walking stick. There he discovered a local government clerk deep in his opium trance. The police officer demanded that the clerk show his smoking permit. The clerk simply stared back at the officer, who went into a fury and started beating him. Then the officer turned on poor young Gao, demanding to know why he would serve a customer without checking his smoker's permit. Gao received blows with the walking stick. A newspaper reporter living in a rented room upstairs came to the shop to see what the commotion was about. The officer boxed the reporter's ears. Only when Gao's cousin showed up could the officer be placated. Gao quit the next day, but finding no other work, he was soon back at his post.[21]

Gotō knew the darker side of the Japanese program. It was a sieve. The Japanese opium monopoly unwittingly supplied as many smugglers as it did licensed shops. Employees of the dispensaries had ways to augment their salaries. They registered nonaddicted fake addicts with whom they split the daily rations. Both portions went into the black market. They gave addicts free opium but kept aside half the amount for themselves. The lamp boys allowed addicts to resmoke the opium residue for a price. Employees bought unlicensed opium smuggled in from China and sold it under the table. All dispensary employees joined together in such schemes and split the proceeds openly and according to rank so as to avoid dangerous jealousies that could jeopardize their illegal operations.

Dispensaries had an even darker side. Manchukuo government officials sincerely wanted to end opium use. Yet the civilian bureaucrats faced a major obstacle within their own organization. Military spy operations liked the unfettered money that came from opium sales. The Peace Preservation Bureau, the secret side of the police organization, liked the dispensaries. Opium dens scattered throughout the country became excellent listening posts. The bureau specialized in placing listening devices in sensitive areas. Local gossip could provide a rich vein of intelligence. What better way to ferret out information about the discontented and the troublesome in Manchukuo than to listen in on conversations in an opium den. Opium dens, as a result, were bugged.[22]

But an addict did not have to bother registering with the police or finding a dispensary. He did not need to put up with inferior drugs or risk the intrusion of spies. Many unlicensed shops catered to the needy clientele. Ge, the bookkeeper at Dispensary Number Thirty-Four, worked in an unlicensed shop before joining the government monopoly. He kept up his personal connections to the underground network, slipping them the government product for extra cash. The unlicensed shops sold opium, morphine, and heroin. Gotō calls them "morphine bootleggers." In fact, their product consisted entirely of heroin. Gotō sent samples from each of the unlicensed shops in the Garden's vicinity to a government laboratory for testing. He learned that out of thirty-six sample packets, only one contained morphine. The rest were heroin and complementary procaine to be mixed with it.

The unlicensed dealers weaseled supplies from the monopoly. They bought drugs from dishonest dispensary personnel. The precinct police, most of them Chinese in origin and corrupt by nature, sold opium licenses to nonaddicts for a bribe of between M$10 and M$20. The practice was so widespread that early in 1940, when the authorities changed the license forms, in an attempt to solve the problem, the street price of heroin increased immediately. A nonaddicted permit holder could acquire a daily supply from the government dispensary and resell it on the black market. A person could support a family in this way.

Addicts bought their dope from the lodgings of the unlicensed dealers, who lived and worked in the better rooms of the same flophouses that their clients patronized. They sold drugs in M$0.50 packets. Gotō Reiji was not precise about weights, but judging from the legal competition, we can guess that a packet held a quarter gram or so. With each purchase, a customer also received a gift packet of procaine, a local anesthetic mixed with the heroin or injected first to ease the sting of the injection. The narcotics dealers perhaps picked this social nicety up from Japanese shopkeepers who customarily did good customers a small favor. Desperate addicts with little cash could buy the procaine packets for M$0.02. The morphine source was often Japanese factories. Once the product reached Harbin, it would be watered down in much the same way drugs are stepped on in the American market of today. Materials used to cut the product ranged from the obvious to the exotic. Sugar, flour, lactose, boric acid, and tooth powder might be used as easily in New York City today as in Harbin in the 1940s. According to the lore of the Fujiadian streets, the best additive was a powder made from the bones of dead addicts, a commodity that would have been plentiful in the neighborhood.

For M$0.50 an addict in the Garden of Grand Vision would receive a packet of heroin weighing a half a gram. If a resident had enjoyed a profitable night's pilfering, he could get a larger amount in M$1 or M$2 bags. As a courtesy the dealer would throw in a packet of procaine. Addicts like to mix the two substances together for a smoother high. All of the packets came wrapped in old, dirty newspaper.

Heroin was smoked or injected. Some addicts rubbed it into their gums or any bodily orifice or mucus membrane. Gotō describes with a voyeuristic eye prostitutes with syphilis rubbing heroin on their genitals or addicts in the rafter rooms smearing opium residue on paper so as to rub it into their rectums. Addicts who injected heroin were not particular about their equipment. Several of the people living in the Garden supported themselves by renting out syringes for M$0.10 a shot.

The unlicensed shops were unwanted but unavoidable competition for government-sponsored narcotics dispensaries. Unlicensed shops were illegal but operated freely. Police rarely bothered to raid them. If such a raid occurred, the smaller dealers and their suppliers might be shut down for a time. Like modern narcotics cops, Gotō lamented that the big fish always found ways to survive.

Few fortunes were made selling drugs on the streets of Harbin. The existence of municipal dispensaries kept the price of street heroin competitive. Successful narcotic dealers at all levels had made financial agreements with officials; the street dealers paid off the local Chinese police. Larger illicit heroin manufacturers shared their profits with particular Japanese personnel, especially at the middle levels of the espionage units.[23]

Thirty-nine of the forty unlicensed morphine dealers in the Garden area were Korean. Gotō calls them blood-sucking ticks. He considers them greedy evil gods who spin their webs throughout the Garden, waiting for the small amounts of wealth the residents will bring them. In fact, the many Koreans living in Manchukuo came in the wake of Japanese expansion. In their homeland, Koreans were colonial subjects of the Japanese Empire. They suffered under that rule as they saw their customs, political rights, and property stripped away by Japanese rulers. Outside Korea, they became second-class citizens. As colonial subjects, they were not considered the equals of Japanese abroad, who constituted a privileged foreign elite. Gotō's comments about Koreans in Fujiadian can be considered mild in comparison to what these people usually faced from Japanese abroad.

Protection from Chinese law was a benefit for the business of smuggling. Korean traffickers could be found throughout North China. When Manchukuo was created in 1931, Japanese authorities encouraged Korean emigration to the new state. In the early days of the new nation, the American consul in Harbin reported to his Washington counterparts that Japanese authorities gave Korean migrants lucrative morphine and heroin shops. They hoped Korean shopkeepers would use their profits to buy agricultural land and take up farming. But with Chinese bandits actively working against Korean migrants, the plan showed little progress. After 1937, when the Manchukuo government ended special privileges for Japanese and Koreans alike, a new effort to end morphine sales got under way. But the results remained limited.[24]

Korean morphine and heroin sellers obtained supplies from the Manchukuo opium monopoly itself. Opium and morphine came to the unlicensed market from Manchurian fields. Gotō calls this smuggling, although few borders were crossed. Farmers grew the crop to supply Japanese opium monopolies in Manchukuo and elsewhere. The problem, however, was one of pricing. The Japanese authorities paid a set price of M$2.80 per ounce of opium. Farmers could get between M$5 and M$6 for opium on the black market. If they could get their product to North China, they could receive M$30 or more. As a result Manchukuoans in the know cornered the black market, buying up all the excess opium that the industrious farmers could produce.[25]

Gotō estimated that the government was only buying 50 to 60 percent of the crop. In 1936, in an excess of zeal, the Manchukuo government mobilized the Concordia Society and any police recruit it could find in the police academies to confiscate unlicensed opium crops. Gotō describes a campaign in which overzealous police beat and kicked farmers. Enthusiastic young men patted down the stomachs of pregnant women and deflated bicycle tires in their quest to eradicate unlicensed opium crops. As a result, searchers confiscated 73,000 ounces of opium. But the movement served only to alienate the farmers involved, who raised complaints all the way to the central government in New Capital. More to the point, two years later Gotō estimated that in 1938, 7 million ounces of illicit opium was going into the black market.[26]

Gotō Reiji began his investigation following the trail of Manchurian opium into the black market. This was the realm of the so-called small goods. While following his leads, he and his colleagues came across informants who provided inside information about large goods, in other words, people who smuggled Manchurian opium across the boundary into North China. The informants remained anonymous, but they named smugglers by name and location. Tang Songshan was a major ringleader. He worked with Guo Zhanshu and Xie Shujun. These men moved drugs, but they also dealt in weapons. They worked out of the Rehe region, where the strongest opium was grown.[27]

Gotō outlines a typical journey. In Ningcheng County, Tang and his men purchased opium from farmers for M$5 per tael (Gotō put the weight at fifty grams; a tael is usually calculated at 1.3 ounces). They then hired twelve local farmers to help them. They packed the opium into burlap bags. Eight farmers handled the opium, and four tended to provisions for the journey. Once packed, they took off. The group traveled through the mountains at night, sleeping during the day. Once in a while they might enjoy the hospitality of a family on route; most of the time they slept outside. When they came to the border, the smugglers paid the farmers off, sending them back home. Gotō points out that while he, his compatriots, and the governing authorities considered the border, any border, to be a solid political entity, in fact borders were optical illusions. Despite the

Great Wall separating North China from Manchukuo, smugglers slipped in and out with illicit goods at will.[28]

In North China the risk decreased as the smugglers entered the rough-and-tumble world of morphine and heroin producers working under the tacit protection of the Japanese military. Yamauchi Saburō was one of these entrepreneurs, and, yes, he was Japanese. The higher up a person traces the morphine network, the closer he comes to Japanese backers, the big fish of Gotō's report. Yamauchi Saburō left a description of his life as a heroin producer in North China during the war. Writing in the safety of Tokyo well after the war ended, he openly described the freewheeling life of Japanese adventurers running drug factories in North China. These men made hefty contributions to the Kempeitai and the Special Service Agency. They openly ran their businesses with little fear of police raids. Their biggest risks came from each other, for rivals might attack their operations or undercut their price. Factories blew up, sometimes due to misused chemicals, sometimes due to vandalism. The result of this cut-throat rivalry was the delivery of high-quality, cheaply priced heroin to the market.[29]

Japanese adventurers were actively involved in heroin sales in Harbin and the countryside. Gao from a small town outside Harbin tells of the Great East Pawnshop owned by an adventurer named Fujita, who sold morphine and heroin from the back room. He had done so before the creation of Manchukuo and continued to do so after the government changed. A townsman everyone called Fatty Ding visited this pawnshop often. Fatty Ding's family was wealthy. He was a landlord himself, at least in his early years. But Fatty Ding loved heroin. He also loved to show off his riches. People in the town often saw him coming out of the Great East Pawnshop, accompanied by two servants, with a box of heroin. Fujita often gave some of the heroin to Fatty Ding as a present. In the end Fatty Ding faced bankruptcy.

Not just Chinese people suffered from addiction. Gao remembers a Japanese police captain assigned to the town. This captain also enjoyed heroin. He would send his Chinese underlings to purchase drugs for him. If he had to venture to the Great East Pawnshop himself, he wore glasses and a muffler to hide his face. The ruse did not stop gossip.

By the time Gotō wrote his report, Japan was already three years into war with China. The Japanese army occupied most of the North. If narcotics flowed smoothly into the area, blame rested squarely with the Japanese organization itself. Before war broke out in 1937, Japanese agents moved narcotics and opium into the area because drugs played a role in military adventure in the region. Katō Toyotaka admits that smuggling was part of the strategy of invasion. He cites a report from September

1936 in which General Matsumoro Takayoshi advocated a "secret trade" to weaken the Chinese economy. Local powerbrokers on all sides of this multi-faceted conflict used drugs as a hidden income source in a fluctuating situation. In many parts of our contemporary world, it still does. Thus when Japanese agents smuggled a high quality, cheap product into a robust Chinese drug market, one in which opium and its derivatives provided the currency for espionage and intrigue, it was a strategy of war. It became a stable measure of value in a fluctuating economic situation. As a consequence, supporting Japanese sympathizers with opium made sense to Manchukuo authorities. The problem arose once the trade needed to be controlled.[30]

Gotō had to realize that his own superiors, or people they knew, had interests in the drug trade. He takes the diplomatic approach in his report by blaming the traffic on Chinese addicts' appetites and Korean traffickers' greed. This would sit well with the image of Japan as a guiding mentor in East Asia. But he also mentions the big fish who always get away. And he points out that opium is legal in Japanese controlled North China. He is leaving unsaid the larger truth: if the government wanted this traffic ended, it needed to clean up its own leadership.

Police inspection (Seki Hiroshige, Seki Paper Company, Matsuyama, Japan).

Japanese soldiers surrender their weapons to Russians in Harbin, August 30, 1945 (permission granted by Times World Wide Prints/The New York Times/Redux).

11

⁂

Harbin Vice

Gambling

The Chinese are all fatalists. They enjoy life by tempting fate as they gamble. Gambling is their life. It seeps into the very marrow of their bones.

—Gotō Reiji[1]

From the time that the Peace Bridge Gambling Club opened, almost every day we hear of families falling into bankruptcy, crime, theft, and suicide.

—Police chief Wang Xianwei[2]

It is true. Chinese people gamble with abandon. Go to Macao, the former Portuguese colony across the bay from Hong Kong. The city's landmark casino, the Lisboa, lights up the nighttime harbor, a gaudy monument to gambling. Since Portugal returned its colony to China in 1999, other entrepreneurs have joined the Lisboa, including Sheldon Adelson's Venetian, today the world's largest gambling mecca. But the pursuit of risk is not limited to former colonies. Walk down a Taiwan alleyway on a sultry weekend afternoon, and chances are you will hear the clicking of mah-jongg tiles. Such comfort with financial risk and the steely nerves required as money rides on the turn of a card or the click of a mah-jongg tile could explain China's present entrepreneurial success.[3]

Gotō Reiji described this zeal for gambling as he watched the Chinese in Fujiadian join in games of chance. With his imperialist eyes he found the passion for risk in such a poor neighborhood one more piece of evidence demonstrating the character flaws of an ancient culture mired in the past. Gotō noted that all Chinese were fatalists. When writing about Chinese and vice, Gotō reinforces stereotypes. He is not at his analytical best, at least not to our twenty-first-century minds. Nevertheless, Chinese people will all admit to a fondness for a game of chance.

As Gotō tries to explain this fixation, he tells his readers that the Chinese, as a race, make no romantic attachments. Sex might be enjoyed, but reproduction remains a basic instinct, necessary to continue the family line. Instead of love, Gotō reasons, gambling provides a meaningful emotional attachment to the world. Gotō did not live to witness China growing into the financial powerhouse we know today. Instead he assures his readers that the Chinese passion for gambling engenders in the population at large a general detachment from the business of nation building. They remain unconcerned and given to pleasure while their nation falls apart.[4]

Gotō and his colleagues saw the ancient Chinese Empire shattered into pieces. The image of ineffective leaders unable to cope in the modern world as their own citizens played at dice reinforced the Manchukuo creation myth. Japan would take on the task that Chinese warlords could not: building a modern Asia. But a vexing question remained: What part would gambling revenues play in building a new society?

Gambling came to Harbin with the first residents as they began work on the city. The Chinese boatmen, dockworkers, and laborers used gambling to while away a few free hours in the absence of much else in the way of entertainment. But Chinese were not the only Harbin pioneers to enjoy games of chance. Russian engineers brought horses with them. Harbin's racetrack, opened in 1905, operated from April to October each year and sponsored both harness and flat racing events. Sporting conditions improved considerably after the Russian Revolution in 1917. An influx of good horses followed White Russians into exile. In 1928 Japanese money poured into the organization. The track closed between 1931 and 1933 after the Mukden Incident and the 1932 flood. When it reopened, the facility was even bigger and better.[5]

Liu Shouyi worked for the racetrack from 1938 until liberation in 1949. He came from a poor family. A friend of his father had the connections to get him the job. He worked in the main office for a short man named Yamamoto with a loud mouth and a sharp temper. The office maintained the track and grounds, renting stalls to the owners of the racehorses. Horse owners hired their jockeys, mostly Russians, and grooms, mostly Chinese.

Race days could provide quite a show. Races attracted the wealthy in the town. Gamblers, mostly Japanese and Russian enthusiasts, showed up in their finest clothes. They arrived in carriages with their families in tow. Chinese Harbiners came as well, if only to watch the spectacle. Bettors bought ticket slips at M$5 apiece. Each slip carried the name of a horse entered into a specific race. Those holding tickets for the winning horse divided up the total amount of money placed in bets for the race—minus a cut for the track, of course. Bets on the horses could be high. Liu overheard one owner and his jockey celebrating a victory by the colt Little Crow. The horse had never won before. The two men had over M$2,000 worth of tickets between them. Such high stakes were out of the range of most Chinese gamers, who went elsewhere to risk a few dollars to chance.[6]

Before the creation of Manchukuo, gambling kept the provincial governments afloat. Local officials working under Zhang Zuolin, the warlord of the three northeastern provinces, taxed gambling, ran provincial gaming houses, and covered a third of local budgets with the proceeds. Once Manchukuo came into existence, Japanese authorities declared that gaming conflicted with the values of the Manchukuo Kingly Way. This puritanical program, we have seen, combined moral uplift with political indoctrination. Under the slogan "Kingly Way," Manchukuo authorities discouraged gambling as a vice in a time of nation building and war. In 1932, the new government closed all provincial gaming halls. Manchukuo state income dropped as a result.[7]

Members of the new government debated means to make up the difference. Chinese serving in the government advocated reopening the halls. Their Japanese counterparts overrode any suggestion of state-sponsored vice, preferring to tax income directly rather than to operate casinos. Gotō Reiji, always with his ear to the Chinese street, questioned the logic of this decision. He dared to point out to his Japanese superiors in the police bureau and the General Affairs Office two problems created among the Manchukuo population by the state's rigid policy.

The first problem involved national image—winning the hearts and minds of the Manchukuo population, we might say. After the old state-run gaming houses closed, the Manchukuo government had to make up revenues. To do so it imposed new direct taxes. As a result, Gotō heard Chinese on the street complain that their taxes had gone up two or three times under the new regime. Gotō points out the basic irrationality of this Chinese attitude. The same people who complained bitterly about direct taxes were more than happy to hand over large amounts of indirect tax to the state through game bosses—as long as they could place a wager.[8]

One county government official told Gotō the following story. His government building was old and in bad shape. He decided on his own to look the other way while he allowed gaming to go on in his office. Within half a year, he was able to build a fine new government headquarters. Gotō puts the dilemma this way: "The indirect tax is enjoyed, the direct tax is hated. . . . While we sing about the Kingly Way, we are alienating the people."[9]

The second problem Gotō described to his superiors lay in the absurd failure of the policy. Gambling persisted everywhere. Elementary school children gambled on their way to school. Innkeepers ran games in their hostels. The local Chinese police protected the action, reaping rich rewards in return. With such a pervasive gambling culture, it comes as no surprise that when we join Gotō on his rounds in Fujiadian, gamers openly do business in the corners and alleys of the neighborhood and the hallways of the Garden of Grand Vision.[10]

Gambling games required little in start-up capital. They were not located in shops or stores but rather were scattered along the hallways of the Garden and in the streets of Fujiadian. Gambling operations may have been small, but they were highly organized. Gambling crews comprised between two and six people, each of whom had staked an equal start-up share in the business. Crews included a lookout, a shill, several henchmen, and a dice thrower. A talented dice thrower brought skill to the group; he would not need to put up a monetary share. Usually the dice thrower was the boss. Gambling crews preyed on people passing along the road. Their customers came from the laboring and shop-keeping classes, as well as loafers and tramps.[11]

Han Ziming ran a gambling crew. At forty years old, he had been living in Harbin for ten years, having moved there from Shandong Province. He lived in a building called the Old Bean Curd Factory with a wife, daughter, and son. The building also housed Xu Guodong, known on the street as Big Gold Tooth, who was also from Shandong. Ma San, thirty-seven years old, had no family. He lived on the street behind the Garden of Grand Vision. Several years before he had been a bureaucrat in the Manchukuo government, as had Liu Jinsheng. Feng Desheng and Li Ziming both ran games in the northern market area of the Garden of Grand Vision.[12]

Ingenious varieties of games flourished along the streets. One game was called "Shaking the Precious Dice." Play involved an intricate combination of dice and roulette. The game boss would set up his equipment on a table near a busy street or intersection. Sheets of paper with numbered sections provided a tableau for players to lay down their bets. Once punters placed their bets, the boss would throw the dice. The resulting numbers combined to calculate the winners. Another game was called "Herding the Old Sheep." The first player would roll six dice. All dice showing a number that came up more than once were taken away, and the rest were added up. The resulting number became a benchmark. Those throwing higher would win; those throwing lower would lose.[13]

The working girls in the Garden of Grand Vision turned sex into a game of chance. They would challenge their customers to extra stakes based on performance. A willing customer would set a time limit. If he ejaculated before the agreed time elapsed, the woman collected the stake. If he could hold out, his time with the woman was free. Gotō noted that the man in question won out either way. Either he enjoyed sex for free or his pleasure increased as the woman he bet with would use all of her skills, hoping to gain extra payment.[14]

Gamblers survived on the streets because they had ties to the local police. But they also needed the help of the villains. Ten villains lived and worked in the alleys around the Garden. They were the bosses of the area. They strolled the neighborhood with the swagger of dandies. They survived through violence, extortion, kidnapping, theft, and blackmail. The villains maintained protection for gambling, prostitution, theft, and loan sharking. They ran the dark underworld. They became local power brokers. They worked in collusion with the local police and the flophouse owners and the spies of the Japanese Special Service Agency. Even the Kempeitai, the Japanese military police who inspired fear throughout the Japanese Empire, had to tip their hats to the villains in Fujiadian.[15]

The relationship among gambling, villains, and loan sharking was symbiotic. Gamblers in Fujiadian provided a source of unending wealth for loan sharks. These moneylenders also provided small loans to the desperate souls trying to make it through another day. Most of the loans in the Garden were for M$0.30 to M$0.50—the price of a meal or a package of narcotics.

King of Hell Sha was a loan shark living in the Spring Forest Lodge. He once lent money to a boy working in the Harbin Opium Dispensary. In return the boy supplied Sha with residue opium ash. This potent dross Sha resold for his own profit. There were two kinds of loans. Those where no goods served as collateral brought in 10 percent interest per day. The second kind of loan—the King of Hell loan—was a pawn. A person left a possession, usually clothes, and received one-fifth of the sale value. If the loan was not repaid in five days, the item was sold.[16]

Gotō introduces us to three of the villains who specialize in white slavery. One is Zhu Chengguang from Shandong Province. Zhu is forty years old. He lives in the Prosperity Lodge in the Garden of Grand Vision. Zhu makes contact with women through flattery. If that does not work, he simply kidnaps them. He acts as a middleman for local pimps. For his trouble, he can earn 20 to 30 percent of the price paid for the women as a transaction fee. This kind of operation is called "pulling the rope" in the local slang. Li Jinsheng had been in the same business. Li's given name translates as "born to gold." It is a misnomer, however. For the past several years Li has been in the clutches of narcotics, and he has become a mere shadow of his former self. His life has gone to ruin. He is now begging in an alley. He resides in a charity ward.[17]

Villains live by stealing anything they can. One fellow living in the Prosperity Lodge robs and runs a crew of pickpockets. His neighbors call him Iron Jaw Liu. Gotō explains that Liu got the name after he robbed a fellow lodger, a Korean named Ko, of his clothes and money. Ko, furious, caught Liu, beat him, and kicked him until his rage passed. Liu refused to confess to the crime and made not even a groan the entire time he endured Ko's rage. The next day, Liu went to the pawnshop where he had stowed the Korean's things. He redeemed the stolen goods and sold them in the ghost (thieves') market behind the Garden of Grand Vision. When Ko learned about the sale, he rounded up a crew of Korean friends. They pounced on Liu, all of them beating and kicking the fellow, leaving him for dead. Unfazed, Liu returned to the lodge, earning the nickname "Iron Jaw."[18]

Big Liver Li is thirty years old. He hails from Mukden and lives in the Garden. "Big liver" implies that the man has guts, and so he has. Li earns his living strolling the streets of Harbin. He follows trucks and bicycles, deftly stealing goods from the back. Once he was on the street waiting for a trolley. A truck speeding along had to slow suddenly to avoid the crowd at a tram stop. In a flash, Li, agile as a cat, darted through a narrow gap between the trolley and the truck and helped himself to goods carelessly left in the truck's cargo hold.[19]

Some villains have no visible means of support. Wang the Carpenter appeared in the Spring Forest Lodge a year ago in March. He is tall and thin, and all day he does nothing but gamble and enjoy the company of women. He likes to brag that the women in the brothels on Sixteenth Street are his family members. Gotō asks him how that could be? The women come from Tianjin. Wang, judging by his thick accent, is a Shandong man. Wang says nothing and merely smirks at Gotō. But Gotō knows that Wang belongs to a secret society called Inner House Teaching. The women have been coerced into a life of prostitution. Wang most likely acts as a protector in the brothel.[20]

The corruption and bribery that kept the gambling operations alive in the Fujiadian neighborhood amounted to small change, hardly noticeable in the larger scheme of Manchukuo enterprises. Yet it was a micro economy that reflected the larger Manchukuo enterprise. Bribes to local police and spies rarely made it above the precinct level. In fact, Gotō implies that villains took money from the police even as the police and spies took money from the villains. Gaming operations obviously made money. In the late 1930s, as Japan's war with China expanded, the Japanese military needed money. Gambling remained illegal in Manchukuo, but quietly sanctioned gamings appeared. The profits from large gambling centers slipped quietly into the coffers of two intelligence services, the Kempeitai and the Special Service Agency. Following the example of occupied Shanghai, where a casino economy helped to maintain the control structure after 1937, Harbin acquired its own casino.[21]

In 1939 a gambling hall opened near the Peace Bridge in Harbin. It was simply called "the Club." This was no small side-street game run by neighborhood bullies. The Peace Bridge Gambling Club offered several rooms where customers of all races could enjoy opium, women, food, tea, and alcohol in addition to gambling games ranging from mah-jongg, poker, and dice to variations on roulette. Services included a barber, should a customer wish to make himself presentable before joining a game.[22]

Wang Xianwei became Harbin City Police Department chief in 1940. He brought to his office both integrity and dogged curiosity. Wang detested gambling. He hated the way that the vice destroyed families, bringing with it the danger of bankruptcy, crime, and suicide. On the books, gambling was still illegal in Manchukuo. Wang made it a personal crusade to close down the Peace Bridge Gambling Club. A large, square, hurriedly constructed wooden building, the Club featured a central atrium surrounded by small rooms on all four sides. The west hall had merchant stalls selling food, tea, and opium. Female entertainers frequented the place. Money exchanges lined the east hall. Punters could not play for cash; they had to exchange money for chips provided by the establishment. Every kind of game was available: mah-jongg, poker, roulette, and other local favorites like the flower assembly, a form of gambling involving betting on cards drawn from a basket. Each day several thousand Harbiners—Chinese, Japanese, Korean, and Russian alike—might visit the place. It was a lure to the multinational population of the city, one place where the paradise of races seemed to work.[23]

Wang raised his concerns about the Club with his assistant chief of police, a man named Maruta. In the upside-down world of the puppet regime, Maruta, although lower in rank, was in fact Wang's boss. Of course Maruta knew the Club existed. He told Wang, if he was so concerned, to go and ask the provincial and city authorities about closing the facility.[24]

Wang did just that. He visited the provincial governor, Yu Jingtao, who said, "There is nothing I can do." Yu told Wang that the year before he had attended a meeting with the Harbin mayor and the previous chief of police. The group met with the provincial police chief, Akiyoshi Toshiro. Akiyoshi announced that the Kempeitai wanted to set up the gambling operation. This was not an advisory consultation. The cooperation of the three officials was mandatory. When Wang reported what he learned to Maruta, the Japanese officer warned his Chinese colleague to be careful of the kinds of people behind the scheme.[25]

Wang was not so timid. On a business trip to Manchukuo's New Capital, he visited the central police commissioner. At the time this was

Commissioner Shibuya Saburō, newly promoted from Harbin. Shibuya, who, we remember, was held in esteem by his Chinese colleagues, told Wang that he knew about the gambling hall but had not heard that so much crime was associated with the place. Wang then visited the Chinese prime minister, Zhang Jinghui, who said he would look into the problem.

When Wang returned to Harbin, Maruta called Wang into his office. While Wang was gone, a Special Service Agency chief had contacted Maruta. He was furious. A minor cop, a Chinese cop no less, had gone over his head asking embarrassing questions in the capital. Maruta passed on his warning to Wang: "You do not understand the situation. Raising problems is really detestable."[26] These words, coming from the Special Service Agency, carried with them a not-so-veiled threat.

Wang was not deterred. He told Maruta he would like to talk to the officer in charge of the Harbin Special Service Agency. The man would not meet Wang. Maruta arranged a meeting between Wang and provincial chief of police Akiyoshi. The interview did not go well. Akiyoshi warned Wang in no uncertain terms that his trip to the central authorities had been noticed by both the Special Service Agency and the Kempeitai. This could be dangerous for a person's health and well-being. "You do not understand the situation," Akiyoshi continued. "People call Harbin a little Shanghai. All nationalities are here and they all like to gamble and smoke on their days off. The gambling hall is a good place to keep watch over them. Don't cause trouble again."[27]

Then the truth came out. The gambling hall paid a monthly sum to the police espionage branch, the Peace Preservation Bureau. Money also went to the Kempeitai. When Wang asked, "What is the Peace Preservation Bureau?" he was told, "If you don't know then forget about it."[28] Wang knew that Akiyoshi was a spy of the highest order and very much involved in setting up the local Peace Preservation Bureau. The incident drove home how much income from vice went secretly to financing undercover operations.[29]

Manchukuo was meant to run and prosper on its own economic resources. But the need for untraceable funds increased as the war in China bogged down. Shanghai fell to Japanese control in 1938. In Japanese hands, the city, famous for its easy virtues and called by many observers a casino economy, became an open source of revenue for the expanding war effort, even as the greater commerce of the city ground to a halt. Manchukuo made its own contributions to the dark side of the government account books. The vast and fertile poppy fields of Rehe were the most lucrative. But like the poppy trade, gambling contradicted the notion of the Kingly Way. Gotō's solution to the problem—at least as far as gambling was concerned—was outright legalization.

Gotō Reiji begins his report about gambling and villains by telling his readers—the same men Wang visited in New Capital—that the antigambling laws are tarnishing the image of the Manchukuo state. We talk about the Kingly Way, but we are alienating the people. For Gotō, the gamblers and villains of Fujiadian controlled a small piece of the Manchukuo pie. That some of his own superiors implicitly allowed open gambling to such an extent, taking money for undercover operations while preaching the evils of gaming, could only increase the sense of alienation that he addresses at the beginning of his chapter.

Both Wang and Gotō wrestled with a dilemma that even today we Americans have yet to resolve. Recently several lawsuits against American casinos illustrate the complexity of the question. In one such case, Arelia Taveras lost millions playing blackjack in Atlantic City. She forfeited her home, and her legal career ended in disgrace when she embezzled money from clients. Early in 2008, Taveras sued the casinos. She claimed, just as police chief Wang might have, that the casino system provided a dangerous atmosphere, similar to a toxic-waste site. While she gambled, the management of Resorts International and the Taj Mahal Hotel gave her complementary drinks and other perks to keep her playing and losing in the casino. This, she argued, fed her addiction to gaming.

Federal judge Renee Bumb threw the case out, ruling that gambling can be a safe activity. It is not equal to dumping toxic waste, as the suit claimed. Moreover the plaintiff, Arelia Taveras, entered into the activity in the hope of winning at a game of chance. She did not negotiate a contract.[30] As such Taveras was responsible for her actions. This is the position that US law takes in such cases. Is gambling a moral weakness? An addiction? Or is it an acceptable, if risky, diversion? Should the state regulate risky, even immoral behavior with legal sanctions? Or should the state cash in on a revenue source. Judge Bumb's ruling separates morality from the law. The Manchukuo government straddled the dilemma with formal bans and underground taxation.

Police chief Wang Xianwei would have sided with the Taveras claim that gambling is a dangerous activity. He preferred legal sanctions to curb risky behavior. In a move we can only admire as gutsy, he called the Japanese authorities on their two-faced policy. He lived to tell the tale, most likely because many of his Japanese colleagues agreed with him. Gotō, had he lived to join the argument, would have sided with Judge Bumb. He preferred gambling be open, legal, and taxed. Yet in his own way, he raised a different side of the same challenging issue with the Manchukuo police authorities as he described the games of chance in the Garden of Grand Vision. Can gambling really be eradicated from society?

12

The End of the Road

Their behavior is truly spooky. They have no fear of hell in the next world, since they live in hell here and now.

—Gotō Reiji[1]

Opium has three pleasures: happy poverty, happy death, happily carrying the coffin along.

—Local saying[2]

One cold morning, Gotō Reiji escorted a writer, newly arrived from Tokyo, on a tour of Fujiadian. The man and his traveling companion were both new to Harbin. Who better to show them the city than a local policeman?

It was a beautiful, sunlit morning. As Gotō led his guests into Long Spring Street behind the Garden of Grand Vision, they stumbled upon nine naked corpses littering the roadway. Finding three more corpses further along the street, Gotō flopped one over, showing his guests how the unfortunate victim had been murdered. Dark blood at the back of its head betrayed death by a violent blow. This corpse lay among others in the middle of the sunny street. Off to one side Gotō found a dust heap. A skull and a human shin covered with skin abrasions protruded from the rubble.[3]

Like his Tokyo guests, we see corpses everywhere we go with Gotō Reiji. Dead bodies clutter the stairs in the Garden of Grand Vision; bodies pile up near the food stalls; bodies fall into the street. In the Garden, death and the smells that accompany it are ever near to hand.

Watching people go about their lives, buy and consume their food, and barter for daily necessities in a street littered with death never ceased to amaze Gotō Reiji. He poked around the food stalls, eavesdropping on conversations like the following:

"When did that corpse turn up?"

"Yesterday, no?"

"What brought him down?"

"Don't know. Began to die after a morphine injection."

"Does anyone know who he is?"

"Don't know. Wasn't it yesterday? Some time? He was reeling in the yard of the Li Family Flophouse?"

"And was he naked then?"

"Surely not! Ha ha ha. Say, doesn't that soybean milk look yummy?"

"It is. Let's have some."

Amid the corpses, people ate meals and drank tea or liquor. They bought and sold goods, stolen and otherwise. Merchants offered rags for sale, laying them out along the curb. An old woman sat cross-legged by the fence with sewing in her lap. She took in mending for a living. As people walked through the filth, laughing as though the corpses were not there, Gotō could not help but ask the oblivious passers-by about their lives. They answered briefly, not wanting to engage a Japanese police officer.

"Why did this person die?"

"His stomach was empty." "Dirty heroin." "He froze stiff." "He was sick." "Old age."

"Why is the corpse naked?"

"What use do the dead have for clothes?" "He sold his clothes for drugs." "Someone stole them."

"When were the clothes stolen?"

"Just before he died." "When he was drunk." "While he was groaning with pain." "While under the spell of heroin." "He sold them for lodging." "The Korean heroin dealer took them as payment for drugs."

Feng Dengdiao, the police informant, described his life under the eaves of the flophouse. He assured Gotō Reiji that a fellow's life there would be short. Feng lived in a fog that reeked of death in its most physical form. His fellow lodgers drooled, vomited, and suffered from diarrhea; their genitals bled even as they enjoyed wet dreams. Feng figured a person could live in this environment no more than four or five days before his own physical and mental health sunk to the same level. Heroin, alcohol, or both provided a way to cope. But once one became possessed by drugs, death was certain. To pay for a chemical escape, Feng and his roommates pilfered and stole.

But as a fellow's habit increased, his condition worsened; he grew too lazy to steal. At the same time, his cravings intensified. An addict could never get enough of his drug. Naturally money went for heroin rather than food. Feng described fellow roomers as creatures with protruding bones, staring into space. A rasping or violent cough, hollow, sucking breathing, and spasms of vomiting all signaled that another poor wretch approached the end of the road. His companions, showing little sympathy, morphed into covetous vultures. Like vampires, they would grab for his clothes even before he gave up the ghost.[4]

Feng described the way of death as he saw it in the Garden. He left out none of the gory details. When a lodger's end was near, management chose two men from among the guests. Their job was to wait until 2 a.m., then to move the corpselike body—the lodger might be dead or still living—from the Spring Forest Lodge into the latrine at the bottom of the stairs or to pitch it out the window into the street. For this service the two lucky fellows would receive a free night's lodging. People in the Garden called the ritual "passing" or "guiding" a person over into Buddhahood.[5]

Gotō sometimes ventured through the neighborhood in the deep of night. Once, around 2 a.m., in front of the East Rising Bubble and Fry Pot, he came upon a corpse recently tossed into the street. Looking closer, Gotō found that the poor fellow was in fact just barely alive. The living corpse, as Gotō called him, was completely naked.

Gotō, referring to his notes of February 24, 1941, relays the following scene. He came across a body in the room that served as a toilet for the Spring Forest Lodge. The corpse lay sprawled on top of the frozen piss and shit. Covered in filthy rags, the man had sunken eyes, dull with the color of death. Gotō assumed the man was indeed dead until a spasm made his teeth chatter, a sound something like dry leaves rustling. People passing by gathered around the room. Following the custom in these cases, the group watched the man's last moments, showing no signs of pity. Instead, they lusted after his clothing. Someone grabbed at his middle. Gotō explains that Chinese peasant men kept money hidden in their waistbands. Perhaps there was a treasure there in the cesspit. Needle tracks covered the body lying in the filth. They were swollen and red, but no puss ran out of them. A black line of vomit ran across his cheek. He most likely threw up while his neighbors robbed him of his clothes.[6]

The Harbin City Board of Health sent a truck around on a daily basis to collect the remains of the unfortunate. It often drove right into the front gate of the Garden. The city employees who manned the trucks came from local fishing communities. With a movement smooth from long practice, they thrust large fishing spears into each corpse's head, pulling the body from the roadway into the back of the truck. The cadavers looked like piles of dried cod as the truck passed through the street.[7]

The truckers carted the bodies to a charity graveyard in Nangang, a potter's field. Officially the graveyard was called Nangang Dayou Ward Pauper's Burial Ground. Local people called it the Hill of 10,000 Bodies. In the graveyard, a pit seven meters by two meters by two meters would hold from eighty to one hundred of these bodies. Covered with a thin layer of soil, the pits reek of decay in the summer time.[8]

There were worse stories to be told. Gotō heard, on one trip to the Fujiadian neighborhood, that a tobacco pouch filled with human intestines had been tossed into the front door of the local police precinct. He also heard reports of Japanese-looking men seen among the corpses in the street. Unidentified bodies got carted off to the Hill of 10,000 Bodies. Any dismembered bodies went to the Ghost King Hall, where they were crudely bundled in reeds to wait for the spring thaw. In warmer weather the remains were tossed with little ceremony into the Songhua River.

The Ghost King Hall was a temple located inside the Lu Family Charity Burial Ground near Peace Bridge. The Lu family provided the money to establish the cemetery. Contributions from Manchukuoan Catholics went to maintaining the grounds. Gotō could not say if the Lu family itself was actually Catholic.

In keeping with the ecumenical blending of beliefs that gave Harbin its eccentric architecture, local residents in the Peace Bridge neighborhood took up their own collection to build the Ghost King Hall on the burial grounds. There people far from home could burn paper god money and charms for their ancestors on commemorative holidays. Gotō adds that Chinese customarily burned paper god money for ancestors during funerals and days of remembrance. This currency, of course, was not legal tender but more of a talisman, money to help the departed in the afterlife.[9]

By tradition born of ancestor worship, Chinese people buried their dead with elaborate funerals. Before a burial, they consulted a geomancer or a sorcerer—and often both—to determine the proper direction in which to place the grave and the proper date for the funeral. Gotō has seen funerals of the well-to-do held in tents or lodges large enough to entertain an entire community or clan. He assures us cynically that the geomancers who set the lucky date for interment are in league with the burial agents. The longer the mourning family has to wait for a lucky day, the more money the grave keeper can squeeze out of them for preserving the remains of their loved one.[10]

When possible, a bereaved family that had settled in Harbin paid to send the body of a loved one back to the native village for a proper funeral. Gotō, himself living abroad, points out that anyone from any country whose loved one meets with tragedy abroad can understand the practice. We all need the comfort that bringing the body home to rest engenders. For Chinese people, with their firm belief in the foundation of the family and village, the desire for a final resting place close to their ancestors was even stronger. Most of the residents of Harbin considered some foreign place to be their hometown. As a result many bodies traveled the rails from Manchukuo south into China proper. This created a thriving industry in corpse transportation. Gotō points out signs and fliers posted around Fujiadian, such as the following: "This store contracts to send coffins or funeral urns by car and by sea with prompt service and proper handling of transit procedures. For a reduced price a coffin or urn will be delivered to a designated gravesite in the place of public registration [the home village]. Should you have a loved one pass away, please come in and discuss this with us. Contact Yang Jiuchang, #60 South Peace Street West, Phone 9127."[11]

Satō Shin'ichirō, with his scholar's curiosity, studied funeral arrangements to satisfy his interest in Chinese customs. But Gotō the policeman had a practical, forensic reason for his research. Sending a corpse back to the home village may be a common Chinese practice, but it was also an opportunity for crime. Opium, heroin, weapons, and gold traveled inside the coffins along with the bodies. Smugglers could and did harvest corpses from the bountiful crop of bodies littering the streets of Fujiadian. A frozen cadaver might disappear into a lovely coffin to be sent on its way back through the Great Wall along with contraband. For a small bribe to the local police, the coffin would receive the proper paperwork for a trip to a fraudulent hometown. For a small fee of M$150 to M$200, the coffin, with its body and contraband inside, traveled on the Japanese-owned South Manchuria Railway straight to Tianjin or Jinan and a lively and lucrative drug market. What official was going to inspect a heavy coffin reeking of death?

In a bit of irony the poor devil, picked naked off the street, received in death the kind of clothing denied to him in life. The drug that controlled his existence accompanied him to his final resting place. Gotō admits that it is hard to determine the truth of these stories, but since between 2,000 and 3,000 corpses traveled back to North China every year, the Manchukuo government had tried to ban the practice. It would seem the authorities took the rumors to be true.[12]

So many corpses lay strewn along the streets of Harbin. Official numbers put the annual death toll at between 2,400 and 3,000. The Harbin city hall favored the lower number; the city police bureau provided the higher. The problem did not go unnoticed beyond the halls of government. Although most of the dead littered the Chinese Fujiadian section of town, Japanese residents complained about the problem from their more comfortable neighborhoods. Throughout the 1930s, reform fell under the aegis of local charities. By 1940, Manchukuo authorities had begun to gather such organizations under their control.

Gotō Reiji describes one attempt to reform the poor. Harbin had a charity for beggars and the homeless run by private donation and in Chinese hands. The asylum was more of a workhouse than a refuge. The people who took advantage of the asylum found they had to endure a limitless sentence of hard labor. On April 1, 1941, Harbin City authorities took over the charity. By October the number of inmates had risen from 450 to 1,600. But in the six-month interval, 500 of those seeking shelter died. Gotō blamed the Chinese staff. Like their compatriots in the flophouses, they stole from the dead. Plunder became one of the perks of the job. In truth, the problem had more to do with the institutional structure than the employees' avarice.[13]

Gotō remarks on the confiscation of only one local charity. The action was part of a larger Manchuria-wide effort to bring the problem of drug addiction under control and to address a labor shortage. It began with a body count. In 1940, at the same time Manchukuo authorities announced a new drug-reduction law—their third revision—the government set up centers for addicts. These institutions, as we have seen, sported the hopeful name "healthy-living centers" or "guidance halls." Reform of addicts, drifters, and the down-and-out was the stated goal of the program.

The reality was harsh. One Manchukuoan remembers the healthy-living centers as a fraud. In his town people caught smoking without a license were sent to one of those halls. But when the person arrested paid a bribe, he entered through the front gate and exited immediately through the rear. If no money was forthcoming, the hapless smoker found himself in a labor camp. The institutions quickly became a blackmail scheme for local authorities. The problems reached into the higher levels of government.[14]

Gotō's study of the poor in Fujiadian coincided with a larger Manchurian census survey that initiated programs geared toward both military preparation and enhanced social control. In 1940 Manchukuo authorities undertook a nationwide census count. Arranged through the Manchukuo Home Ministry, the census aimed to gather details about the residents of every city, county, and banner in the territory. Representatives from local government offices gathered for training in New Capital that summer. They received forms to fill out, which, when completed, would give the government detailed statistics about the makeup of the Manchukuo population, including its age, gender, race, occupation, religion, and assets. The official count took place on October 1, 1940, after which the forms were tallied and sent off to the central government. One official who participated recalled that by October 10, census forms filled his office, coming in like a blizzard.[15]

Officials stated that cataloguing the many peoples of the diverse nation drove the need for the census. In fact, by 1940 the war in China had stalled, draining supplies and energy. The Japanese military needed to identify all able-bodied men for service to the state. More importantly, they sought information about any wealth or talents that might be appropriated to the war effort. Japanese authorities needed to strengthen the *baojia*, or mutual guarantee, system of neighborhood and village control. They hoped to identify "black individuals and black families"—in other words, those Chinese who remained outside Manchukuo control.

On the surface the goal of the census was reform. As such, information about the dispossessed played an important role. Indeed, such reforms immediately touched the lives of those living in the Garden. In the early 1940s narcotics-reform laws converted the licensed opium shops, including the one in the Garden of Grand Vision, into opium recovery centers with health clinics attached.[16] Such social engineering, however, barely disguised a pragmatic wartime necessity: shortage of labor and materials.

In 1943 Nakaii Hisaji, head of the Police Bureau Intelligence Section, led a campaign called "Clean the Capital; Strengthen Public Safety." He set up reed huts surrounded by iron fences and called them reform training facilities. Such institutions spread throughout Manchuria. The posts were meant to reform vagrants by giving them meaningful work. In fact they funneled unlucky arrestees into barracks in the countryside. By the late 1930s Manchukuo needed labor. The war with China after 1937 put a damper on labor migration from the south. From 1938 on, Manchukuo authorities initiated labor conscription, the duty for which fell more and more to the police. Under these conditions reform facilities became no more than slave labor camps. Katō Toyotaka calls the practice a "labor snatch."[17]

Autopsy of the Garden of Grand Vision contributed to this roundup of vagrants. Gotō Reiji, as a member of the Peace Preservation Bureau, was meant to study the Garden to find spies. Instead he found every other sort of antisocial behavior. Katō tells us that as soon as the report went to the Hinkō County police commissioner, his office issued orders to have the Garden purged in a clean sweep. Since the residents of the Garden had no regular employment to speak of, they got caught up in the labor roundup that would condemn them to a living death in the vagrant barracks.[18]

Survivors of the vagrant barracks remembered them as hell on earth. Once there, inmates lost all contact with the outside world. They mined coal, cut logs, or moved rock to build roads. Electric fencing and sentry boxes surrounded the camps. Work hours were long, food was scarce, and rules were strict and arbitrary. Guards permitted no talking at night; while working or marching to the work site, all inmates had to face forward looking straight ahead. In the morning they woke to sing the pledge song; they sang the words instead to mean the "present-day song." Inmates wore yellow clothing, making it easy to spot an escapee.

They referred to the clothes as "modern clothes." Clearly these inmates had good reason to prefer tradition to the kind of modernity that was the watchword of Manchukuo.[19]

Inmates indulged in gallows humor, despite the hardships. One survivor recalled that his fellow internees described the camp's electric fence as having two doors. One door, by which they all entered, had no exit. The second door had an exit but no entrance. Through this second gate, those who had succumbed to starvation or mistreatment were dispatched with as little sympathy as the naked near-dead forced out of slums like the Garden of Grand Vision.[20] The gruesome end-of-life ritual for the nation's poorest moved from the public street into the rural stockade.[21]

The end of the road did not come gently for other players we have met in and around the Garden of Grand Vision. Feng Dengdiao, the police informant, made daily visits to Gotō's office, even though his residence changed often. One October night, he got a fright. One of the boys working at a charity where Feng bunked down to pass a cold snap learned that Feng could write. The boy, probably a spy, pressured Feng to pen a letter to an agent of Chiang Kai-shek's Blue Shirts. These fearsome agents worked out of China proper, spying against the Japanese invaders and Chinese Communists alike.

Caught between a rock and a hard place, Feng produced the letter in a shaky hand, reported the adventure to Gotō, and promptly disappeared. Gotō made inquiries about his friend. He heard conflicting stories: Feng had returned home to his village and family, Feng was living in a culvert near the river, Feng had been beaten to death, Feng had joined a robber band. Whatever the truth, Gotō never saw his friend again. He assumed Feng had died the same miserable death as his fellow lodgers in the Garden of Grand Vision, that he had passed into Buddhahood through the same grim ritual that he had described so well.[22]

Amieto Vespa, the spy, did not survive the war. Vespa had known from the start that Manchukuo would be a hell on earth. From the day of the new nation's inception, he began planning his escape. He had two problems: first, the Japanese authorities needed his local knowledge; second, to keep him under their control, these same authorities held his wife and children hostage. At the very outset of the Manchukuo experiment, Vespa found he had Japanese military officers as handlers. After only a week of interviews with his new Japanese intelligence bosses, he realized that life in Manchukuo would not be the paradise of racial harmony painted in propaganda broadcasts. He called his first handler "the Boss" and his second, ominously, "Torquemada."

Vespa thought it would take only a few months to arrange for his family's safe passage out of Manchuria, after which he planned to leave himself. Instead he remained in Manchukuo for another four and a half years. In early spring 1936, he had to plot his escape in earnest. As the chief investigator in the Simon Kaspe affair, he became a target for both Japanese and White Russian agents. That year he sold all the property he owned in the Harbin area. In order to do so, he had to pay bribes and kickbacks that cost him M$7,000. He took a loss on the real estate—and not a moment too soon.

By the autumn of 1936, his affairs still not completely settled, he received from his handler an assignment in Qiqihar. This would take him away from his home base into a remote border area of Manchukuo. He understood that the order was a death sentence. Instead he flew secretly to Dalian, where he took a steamer to Qingdao in China proper. His wife and children followed him the next day. Unfortunately, when his wife's steamer pulled into Qingdao port, Japanese intelligence officers arrested her, sending her back to Harbin on the charge that her husband had committed treason.

It took Vespa six more months to secure his wife's release. He managed to do so only because an acquaintance from his warlord years, a man who fought with bandits in the Manchurian borderlands, kidnapped a Japanese national and arranged a hostage swap. Vespa, in the meantime, waited for his wife's return in Shanghai. Japanese and Russian agents followed him there. Once Mrs. Vespa had truly escaped from Manchukuo, Amieto Vespa felt safe to write his tell-all book about his adventures and life in Manchuria.[23] Yet, he did not live much longer. His end, like his life, is wrapped in mystery. He died either in Shanghai in 1941 or perhaps in Manila in 1945, presumably murdered by those same Russian and Japanese thugs who had followed him through the Shanghai streets.[24]

Consul George C. Hanson, "Mr. Manchuria," did not survive the war either. As Manchukuo began its history, things began to look up for Hanson. Some of his colleagues in the US State Department recognized his linguistic abilities. After so many lukewarm career reviews, one of his department supporters wrote in his favor. "He has been a class five diplomat forever," the man wrote. "How easy is it for us to nit pick as we sit in beautiful Washington on a sunshiny day." Granted he is a non-conformist, but "his territory consists of 222,000 Square Miles, larger than France or Japan."[25]

His abilities acknowledged, George C. Hanson became the first American consul general to serve in Moscow under the Soviet regime. He was in the right place at the right time and with the right talents. When America recognized the Soviet Union in 1933, it was logical to move a Russian-speaking consul from North China to Moscow. Hanson was the perfect choice for the post. Of course, when he arrived in Moscow, he was not pleased with his accommodations. He had to beg, once more, for a post allowance, including a table setting for eighteen, which would allow him to entertain in the proper style.[26]

Yet fate worked against him. On November 7, 1934, while on home leave, Hanson stopped in New York, where he gave a talk at the Russian-American Chamber of Commerce. He did not come with a prepared lecture. Instead he made general observations about doing business in the Soviet Union. The talk was, by all accounts, well received. Later that evening he attended a social gathering at the Soviet consulate. All seemed well.

Suddenly Hanson was called to Washington, DC. When he arrived at the State Department, he faced an unexpected inquiry. Some who attended the talk at the Russian-American Chamber of Commerce had accused him of making insulting remarks about the Soviet Union. To add to his troubles, he was admonished for being openly drunk at the Soviet party later that evening. To his dismay, he learned he would not return to Moscow. Instead he was to be transferred to Addis Ababa, Ethiopia.

When news of the demotion became public, scores of influential businessmen and friends wrote directly to US Secretary of State Cordell Hull in Hanson's defense. One among many letters came from Karl Bickel, a United Press reporter, who called the allegations false. Both Bickel and his wife had attended the same evening party at which Hanson was said to have been rowdy with drink. Both had talked with Hanson several times over the course of the evening and swore that he had not been drunk. A second reporter, from Scripps Howard News Service, claimed to know that the charges brought against Hanson came from "interests having private axes to grind." Even Will Rogers, the social critic, comedian, and sometimes cowboy, wrote in support of Hanson. Rogers had spent time with Hanson hunting in Manchuria and admired the man who shared his interest in the outdoors.[27]

Public news coverage of the transfer helped Hanson begin to look forward to the new situation. In 1935 Ethiopia (Abyssinia) was a global hot spot. Newspapers featured headlines that warned of impending Italian meddling in the nation. Next to headlines accusing Italy of planning an attack, the *New York Times* informed readers that "George Hanson, renowned troubleshooter in Far East" would be on hand to observe events. Hanson privately looked forward to hunting in Africa.[28]

Yet again, disappointment awaited the consul. While traveling to his new post, during a layover in Alexandria, Egypt, he received sudden notice that he would not be going to Ethiopia after all. He should reroute to Salonika, Greece, to take up a consular post there. An expert in Middle East affairs would take his place in Africa. With Italy rattling swords in preparation for its October 1935 invasion, the US State Department wanted a cooler head in the consulate. This time there was no favorable newspaper coverage to assuage the sting of another clear demotion.

Hanson arrived at his new post in a state of severe depression. Instead of going to work, he took an overdose of sleeping pills. A doctor who later examined him wrote to the department in Washington, DC, to dispel any rumor that Hanson was an alcoholic. But, he added, "Hanson's nervous disorder is primarily due to excess sugar in the blood" and secondarily to "emotional shock." The doctor recommended a month of rest. The State Department ordered him home. "This assignment not made at your request nor for your convenience," read the telegram—not an overly sympathetic note of concern from his secretary of state. State Department colleagues got him from Salonika to Marseille, France, putting him up and watching over him along the way. From Marseille Hanson embarked on the liner SS *President Polk* for America.[29]

On September 1, 1935, while ocean-bound for home, Hanson met with the ship's surgeon, who found him to be doing well. He gave Hanson something to help him sleep. Later that evening Hanson passed a pleasant hour chatting with W. H. Weaver, master of the ship. They talked about Moscow, China, and world affairs. Weaver saw Hanson later at dinner. He was therefore surprised when the next morning a cabin boy reported finding Hanson's body on the floor of his cabin. Weaver went to Hanson's stateroom and found him lying prone in a pool of blood. When Weaver moved the body, he found Hanson's small pistol on the deck. Pronounced dead, Hanson was placed in a refrigerator room to preserve his body for the rest of the journey.[30]

As soon as the news made the papers, there was another public outcry. The *New York Times* published a letter from Hanson himself, answering the accusations made against him the year before.[31] Friends who had supported him then came to his defense once again. William Simms, a lawyer from Pennsylvania, sent a telegram summing up the feeling. "Stunned— have just heard of Hanson suicide—score one for Departments persecution of this faithful servant of our country." This sentiment went public when an impassioned defense of Hanson appeared in *Time* magazine. The article denied the government claim that Hanson had suffered a nervous breakdown. Instead the writer sided with Hanson's many friends, saying that he suffered from "despair over a career deliberately ruined by enemies in the State Department."[32] An editorial in a Japanese-language Harbin newspaper blamed the suicide on "certain [American] bankers and businessmen having Bolshevik connections" who persecuted him for disclosing some of the less-than-ideal economic and labor conditions in the Soviet Union.[33] Perhaps the final insult came several years after his burial, when Hanson's heirs tried to settle his estate. Although dead and buried, he was still being dunned—through the State Department—to repay the train fare for the trip that took him from Harbin to Moscow.[34]

13

Punishing the Police

The Soviet side sentenced prisoners of war, including police officials and other detainees, to hard labor. In an area stretching from the Kamchatka Peninsula in the east to the banks of the Black Sea in the west, from Central Asia in the South to the Arctic Circle in the North, in seventy areas there were around 1,200 to 1,300 detention centers.

—Katō Toyotaka[1]

Eat, shit, and then sleep. This is the life of the internee.

—Satō Shin'ichirō[2]

Both Katō Toyotaka and Satō Shin'ichirō remember August 1945 vividly. The countdown to the end of the Manchukuo experiment came with dreaded certainty. On August 6 the American *Enola Gay* dropped the first Atomic bomb on Hiroshima. On August 8 the Soviet Union declared war on Japan. The Red Army moved into Manchukuo the next day, the same day a second atomic bomb leveled Nagasaki. Flair bombs fell into the Fujiadian neighborhood early on the morning of August 9. Airplanes of uncertain nationality flew over Harbin, heading south. More flair bombs lit up the sky over Fujiadian. The first skirmishes of the final days of World War II in Asia had begun. The Chinese civil war would continue for another four years.

On August 10 Harbin was placed under martial law. The Harbin police chief announced that an all-out attack on Manchukuo's eastern regions was under way. The next day, Katō and other police in Manchukuo received orders from the Kempeitai to burn all secret documents. A

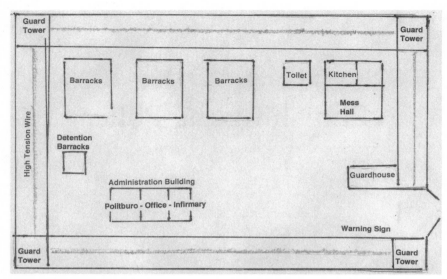

Prison Camp Layout

summons from Tokyo repeated the command two days later: burn all documents, including photographs of the emperor.[3] The Kantō Army moved two divisions of the Fourth Army into the area in response to the expected invasion. Before they could engage in battle, they received the order to surrender. On August 15, 1945, Japan's emperor told his nation that they would have to bear the unbearable and endure the unendurable. Japan had lost the war.[4]

Dismantling Manchukuo turned into a long and messy affair. There would be no orderly withdrawal of the Kantō Army; nor could there be a clear occupation. Soviet troops easily swept into China's Northeast. They would use their time in the area to strip Japanese-built facilities of machinery and heavy equipment. The Chinese Communist base camp in Yan'an was in the North and closer to Manchuria. Some Chinese Communist units were already there, having been active underground during the Manchukuo period. Harbin would become a Chinese Communist stronghold. Nationalist soldiers arrived from the south aided by American transport.[5] Although the two sides in the Chinese civil conflict kept up the pretense of the truce that carried them through the Anti-Japanese War for another year, in fact the long Chinese civil war was about to enter its final phase. Japanese citizens left behind found themselves at the mercy of three armies. With the Kantō Army all but gone, personnel in the police and the civil administration—including Katō Toyotaka and Satō Shin'ichirō—would face chaos.

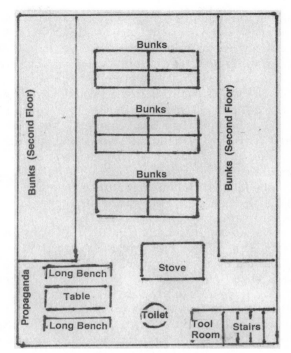

Barracks Layout

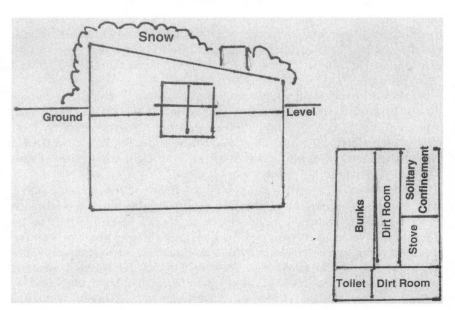

Detention Barracks Layout

Japanese families living throughout China's Northeast all faced immi-
nent danger. Manchukuo was more than a military base; it was a Japanese
settler colony. The home government had encouraged young men and
women from rural Japan to set up farm communities in the Manchukuo
countryside. In pamphlets and speeches, they promised young farmers a
rich land of opportunity, a settler's paradise. Instead young farm families
struggled bravely to eke out a living in the harsh climate of North Manchuria. Japanese merchants brought their families to the cities seeking a
living in the new land. Civilians working in the Manchukuo bureaucracy
never expected they would have to leave. They married, bore and raised
children, sent them through a school system created for the Japanese community, and lived with the full expectation that future generations would
continue to populate the new nation. In 1945 this dream shattered.[6]

And what of the Kantō Army? By 1945, necessity forced the General
Staff to redeploy many units south to the China front or even further
afield to Southeast Asia. Katō tells us that as early as March 1945, the
Manchukuo border area had been all but abandoned. In a strategic re-
deployment south that began even in 1944—code-named "Operation
Flash"—the Kantō Army forces moved toward the Korean border to
prepare for a decisive battle with Russia. Chinese working for Manchukuo police who came under suspicion of being Nationalist spies were
arrested and investigated. Dummy companies appeared to control war
supplies. One such company, the Eastern Border Company, was located
on the fourth floor of the Hotel New Harbin. The Kantō Army controlled
the business. When the Soviet army penetrated the Manchukuo border, it
faced a few scattered divisions situated around Harbin and the northern
areas. Katō lists the units: the 149th outside Qiqihar and the 13th and
136th in Harbin.[7]

As the end drew near, some enlisted men deserted. The life of the ordinary grunt in the Japanese army was harsh. When the system failed,
many got out. Satō ended up helping a deserter navigate postwar Manchuria. Some Japanese army units tried to surrender to Chiang Kai-shek's
Nationalist Army, hoping that they could help fight the Chinese Communist foe. This did not always work out well.

Both Katō and Satō mention the Tonghua Incident of February 3, 1946.
At that time Japanese living in Tonghua City in Manchuria's Southwest
rioted against a Chinese Communist occupation. They did so at the request of the Nationalist Army, with which they sided in the civil war that
was heating up, soon to reach its pre-truce level. As a result Japanese living in the town were massacred. Between 2,000 and 3,000 men, women,
and children died. Satō learned about the massacre in his prison cell.[8]

Katō remembers the last days of Manchukuo as a cold wind of change
blowing through Harbin. People deserted the once bustling streets. The

Soviet Red Army reached Harbin on August 16 and moved into the Soviet consulate building. From this base it began confiscating Manchukuo government buildings.[9] Even before the Soviet army reached the city, before the surrender, Katō began to hear about the deaths of his fellow countrymen and -women. Some died at the hands of Russian soldiers, some were killed by Chinese, others starved as they fled the city, and many committed suicide. Katō chronicled the deaths that came to his notice. For instance, days before the surrender the vice county commissioner living in a city just north of Harbin found himself without food or funds. The Soviet army cut off any escape to Harbin. Seeing his luck run out, the man killed himself, his family, and his dependents—thirty people in all. Residents of a farming village in the countryside tried several times to head south. Their escape blocked by mobs that looted and raped, they committed suicide.

Once the surrender was announced, the Japanese death count rose. On August 16, for instance, a group of 299 men, women, and children, all members of a farm community outside Harbin, suffered a ferocious attack. With no way to save themselves, the entire group committed suicide. Another group of farmers left their village. As they crossed the Songhua River, Chinese police, who had once worked for Manchukuo, sprayed them with gunfire. They all died, either of their wounds or exposure. A vice mayor serving in a town north of Harbin was shot by renegade police. On August 17, another group of farm families threw themselves into the river. The vice mayor of a village in the Harbin jurisdiction was arrested and shot.

Reading through Katō's stark list of the dead, it becomes clear that some Chinese who once worked with the Manchukuo government murdered their old colleagues. The record is full of turncoat police or soldiers who attacked their former bosses. Such was the case of Saitō Taniyoshi and ninety-six of his colleagues. Serving outside Harbin, they were shot by their own police force. Shimogaki Ka'ichirō was arrested and shot by renegade river police. Erstwhile Manchukuoans might have good reason to take revenge for previous mistreatment. More to the point, at the time of surrender, their status shifted from the artificial label "Manchukuoan" to the dangerous designation "traitor Chinese." An aggressive stance could be proof of loyalty. Katō does not comment on the situation.

A personal tragedy for Katō came on August 21. On that day Shibuya Saburō, former police chief then serving as head of the Harbin school, committed suicide, taking his family with him. In his last letter he declared, "To die is easy; to live with true meaning is hard. I will watch my student's future path from the shadows beneath the grass." Numbers of White Russians joined his funeral procession. Shibuya had served as Harbin police commissioner before moving to the central police. He ended his life as head of the Harbin Russian-language school where Katō had studied.[10]

I fear a reader may think that these mass suicides are examples of Japanese wartime fanaticism. Such is not the case. Once the Soviet army burst through the northern Manchukuo border, it did so with a violent fury that made little distinction between soldier and civilian, Japanese and Chinese. Villages and families made the choice to die quickly, even honorably, on their own terms, rather than face unknown torments at the hands of a frenzied enemy. This menu of terrible choices lies beneath the sorrow buried in Katō's lists of the dead.

Then, on August 24, Soviet soldiers came for Katō. He and Tomida Naoji, the unlucky man who was serving as the Harbin police chief at the time of surrender, were arrested. Soviet authorities held Katō, along with his colleagues, in the basement of the Japanese consulate for a few days, then transferred them to the Harbin jail. On December 12, Katō shipped out to a prisoner of war camp deep in the Ural Mountains. Three months later, he was transferred to the Kazak Republic and later to Central Asia. He passed from one camp to another, always being hauled in the back of a truck, locked in with other prisoners, and secured by an iron grate held tight with a sturdy lock. During the day he suffered under hard labor, building roads and rail lines. At night he slept in a prison barracks. He was never a model worker, so he endured poor housing and food rations.

Katō provides a brief but graphic description of life in the camps. He includes sketches of the gulag camp arrangements that are so reminiscent of the building layouts in the *Autopsy* report that it leads one to assume that, as a young officer, Katō drew the short straw and got the job of mapping the Garden of Grand Vision's interior setup.

In Katō's memory, walls of wood and barbed wire surrounded the prison camp area. A high-tension electric wire secured the area, as did four lookout towers, one at each corner. The towers reminded Katō of fire-prevention towers seen in the Japanese countryside. Sometimes at night the guards would sing. A guard post protected the entrance. On the wall opposite the guard post, a warning sign announced in both Russian and Japanese, "If you approach this point, you will be shot." It was here, in front of the guardhouse, that the prisoners lined up in five parade rows each morning before marching off to their work assignments.

Barracks consisted of many units of bunk beds. Each unit provided wood platforms that slept eight men. There was a stove and a toilet, which in fact was no more than an oil drum emptied morning and night. On days when severe cold or too much blowing snow made work impossible, the men stayed in the barracks. On those days anyone with a talent became a star. One man had memorized an epic samurai novel, which he could recite by heart. Several others were good at parlor tricks. Katō remembered two German prisoners who believed in the teachings of Martin Luther. At night they would sing "A Mighty Fortress Is Our God." These men were considered political prisoners.

The camp included offices for the Politburo. In those rooms prisoners were interrogated. All day long officers with white badges on their collars rolled in and out of the office. Katō adds, with no explanation but perhaps a sly wink, that some of these officers were young women. In this area prisoners had to endure the psychological torture of watching lovely meals being laid out, food they could not enjoy themselves.

The prison camp layout included an underground detention cell, or *zemlianka*. It was half buried underground. A prisoner entered through the roof into a room with only enough room for eight or so men to stretch out on bunks. A narrow passageway with a dirt floor separated the bunks from a stove, which provided little in the way of heat, and a room for solitary confinement. During three long weeks in February 1949, Katō and three other colleagues, including Gotō Reiji, endured life in the detention barracks while Politburo officials grilled them about the details of the Manchukuo Peace Protection Bureau for which they had once worked.

During the day, the noonday sun melted the snow on the roof. Water trickled through the roof, soaking into their padded clothing. At night, the damp clothes froze hard as rock, making sleep impossible. Anyone unlucky enough to find himself in solitary confinement had to endure the time shoeless, wearing only a thin shirt. In detention, the daily ration of black bread decreased from 350 to 250 grams. Katō mentions the kindness of guards who would slip them extra food out of pity.

Katō and his colleagues spent most of the three weeks lying in the bunks. Once a day they came out to defecate and walk about a bit. This daily outing was a torture. The jail was so dark and there was so little room to move about that the daily excursion outside caused intolerable pain. The light blinded their eyes. Their feet, numb from lack of movement, could barely hold them up. They wobbled and tired after walking only a few meters.[11] During their interment they were all questioned concerning minute details about the police.

Katō Toyotaka is reticent about what happened to him at the end of the war. He returned to Japan only after a general amnesty in 1950. Many of his friends and colleagues did not survive the Soviet ordeal. He shares a few scattered personal experiences, giving the details of the gulag in sketches and picture headings. He lists dates and places where the suffering of colleagues occurred. He puts his own emotions, guilt, and regrets into his novel about the Garden of Grand Vision. Although most of the plot follows the original report, adding color and commentary, the novelist in him comes out in the last chapters. There Katō paints a graphic

picture of Manchukuo's final year as experienced by the main character
he calls simply Mr. Gotō.

Katō brings to life scenes of triumph, romance, and gruesome death.
The novel ends with residents of the Garden not in labor camps but joining Mr. Gotō at a banquet to celebrate his promotion to chief superinten-
dent. In the autumn of 1944, they all gather at the Garden of Abundance,
a Fujiadian restaurant. The pretty Chun Fang is present, dressed to the
nines, sitting by Mr. Gotō's side. Zou Xisan, a man Gotō Reiji held in some
contempt, praises the policeman as "a man who speaks our language and
who has always been a friend to us." Zou presents Gotō with a cloisonné
plaque commemorating the event.[12]

Yet the tale turns dark. When August 1945 arrives, graffiti appears on
the walls in Fujiadian. "The Japanese are leaving. Russians, with their
big noses, will come." Zou the landlord proves as fickle in his loyalty
and friendship as he had promised in his earlier interview with the real
Gotō Reiji, reproduced in the front of the top-secret report. Only months
before the Japanese surrender, Zou Xisan had donated M$20,000 to the
Kempeitai, an insurance policy of a sort. He used Mr. Gotō's good offices
to see that the cash reached the right hands. Now, with the Japanese army
in disarray, as Mr. Gotō makes a final visit to the Garden, Zou is the first
to complain. "What is he doing here? This is an outrage."[13]

Lin Jitang of the Spring Forest Lodge calls on the expertise of two thugs
among the many villains he knows so well. The men tie Mr. Gotō up and
dump him in one of the rooms in the lodge. "The Japanese have taught
us a lot of things," Lin says. "One of these is how to torture people. Now
we will apply the lesson." In the novel, Mr. Gotō dies, and his bound and
gagged body is dumped into the latrine at the bottom of the stairs. His
skin has been pierced with an awl. Down his back, using a crude mixture
of soot and hot peppers, someone has tattooed, "Mr. Gotō died serving
his emperor in the Garden of Grand Vision."[14]

Katō admits that this graphic ending is a sensational fiction. In fact
some of his colleagues from those days in Harbin criticized him for his
poetic license. Yet the days of chaos following Japan's surrender brought
many such scenes of retribution. A certain Morigawa, a professor at the
Harbin industrial college, organized his fellow teachers to form a group,
the Japanese Youth Volunteer Corp. The plan was to move south and join
the Chinese Nationalist Army, once an enemy, now an anti-Communist
ally. The Chinese Communist organization moved into Harbin after the
Russians left. The city would become a base from which to fight for Manchuria as the civil war grew violent. Before Morigawa could carry out the
plan, he and several professors were arrested, tried for war crimes, and
publically executed in a Daoli park. Katō included Mr. Gotō's demise as a

kind of symbolic commemoration of so many of these kinds of nightmarish scenes, which he personally witnessed.[15]

Why would a person like Gotō seek refuge in the Garden? I asked myself this troubling question as I read the novel's ending. The choice made sense to me only after I pieced together recollections of the two surviving policemen. The Japanese army had evaporated. The police and civil service bureaucrats had been left to fend for themselves. Any means of transportation to the ports in the South proved hard to come by. The tales of looting, rape, and murder certainly drove many families to choose a merciful death by their own hands rather than face public execution or the cruelty of a mob. In Harbin, refugees from settler communities in the North who made it to the city found themselves in relocation camps. One such camp just outside Harbin held up to 10,000 people. In November 1945 the camp suffered a typhus outbreak; 6,500 people died. The survivors, barely clinging to life, buried the dead in the fields outside town.[16] With such grim alternatives, a person like Gotō might take a chance on hiding in the Garden for a few days.

The Mr. Gotō of the novel was most likely a combination of several police officers, all of whom mentored the young Katō when he first arrived in Manchuria. The Gotō Reiji who appears briefly in Katō's police histories did not die in the Garden. He survived at least until 1949, when he shared the underground detention with Katō. One man who formed the composite character for the novel's Mr. Gotō was Mizoguchi Yoshio, a ranking officer in the Peace Preservation Bureau. He survived the prisons in Russia only to be sent to China to be tried for war crimes rather than being repatriated. Mizoguchi was executed in Beijing.[17] A second model was Kondō Kunijirō, who was from the same hometown as Katō. When the young orphan came to Harbin as a police recruit, Kondō became his mentor. At the end of the war, the Soviet Red Army arrested both men. Along with many other of their countrymen, they were held prisoner in the basement of the Harbin Japanese consulate. In December 1945, they endured a long and frigid forced march to a Siberian camp. Through the ordeal, Katō confessed, he often felt ready to die. Each time he lagged behind in weakness and despair, Kondō appeared by his side to urge him on.

Kondō Kunijirō did not survive the Russian prison camp. Katō Toyotaka did. When he returned to his home in Matsuyama, Kondō's family welcomed him. They treated him as one of their own. Katō studied literature at Keio University. Later he went into public service, taught courses at the local university, and, of course, wrote volumes about the Manchukuo police.

Katō as a scholar has made a huge contribution to our understanding of the Manchukuo experience. Even before he became a historian, he demonstrated enviable instincts for the craft. In the chaos following Japan's surrender, Katō participated in the massive record burning as the Kantō Army destroyed evidence of its activities—except he did not really follow orders. He took as many documents as he could back to his residence and hid them in a desk. Once the Soviet army had occupied Harbin, however, soldiers came to take Katō away, leaving the documents behind. He had no idea what happened to them, but his reconstructions and honest reflections leave a record of a complicated experience at once brutal and filled with good intentions.[18]

Amakasu Masahiko did not survive the war. Had he returned to Japan, he would surely have been imprisoned as a class A war criminal by the International Military Tribunal. He might well have been hanged. Such was the fate of his colleague Tōjō Hideki. Or, like a fellow spy, Kodama Yoshio, he might have made a deal with his captors and left prison to live as a political fixer—still in the shadows—a wealthy and respected, if controversial, man. Instead he followed the soldier's code and took his own life. On the day of surrender, Amakasu moved out of the Yamato Hotel and camped in his Man'ei film studio office. As the Soviet Red Army moved closer to New Capital, he called his movie studio personnel together for one last assembly. He told the gathered group, "Today Japan has lost the war and China has won. The Manchurian Motion Picture Association is a national treasure. We now turn it over to you." He sang a patriotic song. After he finished he bowed and said simply, "Thank you."[19]

On August 20, the Soviet Red Army moved into New Capital. Anti-Japanese partisans wrought havoc in the streets, taking their vengeance on any Japanese or Japanese sympathizers they could find. Amakasu dressed himself once again in his cadet's uniform and polished his boots. He wrote out a simple message, leaving it on his desk: "Everyone, good-bye, Amakasu." Then he swallowed a package of cyanide poison he procured from the storage room in the studio's basement.

Even as the city fell to the Soviet army, Amakasu's closest friends carried his corpse from his office, placing it in a temporary coffin in the courtyard. Honored, if not mourned, by both his Japanese and Chinese subordinates, he rested in a temporary grave until his widow could come to New Capital from Dalian for a formal cremation. Two lines of mourners, Japanese and Chinese, paid respect to the body. As many as 3,000 others came to his funeral. His Japanese friends left a bottle of sake with the body. Even in death Amakasu would have his beloved drink. Zhang Yi, director for the Man'ei film studio, saw the body as it was removed from the office to the courtyard. The skin had a greenish hue. The temporary coffin was too short to hold the corpse gracefully.

Zhang Yi survived the war. He added his story to the Chinese Oral History Project. He maintained that Amakasu really was dead. As with other men who seemed larger than life, rumors that Amakasu had faked his death, that when the coffin was unearthed, his body was not inside, that he had escaped into the Manchurian wilderness continued to circulate years after the war. Zhang contended that the rumors were indeed false.[20]

Satō Shin'ichirō survived the war, but not without spending a year and a half waiting to die. Throughout the last year of Manchukuo's history, the possibility of defeat never crossed his mind. Satō recalled hearing about the Kamikaze Special Attack Force damaging American naval forces off Leyte in 1944. The news touched his heart, but it did not contain the vital information that the Imperial Japanese Navy had suffered severe losses despite the sacrifices of brave young Japanese flyers. He did learn of American air attacks on Tokyo.

The realization that the war would be lost came to him suddenly and personally. One December day at the end of 1944, he strolled into the office of the vice police chief in New Capital, where he was living at the time. He learned that Jin Zhiyuan, a close relative of and personal secretary to Manchukuo emperor Henry Puyi, had vanished with all of his worldly wealth. The amount involved was considerable. Rumor had it that Jin had been using his position to enrich himself and his friends through smuggling over the years. Yet his alleged crimes were not the immediate cause for police concern. The police chief wanted to know from Satō where Jin might have gone. More to the point, was Jin involved in a scheme to take the emperor into hiding with him?

Investigations into Chinese neighborhoods being one of his specialties, Satō traveled north. He met with a friend and colleague, Ikehata Satoshi, who was running the police agency in a county north of Harbin. What the two men learned on this trip had little to do with the intrigue of royal disappearances. Satō arranged to meet a Chinese official working with the Manchukuo government at a local restaurant. The two men arrived at the appointed place and time. Then they waited. Instead of the expected official, an old man, with grief written on his face and looking as though he carried the burdens of the world, came to their table.

For a while the man could do nothing but cry. Finally he explained that Japanese soldiers had rounded up many local officials, all of whom had worked for the Manchukuo government. The reason for the arrests? The officials had allegedly worked for the Anti-Japanese Save the Nation Association, affiliated with the Chinese Communists. The men disappeared. Local gossip maintained that they had all been shot, their frozen bodies dumped in the Songhua River. Three survivors remained in the Harbin prison.

Satō went to the Harbin prison where he found the survivors. They would only tell him that their luck was bad. So Satō went to the prosecutor who had initiated the roundup and asked for the source of the evidence linking the officials to the Anti-Japanese Save the Nation Association. "A correspondence from the countryside," came the answer. But how could Japanese murder their own people? Satō was already disillusioned by Manchukuo. This made things seem much worse. The gloom of his discovery led him to endure the next year and a half in a fog of resignation.

The Anti-Japanese Save the Nation Association was, of course, real. It did actively fight against Japan as an enemy. It had managed to instigate a riot in the North during which prisoners escaped from jail and took off into the hills. But Satō still had to see for himself. He traveled to a village in the North located in a valley where farmers made a living growing and processing opium. No one there treated him as an enemy. What he discovered explained the ugly dynamics of anonymous denunciations. The local Chinese police earned extra spending money taking a cut of the opium profits. The village Satō visited sat close to the border between two counties. The elders of the village in question told him that recently police from the neighboring county had contacted them, looking for "their cut." Because the villagers had only just paid off the police of their own jurisdiction, they were short of funds. They asked the neighboring county police to wait for two months. Instead the neighboring police denounced the villagers as working with the Communists. Japanese soldiers came to the village. Several local men were rounded up and endured torture for several days running. One man could not walk on his own when he left captivity. He had to be carried on a crude stretcher.[21]

During the last years of the Manchukuo experience, Satō lived in New Capital, where he taught at the university and worked for the government. Satō had come to Manchukuo filled with idealism and hoping to help build the multicultural nation depicted in the national propaganda. He married and had four sons. His eldest son attended military prep school in Tokyo. The other three boys attended the local Japanese middle and elementary schools. He clearly intended to make the place his home. As the nation became embroiled in a growing war, however, he lost the certainty that the northeastern utopia would come to pass. In fact, his position in the Manchukuo government brought him into contact with evidence of the atrocities that accompanied nation building even before his investigations in the North. Thus he approached the end of the war feeling he had no way to apologize to the many Chinese people who had died. He carried the burden of what he called a "blood debt." Oddly, this overwhelming gloom made his year-and-a-half ordeal easier to endure.[22]

On August 10, even before the surrender, as the soldiers of the Soviet Union penetrated the borders of Manchukuo, the Kantō Army ordered all of its troops south. Satō went to the barracks just in front of his house and found them empty. He knew that like Katō and his colleagues in Harbin, he was on his own. The civil government ordered all Japanese men to gather for war work. Even Satō's teenaged sons came with lamps and shovels. Barricades appeared in the streets. Phone lines were cut. Satō noted that while the Chinese calmly carried on, having faced disaster so many times in the past, Japanese in New Capital were at a loss for what to do.[23]

On August 12, the General Affairs Office, the civilian center of the Manchukuo government, contacted Japanese families, advising them to evacuate for the South as soon as possible. When Satō received this notice, he made a snap decision. He refused to leave. He later admitted his arbitrary decision put his family through serious hardships. Nevertheless, with his language skills and contacts, his presence was a help to those who could not make it out quickly. And many were left behind, for evacuating from Manchuria was easier said than done. Spaces on the first trains leaving New Capital filled up quickly. One by one the trains disappeared. Few returned. Satō would not get home for another year and a half.

Weather conditions added to the confusion. All through the night of August 13 and the next day, the heavens above New Capital opened up and poured down rain on the lines of Japanese evacuees streaming to the railway station, desperate to board trains headed south. Satō insisted that his wife and three boys leave. He accompanied them to the station, where they waited to board an open freight car. Because of the rain, water filled the bottom of the flatbed. Streams of water poured out of holes in the chassis. When the time came to leave, his children dawdled on the platform. Satō scolded them, hurrying them into the car. As the train pulled away from the station, he stood on the platform with tears streaming down his cheeks. He realized that his angry words might be the last his family heard from him.[24]

Satō need not have worried. His wife and children were every bit as stubborn as he. When the cramped freight train arrived at the Mukden Station, Mrs. Satō made up her mind that the family would share whatever fate had in store for them together. She and the boys left the train, finding shelter with a family friend living in Mukden. They returned home to New Capital within a few days. Finding a train going north was not easy. When they did, it was filled with Chinese refugees who might have done the Japanese family harm but did not. Satō's family traveled without incident, the train stopping only for the hungry passengers to dig ginseng from a trackside field to eat.

Satō would spend the next year and a half, when he was not in prison, helping those Japanese left behind after the first trains disappeared. The first problem he faced was finding food and transportation. Freight trains lined the sidings at a rail yard complex just north of the city, but Chinese scroungers were busy selling off the contents of the trains wholesale. Satō knew that the impending Manchukuo government collapse made money issued by its central bank useless. He remembered a story he heard about the events leading to the First Opium War of 1840. It was said that when Lin Zexu burned the British opium, some of his servants took the ash, which still had potency. Because the penalty for such an act was severe, the servants hid it in shit until they could safely sell it. Satō figured if shit-covered dross could be sold, opium was a good store of value.[25]

Satō hired a horse cart and driver. He took monopoly opium north to the station complex. There he found many freight trains filled with goods on the sidings. Satō borrowed an old desk and set it up along the road as his driver called out in a gravelly voice, "There is opium here! We will trade a pile of opium for the freight train goods. A pile of opium for the train." In this way Satō procured supplies that helped Japanese survive as they waited to return home. As he watched the bedraggled Chinese driver disappear into the distance, Satō had nothing but thanks for that man whose efforts had saved the lives of so many Japanese living in New Capital.[26]

Satō was able to support frightened refugees while they waited to return home. With his language abilities he was one of a crew who went out at night to find and distribute supplies. In his memoir he acknowledges his gratitude to the Chinese people for helping him help others survive. He himself says that the kindness of Chinese helped him forage successfully. The task was tedious. When he was not in jail, he worked tirelessly, finding and distributing relief aid. In fact, he worked so hard that after his third arrest, he found the quiet of his jail cell tranquilizing. He slept like a baby.

The end of the war came on August 15, 1945. On that day Satō was in the General Affairs Office building. As he listened to the Japanese emperor's words, he could not help but weep. At the same time he cleaned out the office, getting it ready for the blue-and-white flag of the Nationalist government, which he assumed would replace the Japanese Rising Sun. When he went out to the street, he found the houses of the Chinese residents shut tight, the streets empty. The occupation process proved much more complicated than he supposed. In New Capital (we can now call it by its original name, Changchun), Satō experienced the occupation of three armies—first the Red Army, then Mao Zedong's Chinese Communists, and finally Chiang Kai-shek's Nationalist Army. The Nationalists would use Changchun as a base for their struggle to claim the Northeast.

As a result, in 1947, tens of thousands in the city, military and civilian alike, would die.[27]

On August 20, 1945, Satō watched as Russian troops marched into Changchun. Over the next several days, groups of Russian soldiers looted Japanese houses. The mayhem only ended when Russian officers appeared to bring things under some control. In the tense atmosphere, Japanese refugees crowded into Satō's house. The wife of his colleague Ikehata Satoshi found shelter there. She delivered a baby boy in the safety of his home. Friends poured into his household, which came to number twenty-one souls, including a deserter, all in a house meant for five. Every night he went out, with his second son and the deserter, to scrounge for food.[28]

In September the Russians left, and the Chinese Communist People's Liberation Army (PLA) took control of the city. Chinese troops, just in from the base camp in Yan'an, arrested Satō along with many of his compatriots. These Japanese government officials faced a Chinese tribunal. For Satō it was only his first. As he watched the proceedings, he felt that he was seeing the future of Manchuria in the PLA. He admired the animation and self-confidence these Chinese soldiers displayed. His Japanese compatriots stiffened their spines in open defiance. One soldier, sentenced to death by the tribunal, faced the firing squad. As blood spurted from his wound, he managed to draw a Rising Sun in blood as he died, a grand gesture of defiance worthy of romantic war stories back home.

Satō did not feel fear or defiance as he watched the tribunal. Instead, he remembered his own private discovery of Japanese war crimes. One long document especially made his blood run cold. While he waited for his trial, he felt that his blood debt was about to be repaid. When his turn came, he told the tribunal, "Japan has been defeated because of the egotism of the Japanese people. We have defeated ourselves."[29]

This first tribunal released Satō with the warning, "We will be watching you." As he left the prison gate, a jailer told him he was the only one who would get out alive. Satō went back to his neighborhood rounds, but release was not a joyous experience, for the Chinese were indeed watching. One day Satō visited the home of a friend and mentor, Takeuchi Tokugai. The next day he found that Takeuchi had been arrested. He never saw his friend again. He only learned of Takeuchi's last days from the man who secured Satō's final escape from China. Takeuchi, arrested along with seven other people who had served the Manchukuo government, endured a year in prison. He was shifted from one prison to another, until, on the one-year anniversary of the Japanese surrender, all the prisoners were executed before a crowd of cheering onlookers.

This news saddened Satō. Takeuchi had been his mentor when he started his teaching career in Lushun decades before. As a young man of twenty-three, Satō had found himself in a difficult situation involving a woman. He is coy about the details—an unexpected pregnancy perhaps?—but the young man was contemplating suicide. He had gone so far as to straighten out his affairs and have a last night of drinking with friends when Takeuchi appeared in his room. The senior instructor forced Satō to pull himself together. Takeuchi was himself interested in Chinese language and culture. He urged Satō put his troubles behind him. Instead of pursuing a melodramatic and ultimately useless death, he urged Satō to concentrate on studying Chinese. The loss of this mentor weighed on Satō's mind as he lived out his days.[30]

A second brush with death arrived by an impromptu tribunal. One afternoon Satō went to visit a friend who lived in a lovely house with a substantial garden in Changchun. Satō noticed a hole torn in the garden fence. He used the makeshift entrance as a shortcut to the house. Instead of meeting his friend, Satō found himself once again held prisoner by two armed guards. The men escorted him to the study, where he found a Chinese officer sitting at the desk. The house had become a command post. With out looking up, the Chinese officer ordered Satō shot. The two guards took him back to the garden. They handed him a shovel, commanding him to dig his own grave.

Satō, resigned to his fate, began to dig. As he worked, he turned passages from the Daoist philosopher Zhuangzi around in his head. Perhaps his resignation saved him; perhaps his ability to speak Chinese drew a measure of pity from his captors. As Satō dug his grave, his guard asked if he had a family. He answered that indeed he had a wife and four children. "Then it will be difficult for them?" the guard asked. "Indeed it will," Satō replied. At that point the tension in the garden eased. Satō escaped death a second time and returned to the task of helping his fellow refugees.[31]

Satō Shin'ichirō was arrested a third time in late October 1946, even as the very last returnees prepared to leave Changchun. This time he ended up in a prison run by the Chinese Nationalist Army of Chiang Kai-shek. After his first night in jail, during which he slept soundly, the military official who ran the prison ordered Satō to his office. As luck would have it, the man was an old classmate and friend (Satō would not give the man's name). He offered to release Satō, telling him that human feelings were more important than national laws. This must have struck Satō as a bit ironic. Was not Zou the landlord condemned for this very same lack of consistent national identity in *Autopsy of the Garden of Grand Vision*? Without hesitation, Satō refused the offer. He told his friend he could not in good conscience leave when so many of his compatriots faced trial and execution.[32]

Within a month Satō and fifty other prisoners were loaded into a freight train to be shipped south to Mukden (today, Shenyang, the city where it all began with a bomb blast on the tracks in 1931). In Mukden, with Satō in the lead and guards all around them, the prisoners marched through the streets as throngs of Chinese gathered to watch the spectacle. Some yelled curses at them; others laughed. After they had proceeded into the prison yard, Satō commanded, "Attention!" "Center face!" The prison warden saluted smartly in exchange, and the men were led to their cells.

Life became a routine of eat, shit, and sleep. The cells were small, with the dreary atmosphere of a bachelor officer's quarters. Broken tatami mats covered the floor where the prisoners could sleep on ragged blankets. A small room with a dirt floor contained a ten-gallon sake barrel, which served as the sole common toilet. When Satō arrived in his cell, he immediately hid a good amount of money he had concealed about his person inside the tattered tatami mat. Just before his arrest, he had been denounced in the press as a first-class rascal. Sympathetic Chinese friends had slipped him money before he went away. Luckily Satō hid the money. No sooner were the prisoners settled in their cells than their guards demanded to inspect their rucksacks. The proceedings turned into a glorified looting.[33]

The prison in Mukden became the center where Chiang Kai-shek's Nationalist military held and processed Manchurian war criminals. Like Satō, people had been shipped in from all over the old Manchukuo territory. The prison held between two hundred and three hundred inmates, including many Koreans and Chinese who had worked for Manchukuo. When Satō arrived, trials and executions were already a regular occurrence. He lived in this limbo for another two months. Then, suddenly, he learned he had been judged not guilty. He was free to go.

In a stupor of disbelief, Satō visited the prison warden just before his release. "We may never see each other again," he told the warden. "We have no connections. Why have you been so kind to me?" The warden explained that they actually had a mutual friend, a certain Mr. Zhang, who once served as a county commissioner for the Manchukuo government. After the fall of Manchukuo, Chinese Communists arrested Zhang and shot him as a traitor. The warden, mourning his dead friend, recalled his friendship with Satō. This was just one of many messy stories that came out of the chaotic situation in postwar Manchuria as it transitioned once again into civil war. This case happened to work to Satō's benefit. After the warm exchange between former enemies, Satō spied on the wall of the warden's office a sandalwood samisen (a three-stringed instrument much like a banjo). It was one of three instruments that had been stolen from his home at the time of his third arrest. Satō sweetly said to the warden, "Actually, that samisen belongs to my beloved wife." The warden replied, "Oh! Is that so! Take it with you then." Satō shook the man's hand in deep gratitude for several minutes before he left prison for the third and last time.[34]

After Satō returned to Japan, he learned of another possible reason for his release. One night he was chatting with his uncle, Yamada Jun'saburō, who had also recently repatriated to Japan. Yamada once worked with Sun Yat-sen, the father of the Nationalist party; thus he knew people in the Nationalist government. When, at the time of his arrest, the press in Mukden broadcast Satō's name, denouncing him as a rascal, newspapers in Beijing and Shanghai picked up the story. Satō's uncle read about his nephew in the local paper. Yamada visited the general in Shanghai and told him that the Satō Shin'ichirō described as a rascal in the article was nothing like the real person. He begged the general to secure Satō's release. The general then wrote, "Release Satō, bring him to the governor's residence." Then he asked Yamada, "Will this do?" Yamada merely bowed, saying, "Please." Did the message secure Satō's release? His uncle would say no more.[35]

Reading through Satō's memories of prison, a person comes away with survival strategies for living through hard times. They include learning to speak the local language, developing and maintaining old school ties, and, perhaps most importantly, resigning oneself to one's fate. All of these worked for Satō.

Satō returned home and regained his strength, He became a professor at the Colonial University in Tokyo. Surrounded by friends and adoring students, Satō enjoyed a more rewarding life after the war than before. How many China scholars can claim such a depth of hands-on familiarity with the subject? As an academic he produced volumes. He wrote about the growing commune system in agriculture in the 1950s, a time when China was closed to the world. After the Cultural Revolution, he wrote about Mao Zedong as a fascinating man but a flawed leader. He wrote about Sun Yat-sen, the Chinese revolutionary with ties to Japanese sympathizers. He never broached in print, however, the subject of his experience during the war or his investigation into the slums around the Garden of Grand Vision. The text of the *Autopsy* would not appear in print until several years after his death in 1999.

Conclusion

Those of our countrymen who lived in Manchuria, whether as adults or as children, were madly drunk on the fine wine of the invader and fully enjoyed international Harbin as an exotic city. But under the skin of the international city there was the worldly hell in the warren of Fujiadian, a citadel of agents and spies.

—Katō Toyotaka[1]

While Japanese people loved Manchukuo, they did not trust Manchukuoans. Especially myself. How many times did I behave arrogantly to Manchukuoans. Japanese people, with their illusion of being a race of leaders, did not believe in the lively life force of the Manchukuoans.

—Satō Shin'ichirō[2]

What did Gotō Reiji and his colleagues make of the people living in the Garden of Grand Vision? In the *Autopsy* report, he is quite blunt in his prejudice at times, claiming that Chinese men are sexual perverts or that Chinese peasants are lazy and hate to bathe. When discussing the residents of the Garden in his concluding chapter, he writes that on Rich Brocade Street people lack any moral compass. They have forgotten all of the courtesies of civil life. He repeats his refrain of a Chinese society unable to reorganize for modern life.[3] This reflects the prejudices of his own organization.

Yet, the people in the Garden, Gotō reminds us, have their own biases. They call the Japanese "Eastern Ocean devils." Any of their own who acted Japanese became "false Eastern Ocean devils." Gotō makes a list of the derogatory names that attach to migrants from every region. The people from Shandong—and most of the Garden residents were from this area—were called "Shandong sticks." They tended to be drifters, worked as day laborers, and were completely lacking in self-awareness—or so it was said.

A person from Hebei, like Feng Dengdiao, might be called a "son of Leting County" if he came from there. Or the individual might simply be identified as someone from inside the Wall. These people were considered to be cripples and idiots. When they worked, they stole and sold the goods from baskets hanging from their shoulders. They had a reputation for immorality.

Koreans, known as "stinking Koreans," were regarded with suspicion in the Garden because of their quasi-Japanese status. They might be police, or spies for the police, or agents for spies. They worked in the neighborhood selling heroin or running gambling operations. Gotō, along with the other residents, considered Korean morphine dealers ill disciplined, self-indulgent, indecisive, and cowardly. Gotō heard such judgments shouted in the dark atmosphere of the Garden of Grand Vision. He tended to agree. He considered them blood-sucking ticks.[4]

Yet Gotō Reiji asks his readers not to be too quick to criticize those who have come to the Garden. He reminds us that any one of us might fall to a level of depravity were we living in the midst of extreme poverty, alongside the maimed, deformed, diseased, and mentally defective, like those in the Garden. People in the Garden had to mingle daily with blackmailers, villains, agents of spies—both from China and from the Japanese Kempeitai—prostitutes, thieves, gamblers, criminals, and smugglers. In such an atmosphere, the normal psyche can no longer function; perversion takes over; the ability to reason is suppressed. So wrote Gotō in "Character," the last chapter in the *Autopsy*, which highlights the latent ambiguity running through the document. Either the residents are coping with extreme poverty that has laid them low, or they are consumed with bizarre perversions that have driven them into extremes.

As Gotō tries to explain to his superiors in the Manchukuo government the causes of and solutions to the problems in the Fujiadian slums, he refuses to blame the victims of poverty. He concludes his report by saying that the stress of life in Manchuria has pushed the residents of the Garden lower and lower on the social scale, until they have ended up with their last hold on life inside the Garden's walls. This comment has the marks of a writer trying to feed his audience uncomfortable ideas buried inside the expected rhetoric.

Gotō had been tasked with ferreting out spies and subversives in the slum. He assures his readers—and, remember, these are senior officers in the Peace Preservation Bureau, the Special Service Organization, and the

Kempeitai responsible for social control at any cost, no matter how brutal—that the people in Fujiadian are too stupid and animal-like to engage in any kind of radical activity. True, there are those who would like to urge them to boycott Japanese goods or create a proletarian movement among the poor of the city. Gotō assures his superiors that the residents of the Garden have little of the kind of self-awareness or intellect needed to organize politically.[5]

Yet Gotō mentions a disturbing potential for problems in the slums. He cautions that if someone were to agitate enough to get this mass of humanity in motion, the sheer numbers would create a physical force that could push Japan into retreat. His veiled warning delivered a truth that readers could choose to hear or not. The scenario he envisaged is exactly what happened between 1945 and the Communist victory in 1949.

Gotō wrote in 1940 and 1941. His readers were more concerned with prosecuting a war inside China that grew larger and more difficult with each day. The expanding battlefield ate away at strategic materials, treasure, and population. Gotō's report—despite his clear statement that, although down-and-out, the residents were not spies—became a justification for immediate relocation of the poor and distressed from the Garden into labor camps, ostensibly for their own protection and rehabilitation. Manchukuo officials did not care if they were spies—they could be useful.[6]

Over time interpretations of experienced events change. The traumas of surrender and imprisonment gave the surviving investigators, Satō Shin'ichirō and Katō Toyataka, a different perspective from which to reflect on their survey of the Harbin slums. More importantly, it lifted restraints present in the first writing. The shift in understanding shows clearly in a comparison of the prewar and postwar texts.

As the authors of *Autopsy of the Garden of Grand Vision* were conducting their research, China's social disorder seemed incurable. In their report, Gotō and his colleagues blame the Chinese people as a race for a lack of patriotism leading to national weakness. Comparing what they saw in Harbin with their own pride in Japan's cultural unity and achievements, they let their sense of national accomplishment tinge their sympathy for their subjects.

Beginning with the statement "Fujiadian is a shame on the triumph of Manchukuo!" the police report repeats the theme of Japanese modern order struggling against chaos. In describing the streets surrounding the Garden of Grand Vision, the authors lament that "the Chinese people have no sense of cleanliness or social order." In explaining prostitution, they again remind us of the overly erotic tendencies of Chinese men. And gambling they characterize as a substitute for the softer emotions of romance and love. Clearly they intended the study to justify an ongoing occupation and invasion of China.

Writing after the war, Katō Toyotaka presents the same details of the Fujiadian neighborhood and its residents as the original report. Yet he comes to a different conclusion. He tells his readers that people coping with war and poverty in the Garden of Grand Vision demonstrate the survival abilities and strength of the Chinese people. In writing his police histories and novel, Katō brings a postwar understanding to his experiences in the Harbin slums.

Katō Toyotaka, as a historian, is admirably open and frank about his viewpoint. He tells us that he hopes to describe a piece of history from the perspective of a police officer who served in Harbin. Katō acknowledges that he is not a neutral observer of the past. He joined the Harbin police in his youth. He came of age as a police officer in Manchukuo. By the end of the war, he was attending Harbin Russian Academy, sponsored by the recommendation of his police colleagues. He worked with dedicated men whom he considered mentors. Had the war not ended, he would have graduated and taken his place as an official of rank in the Manchukuo government. His debt to his police experience is strong.[7]

Katō began his postwar writing hoping to fill in considerable gaps in the known story of Manchukuo. He acknowledged that officials destroyed most public records of the short-lived nation in the days following surrender. As we have seen, his own attempt to save something for the historical record vanished when Soviet soldiers hauled him off as a prisoner of war. It was as if the entire memory of the Manchukuo experience had been obliterated. In the 1960s, as he began work on his police history, he could find little mention of the Manchukuo project. What he did find dismissed it as "a puppet regime of Japanese imperialism." Manchukuo, as a place, always appeared in texts in parentheses. But, Katō points out, it was not simply a plan of the Kantō Army. All sorts of people with an assortment of motives joined in the building of a new nation.[8]

Katō had strong personal links to Manchukuo and its police service. At the same time, he wrote honestly about the role of the police in the darker side of the Second World War. His first volume of the police history is descriptive, detailing tediously the organization of government and bureau, while skirting any mention of torture or abuse. In his second volume, however, he reveals police connections to spy operations in the 1937 creation of the Peace Protection Bureau and its branches, which could and did whisk political prisoners away to certain and horrible ends. His first volume met with praise from scholars and colleagues. When he told these same people about his intentions for his second volume, they reacted negatively. Some actively spit out their disapproval.[9]

In his novelized version of the Garden of Grand Vision, Katō Toyotaka reconciles his presurrender experiences and his postwar sensibility. The novel, as he admits, is firmly based in fact. Its plot, such as it is, follows the outline set by the original police report. Inside the novel, however, characters who appear briefly in the police report give voice to unpleasant facts that Gotō Reiji and his colleagues judiciously ignore in the official document.

Braying Mule Wang becomes a central figure in the novel. With his nasal twang, peasant sensibilities, and prostitute wife, Braying Mule is little more than a curiosity in the original report. In the novel, however, he serves as a Greek chorus to Mr. Gotō's dominating police presence. After Gotō leaves the scene, Braying Mule makes his comments to Zou the landlord and Lin the owner of the Spring Forest Lodge, pointing out inconsistencies in Gotō's attitudes and the hidden horrors of the Japanese rule.

Braying Mule Wang's role as truth teller is clear when the novel introduces prostitution in the Garden. In the police report, Gotō blames Chinese prostitution on the unnatural sexual desires of Chinese men and their grotesque erotic pastimes. In the novel Braying Mule Wang debates this point. As he points out to anyone in the Spring Forest Lodge who will listen, prostitution is not unknown in Japanese culture. In fact, he says, Japan has a history of beautiful, well-appointed brothels with girls brought in to train in the arts of singing, dancing, and providing sexual diversion. After all, Mr. Gotō's own mistress is a geisha in training, is she not?[10]

Braying Mule Wang does not mention the comfort women kidnapped to serve as sex slaves for the men of the Japanese military, a sensitive issue that only came to public notice in the 1990s. He does, however, openly refer to another taboo topic: Unit 731, or the Biological Research and Water Purification Bureau in Pingfang. After meeting with Gotō to deliver the names of suspicious characters in the Garden of Grand Vision, Wang experiences a spasm of remorse about his treasonous act. He warns Zou the landlord that some people might disappear.

Here is something, he says, that will make your hair stand on end. I have heard that in Pingfang they have rooms where they cut people open alive. You might not think it possible, but consider! I have seen Mr. Gotō eat raw fish. The Japanese are not like us. Gotō does not deny this happens either. He says that it is all done in the interest of science.

In little more than half a page, Braying Mule Wang admits the existence and dark doings of Unit 731. At the end of the war, between its surrender and the Russian occupation of Manchuria, the Japanese military bombed the Pingfang facility, reducing it to unrecognizable rubble. During the International Military Tribunal trials that followed the war, which made public every sort of war atrocity, the research at Pingfang went unmentioned. Records of the experiments transferred into American hands. The brigade remained obscure until a Japanese reporter uncovered the truth in the early 1990s.[11]

Katō's writings never became best sellers. They were not carried by any of the mainstream publishers, all located in Tokyo. Instead he published in his hometown through an organization of which he was an officer. But in referring to Unit 731, Katō was two decades ahead of his time. Not until the 1990s, as Harbin approached its centennial, did historians, both in Japan and in English-speaking countries, begin to look at Manchukuo as an organization. Until then scholars had studied in detail the factions and alliances within the Japanese military that gave rise to the creation of Manchukuo. They had analyzed the effect of Manchukuo on Japan and the international community. But not until many decades after the close of the war did anyone, scholar or not, treat Manchukuo as a state. Instead it had remained an incident, a step in a larger military operation, a place name perpetually enclosed in brackets.

Amakasu Masahiko remains a riddle. No one remembers him as a complex human being. He is painted in memoirs in stark black or white. Police who remember the Manchukuo organization are quick to blame anything that went wrong on Amakasu and his corrupt cronies. One the other hand, people who worked for the Concordia Society and the film studio, Chinese or Japanese, loved him. And so he comes alive in the documents either as a scheming mastermind who plotted against Chinese enterprises using the film studio as a cover or as a lonely soul, haunted by the memory of a political murder—for which he may have been scapegoated—who worked to protect artistic leftists at a time when their politics might have been hazardous to their health. He is demonized as a carousing womanizer; yet he loved his family. His surviving daughter remembers him with deep affection, even though after the war she studied Russian and worked for the Soviet Information Agency.

Reading through the biographies of these officials, I come away with sadness for the depth of the tragedy of Manchukuo. It is not simply that the system was brutal. Rather, quest for power in Asia brought out the worst in men like Amakasu Masahiko, while it wasted the talents and dedication of better men who dreamed of an ideal state. This was especially true for Satō Shin'ichirō, who worked with police officers like Shibuya Saburō in various capacities. Satō related later in his life the disappointment he felt when, halfway through the Manchukuo experiment, he began to realize that darker deeds were being done in the name of Japanese justice. His epiphany came one day when he read a top-secret document from the War Planning Department. The contents woke him from his dream of a utopian Manchukuo. How could the Japanese rule China with out the cooperation of the Chinese? Force would not work in the end. But this thought was best kept to himself at the time.[12]

Satō assumed he would die in Manchuria. He accepted his death as repayment of his blood debt. At one point, while he waited in prison for his trial and execution for a third time, one of his fellow internees suddenly lost his nerve. One day the man passed him a piece of paper with the heartfelt message, "Please get me out of prison." The man begged Satō to do something. Satō knew that he could intercede with the Chinese guards, but he resolved not to. He reasoned that in the long run, Japan would regain its importance in the world. For this to happen, the blood debt had to be repaid.[13]

Satō Shin'ichirō and his family left Changchun at the end of 1946. They were among the last of the Japanese to be repatriated from there. They did not leave a city that would finally find peace. Changchun became a stronghold of the Nationalist Army in its fight with the Chinese Communist Army. Even as Satō left, the anti-Japanese truce between Mao Zedong's Chinese Communists and Chiang Kai-shek's Chinese Nationalists was frayed to the breaking point. As a center for the Nationalist Army, Changchun was a strategic target.

Over the winter of 1948, the civil war in Manchuria swayed in favor of Mao's army, led by Lin Biao. No longer fighting a guerilla-style war, the People's Liberation Army moved from the north toward Changchun and Shenyang (Mukden). Over the summer of that year Lin Biao lay siege to Changchun. When the Nationalist Army finally surrendered after serious battle losses, as many as 200,000 civilians had succumbed to hunger. By November 1948, the Nationalist Army had lost the Northeast. Within a year, the civil war had ended. With Mao's victory, Harbin, the international city of the 1920s that became a failed experiment in pan-Asianism in the 1930s, began a distinctly new course down a dramatically different path.[14]

Harbin today is as Chinese as a city can get. Few of the older Russian families remained in the city after liberation in 1949. Yet Harbin retains its foreign allure. Center Street is still a cobblestone road. Its pedestrian mall is lined once again with fashionable shops. The beer still flows freely. I returned to the city ten years after my first journey following in Gotō's trail. Harbin has clearly experienced constant growth and transition, starting with the laying of the first piece of track, the mortar slathered on the first brick, and the arrival of the first spies. I wanted to see how the city has changed in this new century. I especially wanted to learn how the old-style Chinese baroque and courtyard houses had fared under the tyranny of the wrecking ball. To my delight, the Daowai section retains blocks and blocks of courtyard houses, most with the baroque adornments that give them style. We can all agree that the building that was the Garden of Grand Vision needed to be razed. But when well maintained, these brick houses, with bright courtyards and ornamentation, can be lovely.

I am not alone in this opinion. Recently two architects, one Chinese, one Japanese, made a special study of the Fujiadian courtyard house. The results appeared in the *Journal of the Japanese Society of Architecture*. The authors argue that the trend toward frenzied building in modern cities destroys the kind of public space that nurtures human interaction. They specifically praise the Fujiadian courtyard building style from Harbin as an example of a traditional construction that encourages neighborly interaction.

The authors spent one summer day in 2006 observing activity along a block of buildings not far from where the Garden of Grand Vision once stood. They describe the tunnel-like entrance not as a place that nurtures crime but as a useful area for keeping bikes, mailboxes, and electricity meters. Inside the courtyards they depict a common space for human activity: food preparation, laundry drying, or just enjoying an afternoon reading a newspaper in the sun. Neighbors chat with one another as they go about their daily routines. The community interaction moves from the courtyard into the street.[15]

Perhaps someone in Harbin's city planning office read the article. More likely the beauty of the houses themselves drew the attention of developers. At present, two or three entire blocks of baroque-style courtyard houses are being restored. The area will become a historic district, complete with shopping, restaurants, and nightly crowds. The Oriental King of Dumplings is already open for business on a well-placed corner. Down the street a Russian restaurant occupies a spot where few Russian businesses would have been located in the past. The city is reinventing itself, emerging from its rust belt present to become a lively tourist destination. Its exotic Western character this time appeals to Chinese tourists rather than travelers from Japan.[16]

For more than a century now, Harbin has transformed, grown, and transformed again. This process continues apace. I can see the changes after only ten years. People still fill Center Street. They stroll along the riverbank or plan weddings at booths set up for the purpose. They skate, they fish, they shop, and they gather in beer pavilions to share pitchers of draft, sausages, and noodles. Nighttime still brings performers to stages. But the USA Bucks is gone, driven out by six or seven other coffeehouses, including a real Starbucks. As on main streets everywhere, many of the smaller shops have been replaced by global brands. Both Columbia Sportswear and North Face are prominent on the street. Where once there was a night market, now there is a Walmart. The Tyrant of Dumplings is gone, done in by the wrecking ball—if not by the more successful King of Dumplings across the way.

Harbin thrives. Manchukuo, however, remains a footnote in history, mentioned in brackets, if at all.

Notes

INTRODUCTION

1. Hinkōshō Chihō Hōan Kyoku [Hinkō Prefecture Regional Public Safety Bureau], Keimu Sōkyoku [Police Affairs General Office], *Daikan'en no Kaibō* [Autopsy of the Garden of Grand Vision], *Kanminzoku Shakai Jittai Chōsa* [Investigation into the Social Conditions of the Chinese Race] (Tōkyō: National Diet Library, 1942), 293 (hereafter Keimu Sōkyoku, *Daikan'en no Kaibō*).

2. Kagawa Tetsuzō, *Manshū de Hataraku Nihonjin* [Japanese Working in Manchuria] (Tōkyō: Diamond Publishing, 1941), 118.

3. Well, perhaps a railway car or two will explode.

4. It is hard to grasp the particulars of the Special Service Agency, originally called the Special Services Organization. I have found conflicting explanations of its origin and structure. The best description, and the one that I use as an authority, is found in Nihon Kindai Shiryō Kenkyu Kaigi [Conference on the Study of Modern Japanese Reference Materials], "Sono ta: Tokumu Kikan" [Extras: The Special Service Organization], *Nihon Rikukaigun no Seido, Sōshiki, Jinji* [The Organization, Structure and Personnel of the Japanese Army and Navy] (Tōkyō: National Institute for Defense Studies, 1971), 208–16. The organization originated during the Siberian Expedition (1918–1922), when the Japanese military entered eastern Russia to assist the Entente powers during World War I. Branches of the agency were set up on the spot to provide translation services and spy operations against the newly established Soviet Union. After the Japanese military withdrew from Soviet territory, the organization remained, with a central headquarters in Harbin. Similar organizations located in China grew out of Japanese military advisors sent to help the Chinese warlords. The Chinese-focused Special Service Agency had a headquarters in Mukden.

5. James Carter, "A Tale of Two Temples: Nation, Region, and Religious Architecture in Harbin, 1928–1998," *South Atlantic Quarterly* 99, no. 2 (winter 2000): 97–115.

6. "China Tried to Keep Benzene Spill Secret," *New York Times*, November 25, 2005; "Smog Envelopes and Chokes City in Northeast China," *New York Times*, October 22, 2013.

7. Nishizawa Yasuhiko, *Zusetsu "Manshū" Toshi Monogatari: Harubin, Dairen, Shin'yō, Chōshun* [Illustrated tales from the cities of Manchuria: Harbin, Dalian, Shenyang, Changchun] (Tōkyō: Kawade Shobō Shinsha, 1996), 35. The lineup for enjoying art nouveau buildings is, first, Paris and Nancy in France, followed by Harbin.

8. Nishizawa, *Manshū Toshi Monogatari*, 31–32.

9. Carolyn Hsu, *Creating Market Socialism: How Ordinary People Are Shaping Class and Status in China* (Durham, NC: Duke University Press, 2007), 55–58; "Rust Belt Revival," *Economist*, June 16, 2012.

10. Sumino Yukihiro, "Yamato Hoteru Junrei" [Yamato Hotel Pilgrimage], *SD* (February 1996): 97–100; Yoshimoto Yoniko, *Manshu Ryukoki* [Notes on a Journey through Manchuria] (Tōkyō: Tohaku Hakkojo, 1934), 7.

11. Norman Smith, "Hibernate No More! Winter, Health, and the Great Outdoors" (paper presented at the "The Manchurian Environment: Natural Resources, Climate and Disease" workshop, University of British Columbia, May 18, 2013).

12. Katō Toyotaka, *Manshūkoku Keisatsu Shōshi* [Short History of the Manchukuo Police], Vol. 1: *Manshūkoku Kenryoku no Jittai ni Tsuite* [Concerning the Actual Condition of Power in Manchukuo] (Matsuyama: Man-Mō Dōhō Engokai Ehime-ken Shibu, 1968), 195.

13. Katō Toyotaka, "Daikan'en," in *Shōsetsu: Daikan'en* [Novel: Garden of Grand Vision] (Matsuyama: Ehime Tsushinsha, 1974), 198.

14. Katō Toyotaka, *Manshūkoku Keisatsu Shōshi* [Short History of the Manchukuo Police], Vol. 2: *Manshūkoku no Chika Sōshiki ni Tsuite* [On the Organization of Manchukuo Underground] (Matsuyama: Man-Mō Dōhō Engokai Ehime-ken Shibu, 1974).

15. In fact, a better translation would be "lesser history of the Manchurian police." Katō noted he was paying homage to an earlier *History of the Manchukuo Police*. Katō's work is much better. *Manshūkoku Keisatsu Shi* (Shinkyō: Chianbu Keimushi, 1942).

16. Katō, "Daikan'en," *Shōsetsu: Daikan'en*, 169–242.

17. Satō Shin'ichirō, *Satō Shin'ichirō Senshū* [Satō Shin'ichirō Selected Writings] (Tōkyō: Satō Shin'ichirō Senshū Kankōkai, 1994), 309–12.

18. Satō, *Satō Shin'ichirō Senshū*, 1–5.

CHAPTER 1 IN THE GARDEN

1. Keimu Sōkyoku, "Jo ni Kaete" [In Place of an Introduction], in *Daikan'en no Kaibō*, 1.

2. Katō gives the Chinese of this song in the Latin alphabet with no tone marks. It is impossible to tell if "bi" means bí (nose) or bī (vagina). The Japanese translation merely says "ones." Katō, *Shosetsu—Daikan'en*, 175, 240.

3. Gotō notes that he made the description of the Spring Forest Lodge based on the people present between February and April 1940. Personnel, both owners and renters, changed so often that a return trip gave no guarantee that the same cast of characters could be found even a month later. Keimu Sōkyoku, "Kichinyado no Kōsei" [Organization of the Flophouses], in *Daikan'en no Kaibō*, 25–30.

4. Keimu Sōkyoku, "Daikan'en no Enkaku" [History of the Garden of Grand Vision], in *Daikan'en no Kaibō*, 2.

5. Katō, "Daikan'en," *Shosetsu—Daikan'en*, 172.

6. Keimu Sōkyoku, "Daikan'en no Enkaku," *Daikan'en no Kaibō*, 2.

7. In Beijing today a hotel called Daguan Yuan (translated as Grand View Garden on the English website) re-creates the luxury depicted in the novel *Dream of the Red Chamber* (www.beijingtrip.com/attractions/grandview.htm). There is also a company that makes various delicacies, several parks, and a section of Jinan, Shandong, all bearing the name.

8. Keimu Sōkyoku, *Daikan'en no Kaibō*, quote from the caption under the Garden of Grand Vision entryway illustration.

9. Katō Toyotaka, "Daikan'en," in *Shōsetsu: Daikan'en* [Novel: Garden of Grand Vision] (Matsuyama: Ehime Tsushinsha, 1974), 173.

10. Nishizawa Yasuhiko, *Manshū Toshi Monogatari* [Tales from the Cities of Manchuria] (Tōkyō: Kawade Shobō Shinsha, 1996), 38; Wang Yufei and Goto Haruhiko, "Harubin shi Fujiadian Chi-iki no 'Dayuan' Shiki Kenchiku Airia ni Okeru Toshi Kūkan Keitai to Shūjū Keisei Ryōiki ni Kansuru Kenkyū" [On the Relation between Urban Space and Dwelling Territory in the "Dayuan" House Area of Fujiadian, Harbin, China], *Nihon Kenchiku Gakkai Keikakukei Ronbunshū* [Journal of Architecture and Planning Transactions of the Architecture Institute of Japan] 622 (December 2007): 113–20.

11. Keimu Sōkyoku, "Daikan'en no Enkaku," in *Daikan'en no Kaibō*, 4.

12. Keimu Sōkyoku, "Daikan'en no Enkaku," in *Daikan'en no Kaibō*, 3–4; Katō, "Daikan'en," *Shōsetsu: Daikan'en*, 174.

13. Keimu Sōkyoku, "Kichinyado no Kōsei," in *Daikan'en no Kaibō*, 19–21; Katō describes the setup clearly in "Daikan'en," *Shōsetsu: Daikan'en*, 178–79.

14. Keimu Sōkyoku, "Daikan'en no Enkaku," in *Daikan'en no Kaibō*, 7.

15. Katō, "Daikan'en," *Shōsetsu: Daikan'en*, 178–79.

16. Keimu Sōkyoku, "Daikan'en no Enkaku," in *Daikan'en no Kaibō*, 3.

17. Keimu Sōkyoku, "Daikan'en no Enkaku," in *Daikan'en no Kaibō*, 7.

18. Keimu Sōkyoku, "Daikan'en no Enkaku," in *Daikan'en no Kaibō*, 7; Katō, "Daikan'en," *Shōsetsu: Daikan'en*, 186; reworking the interiors of housing to accommodate more people was common in Shanghai neighborhoods as well. See Lu Hanchao, *Beyond the Neon Lights: Everyday Shanghai in the Early Twentieth Century* (Berkeley: University of California Press, 1999).

19. Katō, "Daikan'en," *Shōsetsu: Daikan'en*, 173; Keimu Sōkyoku, *Daikan'en no Kaibō*, 3.

20. Keimu Sōkyoku, "Kichinyado no Kōsei" in *Daikan'en no Kaibō*, 20.

21. Keimu Sōkyoku, "Kichinyado no Kōsei," in *Daikan'en no Kaibō*, 19–20.

22. Keimu Sōkyoku, "Kichinyado no Kōsei," in *Daikan'en no Kaibō*, 21.

23. Katō, "Daikan'en," *Shōsetsu: Daikan'en*, 187–88.

24. Keimu Sōkyoku, "Kichinyado no Kōsei," in *Daikan'en no Kaibō*, 26.

25. Keimu Sōkyoku, "Kichinyado no Kōsei," in *Daikan'en no Kaibō*, 27.

26. Keimu Sōkyoku, "Kichinyado no Kōsei," in *Daikan'en no Kaibō*, 28–29; Katō, "Daikan'en," *Shōsetsu: Daikan'en*, 194–95.

27. Keimu Sōkyoku, "Kichinyado no Kei'ei" [Management of the Flophouses], in *Daikan'en no Kaibō*, 37–39.

28. Keimu Sōkyoku, "Ishoku" [Clothes and Food], in *Daikan'en no Kaibō*, 199; mooning, which I thought was a universal teenaged prank, is not really practiced in Japan. I called several Japanese male friends to ask about mooning; each was as perplexed by the idea as Gotō. One friend looked the word up in his English-Japanese dictionary and found that "mooning" meant pining for a lost love. When I explained what it really meant, he was completely baffled.

29. Keimu Sōkyoku, "Ishoku," in *Daikan'en no Kaibō*, 199.

30. Keimu Sōkyoku, "Ishoku," in *Daikan'en no Kaibō*, 200.

31. Keimu Sōkyoku, "Ishoku," in *Daikan'en no Kaibō*, 199.

32. The Taiwan Society website, for instance, calls its organization the World Red Swastika Society of Taiwan Headquarter, "Shijie Hongwanzi Hui" [World Red Swastika Society], 2005, www.twrss.org.

33. Keimu Sōkyoku, "Shakuhakunin" [Lodgers], in *Daikan'en no Kaibō*, 55–59.

34. Keimu Sōkyoku, "Shakuhakunin," in *Daikan'en no Kaibō*, 57–59; Katō, "Daikan'en," *Shōsetsu: Daikan'en*, 196–97.

35. Katō, "Daikan'en," *Shōsetsu: Daikan'en*, 197.

36. Keimu Sōkyoku, "Shakuhakunin," in *Daikan'en no Kaibō*, 60–62.

37. Kagawa Tetsuzō, *Manshū de Hataraku Nihonjin* [Japanese Working in Manchuria] (Tōkyō: Diamond Publishing, 1941), 118.

CHAPTER 2   ICE CITY

1. Nagano Sei'ichi, *Kitaman Fūdo Zakki* [Notes on the Topography of North Manchuria] (Tōkyō: Zuyuho Publishing Company, 1938), 118.

2. Yanagida Momotarō, *Harupin Tsuioku* [Remembering Harbin] (Tōkyō: Self-published, 1974), 1.

3. David Wolff, "Bean There," *South Atlantic Quarterly* 99, no. 1 (winter 2000): 241–52. The United States only began to outproduce Manchuria in soy after the Second World War. Contemporary discussions of Manchurian riches can be found in Robert Burnett Hall, "The Geography of Manchuria," *Annals of the American Academy of Political and Social Science* 152 (November 1930): 278–92.

4. Hall, "The Geography of Manchuria."

5. Liaoning, the name of the province today, is larger now than it was in earlier days. It absorbed part of Rehe Province after liberation in 1949. Confusingly, its name changed from Fengtian to Liaoning in 1929 and back to Fengtian in 1932.

6. David Bello, "The Cultured Nature of Imperial Foraging in Manchuria," *Late Imperial China* 31, no. 2 (December 2010): 1–33.

7. Jacques Gernet, *A History of Chinese Civilization* (Cambridge: Cambridge University Press, 1987), 463–66.

8. Valery M. Garrett, *Chinese Clothing: An Illustrated Guide* (Hong Kong: Oxford University Press, 1994), 104.

9. Kangxi left behind a charming diary translated by Jonathan Spence, *Emperor of China: Self-Portrait of K'ang Hsi* (New York: Knopf, 1975). The last of the Qing wrote more of an apology. Henry Puyi, *The Last Manchu: The Autobiography of Henry Pu Yi, Last Emperor of China* (New York: Putnam, 1967).

10. "Emperor Henry Puyi," *Time*, March 5, 1934.

11. The apt phrase comes from the title of the timely book by scholar and political commentator Owen Lattimore, *Manchuria: Cradle of Conflict* (New York: Macmillan, 1932).

12. S. C. M Paine, "The Chinese Eastern Railway from the First Sino-Japanese War until the Russo-Japanese War," in *Manchurian Railways and the Opening of China: An International History*, ed. Bruce Al Elleman and Stephen Kotkin (Armonk, NY: M. E. Sharpe, 2010), 13–36; Olga Bkich, "Origins of the Russian Community on the Chinese Eastern Railway," *Canadian Slavonic Papers* 27, no. 1 (March 1985): 1–14.

13. The possibility of war put the entire Harbin business community at a standstill during the summer of 1929. Hanson to State Department, "Political Conditions for North Manchuria during the Month of July, 1929," August 16, 1929, RG 59, 893.00P.R.HARBIN/27.

14. "A Place for Drying Fishnets" is only one of many interpretations, but it is the one I encountered most often. Koshizawa Akira, *Harubin no Toshi Hattatsu Shi* [History of the Growth and Development of Harbin] (Tōkyō: Nittchu Kaishizai Kyokai Kaiho, 1986), 5–6; James Carter, *Creating a Chinese Harbin: Nationalism in an International City, 1916–1932* (Ithaca, NY: Cornell University Press, 2002), 14–15.

15. David Wolff, *To the Harbin Station: The Liberal Alternative in Russian Manchuria, 1898–1914* (Stanford, CA: Stanford University Press, 1999), 27–37.

16. Yanagida Momotarō, *Harubin no Zanshō* [Harbin Afterglow] (Tōkyō: Hara Shobō, 1986), 65–79; Nishizawa, *Manshū Toshi Monogatari* [Tales from the Cities of Manchuria] (Tōkyō: Kawaderu Shobō, 1996), 43.

17. Meng Lie, ed., *Huashuo Ha'erbin* [Harbin Told in Pictures] (Beijing: Hualing Publishing Company, 2002), 9–15.

18. James A. B. Scherer, *Manchukuo: A Bird's-Eye View* (Tokyo: Hokuseido Press, 1933), 73. Scherer reported being completely stumped by all the name changes going on. He could not pronounce Changchun. He felt it was a bad name anyway since Manchuria does not have anything like a long spring. Because he struggled with Changchun, he was told to call it Xinjing. He mastered that only to be given the Japanese pronunciation, Shinkyo. Scherer, *Manchukuo*, 64.

19. Fu Yingming, "Fujiadian Yu Ha'erbin Chengshi" [Fujiadian and the History of Harbin], Fu Yingming de Blog [Fu Yingming's Blog], July 9, 2007, http://blog .sina.com.cn/s/blog_4bf9cc4101000azz.html (accessed June 7, 1913); for a discussion, see "Xian You Fujiadian; Hou you Ha'erbin" [First There Was Fujiadian; Afterward There Was Harbin], Fu Yingming de Blog, October 30, 2010, http:// blog.sina.com.cn/s/blog_4bf9cc4101000azz.html (accessed September 14, 2013).

20. Mi Dawei, *Heilongjiang Lishi — Fu Ha'erbin Chengshi Shi* [The History of Hei-longjiang: The History of Harbin City Attached] (Harbin: Heilongjiang People's Publishing Company, 2012), 316–17;

21. Ji Fenghui, ed., "Fujiadian," in *Huashuo Ha'erbin* [Tales of Harbin] (Harbin: Heilongjiang People's Publishing Company, 2002), 32–33; the growth of Harbin is described in Carter, *Creating a Chinese Harbin*.

22. Song Hongyan, *Dongfang Xiao Bali* [The Little Paris of the East] (Harbin: Heilongjiang Kexue Zhishu Chubanshe, 2001).

23. Harbin architecture is described in detail in Nishisawa Yasuhiko, "Harbin," in *Manshū Toshi Monogatari*, 12–37.

24. The traditional brightly painted nesting dolls, or *matryoshka*, in the gift shops on Center Street included a few making clever political commentary. Popular in 2004 were dolls whose layers revealed the faces of George W. Bush, Tony Blair, Saddam Hussein, Osama bin Laden, and Vladimir Putin, in various descending orders. By 2013 the lineup had changed. Now Barack Obama has joined Vladimir Putin. Saddam Hussein and Osama bin Laden, both "so yesterday," have been replaced by Syria's Bashar al-Assad and Mohamed Morsi.

25. Ji Fenghui, ed., "Taiyang Dao" [Sun Island], in *Huashuo Ha'erbin*, 280.

26. For a collection of photos of the church, see "St Nicholas Cathedral in Harbin," Orthodox.cn, www.orthodox.cn/localchurch/harbin/nikolai_en.htm.

27. The 秋林 (Chinese "Qiulin" or Japanese "Churin") characters translate as "Autumn Forest." This was a transliteration of the owner's Russian name. Thank you to Olga Bakich for pointing this out.

28. Yanagida, *Harubin no Zanshō*, 17–18.

29. Ji Fenghui, ed., "Fujiadian," in *Huashuo Ha'erbin*, 33; Nishizawa, *Manshū Toshi Monogatari*, 28.

30. Mi, *Heilongjiang Lishi — Fu Ha'erbin Chengshi Shi*, 340.

31. Hoshi Ryōichi, *Manshū Rekishi Kaidō: Maboroshi no Kuni o Tazunite* [The Roads of Manchuria: A Visit to a Dreamlike Country] (Tōkyō: Kōjinsha, 2000), 160–62.

32. Li Yuanzhi, ed., *Ha'erbin Luyou Wenhua Quanshu* [Harbin Travel Culture Guide] (Harbin: Harbin Publishing, 2001); views of the temple, variously translated as "Bliss Temple" or "Paradise Temple," can be found on YouTube, at http://www.youtube.com/watch?v=Q1n_PG4KUjg.

33. Yanagida, *Harupin Tsuioku*.

34. Ji Fenghui, ed., "Riben Langren" [Japanese Ronin], in *Huashuo Ha'erbin*, 76–77.

35. Manchukuo Bureau of Information and Publicity, Department of Foreign Affairs, *An Outline of the Manchukuo Empire, 1939* (Dairen: Manchuria Daily News, 1939), 25–28.

36. Carter, *Creating a Chinese Harbin*.

37. Keimu Sōkyoku, "Daikan'en no Enkaku" [History of the Garden of Grand Vision], in *Daikan'en no Kaibō*, 4–7.

CHAPTER 3 SETTLERS

1. Keimu Sōkyoku, "Fujiadian to Daikan'en" [Fujiadian and the Garden of Grand Vision], in *Daikan'en no Kaibō*, 1.

2. Morikawa Hatsuno, *Aa, Harupin: Morikawa Hatsuno Shuki; kōtei hoki Komiyama Noboru* [Ah, Harbin: The Diary of Morikawa Hatsuno; revised by Komiyama Noboru] (Tōkyō: Katakura Shoten, 1984), 86.

3. A large number of books about the First Opium War are available: Maurice Collins, *Foreign Mud* (London: Faber and Faber, 1947), is a readable and entertaining account of the conflict. Arthur Waley, *The Opium War through Chinese Eyes* (Stanford, CA: Stanford University Press, 1958), has translated Lin Zexu's own impressions of the conflict. The classic study is Hsin-pao Chang, *Commissioner Lin and the Opium War* (New York: Norton, 1964). For the psychoactive revolution, see David Courtwright, *Forces of Habit: Drugs and the Making of the Modern World* (Cambridge, MA: Harvard University Press, 2001).

4. Referring to the territory just beyond the Wall, "Kantō" is the Japanese pronunciation of the characters for "East of the Pass," the pass in question being Shanhaiguan or Mountain Ocean Pass, the point where the Great Wall meets the ocean. In Chinese, the characters are pronounced "Guandong." The name often appears in English texts using the Wade-Giles transliteration of the Chinese, "Kwantung." I have chosen to use the Japanese pronunciation for the sake of clarity.

5. Shumpei Okamoto, "The Japanese Second Army Battles at Chinchou," in *Impressions of the Front: Woodblock Prints of the Sino-Japanese War, 1894–1895* (Philadelphia: Philadelphia Museum of Art, 1983), 35; Okamoto, "After the Fall of Weihaiwei, the Commander of the Chinese Peiyang Fleet, Admiral Ting Ju-chang, Surrenders," in *Impressions of the Front*, 44.

6. For the details of the Japanese decision to go to war, see Shumpei Okamoto, *The Japanese Oligarchy and the Russo-Japanese War* (New York: Columbia, 1970).

7. John Young, *The Research Activities of the South Manchurian Railway Company, 1907–1945: A History and Bibliography* (New York: East Asian Institute, Columbia University, 1966).

8. A concise description can be found in Edward J. Drea, *Japan's Imperial Army: Its Rise and Fall, 1853–1945* (Lawrence: University of Kansas Press, 2009), 124.

9. A picture of the tower can be found in Koshizawa Akira, *Harubin no Toshi Hattatsu Shi* [History of the Growth and Development of Harbin] (Tōkyō: Nittchu Kaishizai Kyokai Kaiho, 1986), 57, or Hamano Kenzaburō, *Aa Manshū* [Ah, Manchuria] (Tōkyō: Akigen Shobō, 1970), 73; Yanagida Momotarō, *Harubin no Zanshō* [Harbin Afterglow] (Tōkyō: Hara Shobō, 1986), 23.

10. South Manchurian Railway Company, *Ha'erbin Annai* [Harbin Guide], Special 276/594 (Tōkyō: National Diet Library); Horikawa Ryūjin, *Ha'erbin Nikki* [Harbin Diary] (Nagoya: Shōtokudō, 1934), 26–29; A. R. Lindt, *Special Correspondent: With Bandit and General in Manchuria* (London: Corben-Sanderman, 1933), 39.

11. Keimu Sōkyoku, "Daikan'en no Enkaku" [History of the Garden of Grand Vision], in *Daikan'en no Kaibō*, 4–5.

12. Ichisada Miyasaki, *China's Examination Hell: The Civil Service Examination of Imperial China*, trans. Conrad Schirokauer (New York: Weatherside, 1976).

13. Tsukase Susumu, "The Penetration of Manzhouguo Rule in Manchuria," in *China at War: Regions of China, 1937–1945*, ed. Stephen R. Mackinnon, Diana Lary, and Ezra Vogel (Stanford, CA: Stanford University Press, 2007), 114.

14. There are not many books in English about the remarkable Kang Youwei. Jonathan Spence, *Gate of Heavenly Peace: The Chinese and Their Revolution,*

1895–1980 (New York: Viking, 1981), features Kang as a main character in the first part of the drama of China's transition to the modern age.

15. Peasant revolt, always against the dynasty, figured in the decline of most imperial houses. Caused by the social disruptions that provide us with the background for the Hong Kong martial arts films we love to watch, peasant revolts came from poverty in the countryside and corruption in the government. The Boxer Rebellion was different in that the dynasty backed the rebels as long as they remained antiforeign. The incident is dramatized in the awful film *Fifty-Five Days in Peking*, starring Charlton Heston and Ava Gardner, both of whom should have known better. It provides background for *Once upon a Time in China III*, staring Jet Li.

16. Keimu Sōkyoku, "Daikan'en no Enkaku," in *Daikan'en no Kaibō*, 5–6.

17. Harold Z. Schiffrin, *Sun Yat-sen and the Origins of the Chinese Revolution* (Berkeley: University of California Press, 1968), gives the most readable account of Sun's early revolutionary activities.

18. Keimu Sōkyoku, "Jo ni Kaete" [In Place of an Introduction], in *Daikan'en no Kaibō*, iv.

19. Katō Toyotaka, "Daikan'en," *Shōsetsu: Daikan'en* [Novel: Garden of Grand Vision] (Matsuyama: Ehime Tsushinsha, 1974), 183.

20. Keimu Sōkyoku, "Jo ni Kaete," in *Daikan'en no Kaibō*, vii.

21. Keimu Sōkyoku, "Jo ni Kaete," in *Daikan'en no Kaibō*, vii.

22. Keimu Sōkyoku, "Jo ni Kaete," in *Daikan'en no Kaibō*, ix.

23. Katō, "Daikan'en," *Shōsetsu: Daikan'en*, 184–85; Keimu Sōkyoku, "Jo ni Kaete," in *Daikan'en no Kaibō*, 7–8.

CHAPTER 4   DIRTY WORK

1. Keimu Sōkyoku, "Tōhin to Tōhin Shori" [Stolen Goods and Distribution of Stolen Goods], in *Daikan'en no Kaibō*, 178.

2. Jeff Ferrell, *Empire of Scrounge: Inside the Urban Underground of Dumpster Diving, Trash Picking and Street Scavenging* (New York: New York University Press, 2006), 33, 161. Ferrell wrote his book after living from the proceeds of dumpsters and trash piles for the year he spent between jobs.

3. Keimu Sōkyoku, "Tōhin to Tōhin Shori," in *Daikan'en no Kaibō*, 175–98.

4. Along with Danny Boyle's *Slumdog Millioniare* (Los Angeles: Fox Searchlight Pictures, 2008), Sudhir Venkatesh made a splash with *Gangleader for a Day: A Rogue Sociologist Takes to the Streets* (New York: Penguin, 2008). Most recently Katherine Boo, in *Behind the Beautiful Forevers: Life, Death, and Hope in a Mumbai Undercity* (New York: Random House, 2012), treats slum dwellers as hardworking people with interesting, if heartbreaking, stories.

5. Robert Neuwirth, *Shadow Cities: A Billion Squatters, a New Urban World* (New York: Routledge, 2005); "Cities of the Poor," *World*, BBC, December 17, 2006; Mike Davis uses the word "mega-slum" in *Planet of Slums* (London: Verso, 2006) to describe the ballooning squatter communities growing up worldwide; Suketu Mehta, *Maximum City: Bombay Lost and Found* (New York: Alfred A. Knopf, 2005).

6. William J. House, "Priorities for Urban Labor Market Research in Anglophone Africa," *Journal of Developing Areas* 27 (October 1992): 49–68; Asef Bayat, "Un-civil Society: The Politics of the 'Informal People,'" *Third World Quarterly* 18, no. 1 (1997): 53–72.

7. Keimu Sōkyoku, "Tōhin to Tōhin Shori," in *Daikan'en no Kaibō*, 178.

8. Keimu Sōkyoku, "Tōhin to Tōhin Shori," in *Daikan'en no Kaibō*, 179.

9. Keimu Sōkyoku, "Tōhin to Tōhin Shori," in *Daikan'en no Kaibō*, 179–80.

10. Keimu Sōkyoku, "Tōhin to Tōhin Shori," in *Daikan'en no Kaibō*, 181.

11. Keimu Sōkyoku, "Tōhin to Tōhin Shori," in *Daikan'en no Kaibō*, 181–82.

12. Keimu Sōkyoku, "Tōhin to Tōhin Shori," in *Daikan'en no Kaibō*, 185–86.

13. Keimu Sōkyoku, "Tōhin to Tōhin Shori," in *Daikan'en no Kaibō*, 187–88.

14. Keimu Sōkyoku, "Tōhin to Tōhin Shori," in *Daikan'en no Kaibō*, 189.

15. Keimu Sōkyoku, "Tōhin to Tōhin Shori," in *Daikan'en no Kaibō*, 190–91.

16. See David Bello, "The Cultured Nature of Imperial Foraging in Manchuria," *Late Imperial China* 31, no. 2 (December 2010): 1–33; for details of the clothing regimen, see Valery M. Garrett, *Chinese Clothing: An Illustrated Guide* (Hong Kong: Oxford University Press, 1994), 30–32; Valery M. Garrett, *Mandarin Squares: Mandarins and Their Insignia* (Hong Kong: Oxford University Press, 1990), 19–21.

17. Keimu Sōkyoku, "Tōhin to Tōhin Shori," in *Daikan'en no Kaibō*, 183, 193–94.

18. Keimu Sōkyoku, "Tōhin to Tōhin Shori," in *Daikan'en no Kaibō*, 194.

19. Keimu Sōkyoku, "Tōhin to Tōhin Shori," in *Daikan'en no Kaibō*, 196–97.

20. Keimu Sōkyoku, "Tōhin to Tōhin Shori," in *Daikan'en no Kaibō*, 194.

21. Keimu Sōkyoku, "Tōhin to Tōhin Shori," in *Daikan'en no Kaibō*, 197.

22. Keimu Sōkyoku, "Tōhin to Tōhin Shori," in *Daikan'en no Kaibō*, 198.

23. Keimu Sōkyoku, "Ishoku," in *Daikan'en no Kaibō*, 203.

24. Keimu Sōkyoku, "Ishoku," in *Daikan'en no Kaibō*, 203–4.

25. Keimu Sōkyoku, "Ishoku," in *Daikan'en no Kaibō*, 204.

26. Keimu Sōkyoku, "Ishoku," in *Daikan'en no Kaibō*, 201–2.

27. Keimu Sōkyoku, "Kojiki" [Begging], in *Daikan'en no Kaibō*, 159; the practice came to Manchuria from North China, where the same organization and legend of the staff predominated. Hanchao Lu, *Street Criers: A Cultural History of Chinese Beggars* (Stanford, CA: Stanford University Press, 2005), 108–13.

28. Keimu Sōkyoku, "Kojiki," in *Daikan'en no Kaibō*, 158; see Lu, *Street Criers*.

29. Keimu Sōkyoku, "Kojiki," in *Daikan'en no Kaibō*, 162–64.

30. Keimu Sōkyoku, "Kojiki," in *Daikan'en no Kaibō*, 164.

31. Keimu Sōkyoku, "Kojiki," in *Daikan'en no Kaibō*, 165.

32. Keimu Sōkyoku, "Kojiki," in *Daikan'en no Kaibō*, 165–66.

33. Keimu Sōkyoku, "Kojiki," in *Daikan'en no Kaibō*, 169.

34. Keimu Sōkyoku, "Kojiki," in *Daikan'en no Kaibō*, 167.

35. Keimu Sōkyoku, "Kojiki," in *Daikan'en no Kaibō*, 168.

36. Keimu Sōkyoku, "Kojiki," in *Daikan'en no Kaibō*, 169–71.

37. George Orwell, *Down and Out in Paris and London* (New York: Harcourt, Brace and World, 1961), 162.

38. Keimu Sōkyoku, "Kojiki," in *Daikan'en no Kaibō*, 157. The debate about beggars was intense in China. Just like American concerns about the "welfare queen," many in China gave evidence that beggars made a good living by begging rather

than working. Tales of beggars enjoying good food and living in lovely houses circulated especially during the modern era. Lu, *Street Criers*, 45–53.

39. Kagawa Tetsuzō, *Manshū de Hataraku Nihonjin* [Japanese Working in Manchuria] (Tōkyō: Diamond Publishing, 1941), 114.

CHAPTER 5   CONTESTED LAND

1. Amieto Vespa, *Secret Agent of Japan* (Boston: Little, Brown and Company, 1938), 12.

2. Keimu Sōkyoku, "Jo ni Kaiete" [In Place of an Introduction], in *Daikan'en no Kaibō*, 4.

3. Satō Shin'ichirō, *Satō Shin'ichirō Senshū* [Satō Shin'ichirō Selected Writings] (Tōkyō: Satō Shin'ichirō Senshū Kankōkai, 1994), 35. For Sun's ideas, see Audrey Wells, *The Political Thought of Sun Yat-sen: Development and Impact* (London: Palgrave, 2001). Paul Linebarger calls the thought of Sun "one of the most ambitious bodies of doctrine ever set forth by a political leader" in *The Political Doctrines of Sun Yat-sen: An Exposition of the San Min Chu I* (Baltimore: John Hopkins University Press, 1937), 20. Harold Z. Schiffrin claims Sun was not a great thinker but rather an improviser. "His style, not his ideas, made him." *Sun Yat-sen and the Origins of the Chinese Revolution* (Berkeley: University of California Press, 1968), 2.

4. Satō, *Satō Shin'ichirō Senshū*, 36–37.

5. Nishiki Masaaki, "Jimmon Hatsuhi—Ban'yū Jidai" [The First Day of Interrogation—Days of Reckless Valor], *Sono Yuku Tokoro o Shirazu* [Travel to Those Places Unknown] (Tōkyō: Shū'eisha, 2001), 51.

6. For a detailed discussion of the complicated shifts in both Sun's thinking and that of his Japanese friends, see Marius B. Janson, *Sun Yat-sen and the Japanese* (Cambridge, MA: Harvard University Press, 1954).

7. Kōmoto Daisaku, "Watakushi wa Chō Sakurin o Koroshita" [I Murdered Zhang Zuolin], in *Bungei Shunjū ni Miru Showa Shi* [Showa History as Seen through the Bungei Shunjū Magazine], ed. Bungei Shunjū (Tōkyō: Bungei Shunjū Ltd., 1988), 1:45.

8. Vespa, *Secret Agent of Japan*, 4, 15.

9. Ronald Suleski, *Civil Government in Warlord China: Tradition, Modernization and Manchuria* (New York: Peter Lang, 2002).

10. Yang Chaohui and An Linhai, "Weiman Shiqi de Rehe Yapian" [Rehe Opium during the Bogus Manchukuo Period], in *Weiman Wenhua* [Bogus Manchukuo Culture], ed. Sun Bang. *Weiman Shiliao Congshu* [Collection of Historical Materials on Bogus Manchukuo] 7 (Jilin: Jilin People's Publishing Company, 1993), 425.

11. For an excellent discussion of clashing drug and alcohol policies in Manchuria and Manchukuo, see Norman Smith, *Intoxicating Manchuria: Alcohol, Opium, and Culture in China's Northeast* (Vancouver: University of British Columbia Press, 2012).

12. Qu Wei and Li Zhuxiao, eds., *The Jews in Harbin* (Beijing: Social Sciences Documentation Publishing House, 2003), provides excellent photographs of old

Harbin as well as a commemoration of the Jewish community. Information about the Harbin Jewish community is all over the Internet. See, for example, Shiri Lev-Ari, "Harbin's Jews: Isle of Calm for Embattled Nation," *Haaretz*, February 9, 2007, www.haaretz.com/print-edition/news/harbin-s-jews-isle-of-calm-for -embattled-nation-1.212454. See also "Finding Family Roots in Harbin's Jewish Cemetery," China through a Lens, www.china.org.cn/english/2004/Sep/106964. htm. The articles all mention that Chinese people like Jews. One article calls it reverse antisemitism. I had several teachers in Taiwan who reacted with this very kind of admiration when they learned that my husband is Jewish.

13. Philip J. Sipkov, *Escape from Destiny: A Biographical Sketch of George E. Prujan* (Washington, DC: Self-published, 1986).

14. Shi Fang et al., *Ha'erbin Eqiao Shi* [A History of Russian Expatriates Living in Harbin] (Harbin: Heilongjiang People's Publishing Company, 2003), 39–90, quotes from 62–63.

15. Yanagida Momotarō, *Harupin Tsuioku* [Remembering Harbin] (Tōkyō: Self-published, 1974), 14.

16. Satō, *Satō Shin'ichirō Senshū*, 191.

17. Satō, *Satō Shin'ichirō Senshū*, 1–5.

18. Suleski, *Civil Government in Warlord China*.

19. Hanson to MacMurray, "Political Conditions for North Manchuria during the Month of April, 1928," May 16, 1928, RG 59, 893.00P.R.HARBIN/4.

20. James A. B. Scherer, *Manchukuo: A Bird's-Eye View* (Tokyo: Hokuseido Press, 1933), 75.

21. William Dodd, a German-speaking history professor, ran into the same problems at a higher level when he served as American ambassador to Germany in the 1930s. See Erik Larson, *In the Garden of Beasts: Love, Terror, and an American Family in Hitler's Berlin* (New York: Crown, 2011); the "pretty good club" comment is on p. 35.

22. Hanson to State, "Request of Consul G. C. Hanson to Be Promoted to Be a Consul of Class Six," June 7, 1917, RG 59, 123.H194/60, Box 1403, Folder 4.

23. Hanson to State, "Request of Consul G. C. Hanson to Be Promoted to Be a Consul of Class Six," June 7, 1917, RG 59, 123.H194/60, Box 1403, Folder 4.

24. Hanson to State, "Request That Consul George C. Hanson's Salary Be Raised to $4,500," May 19, 1919, RG 59, 123.H194/85; Fuller to Hanson, "Consul Hanson's Request for Promotion," July 15, 1919, RG 59, 123.H194/99, Box 1403, Folder 4.

25. Hanson to State, "Request for Travel Expenses," November 10, 1921, and Wilber J. Carr to Hanson, January 24, 1922, RG 59, 123.H194/108, Box 1403, Folder 4.

26. Hanson to Charles C. Eberhardt, February 11, 1922, RG 59, 123.H194/125, Box 1403, Folder 4.

27. "Suicide of a Consul," *Time*, September 16, 1935.

28. Hanson to State, "Reporting on His Absence from Post on a Hunting Trip," February 27, 1923, RG 59, 123.H194/126, Box 1403, Folder 4.

29. Foreign Service Administration, Memo, November 19, 1930, RG 59, 123. H194/327, Box 505, Folder 6.

30. J. L. Curtis to Hon. Sec. of State Henry L. Stimson, March 9, 1931, RG 59, 123.H194/321, Box 505, Folder 6.

31. Hanson to MacMurray, "Political Conditions for North Manchuria during the Months of January–May, 1928," February–June 1928, RG 59, 893.00P.R.HARBIN/1-5.

32. Hanson to MacMurray, "Political Conditions for North Manchuria during the Month of June, 1928," July 19, 1928, RG 59, 893.00P.R.HARBIN/6.

33. Hanson to MacMurray, "Political Conditions for North Manchuria during the Month of June, 1928," July 19, 1928, RG 59, 893.00P.R.HARBIN/6.

CHAPTER 6   CONFLICT

1. Amakasu interview, *Manchuria Daily*, July 13, 1929, quoted in Sano Shinichi, *Amakasu Masahiko, Ranshin no Kōya* (Amakasu Masahiko, Field of Ambition) (Tōkyō: Shinchōsha, 2008), 242.

2. Asahi Heigo, member of the Righteous Corp of the Divine Land, murdered the head of the Yasuda industrial conglomerate in 1921. At his arrest he considered himself a hero and role model for ultranationalist activists who would follow. Asahi Heigo, "Call for a New 'Restoration,'" in *Sources of Japanese Tradition*, edited by William Theodore De Barry et al. (New York: Columbia, 1958), 2:260–62.

3. Shanghai journalist H. G. W. Woodhead mentioned how much healthier Zhang Xuelang looked when he met the warlord's son in 1932 than the young man had looked several years earlier in Shanghai. Although he did not mention the addiction, he noted a distinct improvement in his English. H. G. W. Woodhead, *A Visit to Manchukuo* (Shanghai: Mercury Press, 1932), 108.

4. Hanson to MacMurray, "Political Conditions for North Manchuria during the Month of May, 1929," June 20, 1929, RG 59, 893.00P.R.HARBIN/24.

5. Kōmoto Daisaku, "Watakushi wa Chō Sakurin o Koroshita" [I Murdered Zhang Zuolin], in *Bungei Shunjū ni Miru Showa Shi* [Showa History as Seen through the Bungei Shunjū Magazine], ed. Bungei Shunjū (Tōkyō: Bungei Shunjū Ltd., 1988), 1:44–52.

6. Joshua Hammer, *Yokohama Burning: The Deadly 1923 Earthquake and Fire That Helped Forge the Path to World War II* (New York: Free Press, 2006).

7. One news editor working in Tokyo remembers being forced to drop the well-known story of murder in a report describing Amakasu's appointment to the Special Service Agency. A. Morgan Young, *Imperial Japan, 1926–1939* (New York: William Morrow and Company, 1938), 310.

8. Mutō Tomio, *Manshūkoku no Dammen* [Sketches of Manchukuo] (Tōkyō: Kindaisha, 1956), 196–97.

9. Mutō, *Manshūkoku no Dammen*, 197.

10. For the classic discussion of these treaties, see Akira Iriye, *After Imperialism: The Search for a New Order in the Far East, 1921–1931* (Cambridge, MA: Harvard University Press, 1965), and *Across the Pacific: An Inner History of American–East Asian Relations* (Chicago: Harcourt Brace, 1967).

11. Takafusa Nakamura, "Recession, Recovery, and War, 1920–1945," in *The Interwar Economy of Japan: Colonialism, Depression, and Recovery, 1910–1940*, ed. Michael Simka (New York: Garland Publishing, 1998), 99–143.

12. Young, *Imperial Japan*, 127–30; Richard Sims, *Japanese Political History since the Meiji Renovation, 1868–2000* (New York: Palgrave, 2001), 123–78.

13. Tsunoda Fusako, *Amakasu Tai'i* [Captain Amakasu] (Tōkyō: Chūō Kōronsha, 1979), 123.

14. Young, *Imperial Japan*, 66–75.

15. Satō Shin'ichirō, *Satō Shin'ichirō Senshū* [Satō Shin'ichirō Selected Writings] (Tōkyō: Satō Shin'ichirō Senshū Kankōkai, 1994), 61–63.

16. Mark Peattie, *Ishiwara Kanji and Japan's Confrontation with the West* (Princeton, NJ: Princeton University Press, 1975).

17. Mutō, *Manshūkoku no Dammen*, 143–45.

18. Satō, *Satō Shin'ichirō Senshū*, 61–63.

19. See an interview of Zhang on the Xi'an incident from his point of view on YouTube (with subtitles) at http://www.youtube.com/watch?v=bPK05CcrKiw.

20. League of Nations, Commission of Enquiry into the Sino-Japanese Conflict, "Memorandum on the Japanese Invasion of the Three Eastern Provinces," in *Appeal by the Chinese Government: Report of the Commission of Enquiry Signed by the Members of the Commission on September 4th, 1932, at Peiping* (Geneva: Geneva Research Center, 1932), 79–137; *Memoranda Presented to the Lytton Commission by V. K. Wellington Koo, Assessor* (New York: Chinese Cultural Society, 1932), 1:P86.

21. League of Nations, Commission of Enquiry into the Sino-Japanese Conflict, "Memorandum on the Japanese Invasion of the Three Eastern Provinces."

22. Will Rogers, "Will Rogers Gives His Cure for the Far East Trouble," *New York Times*, February 27, 1933.

23. Mao Zedong, "The League of Nations Is a League of Robbers," *Selected Works of Mao Tse-tung*, available at the Marxists Internet Archive, www.marxists .org/reference/archive/mao/selected-works/volume-6/mswv6_15.htm.

24. Tsunoda, *Amakasu Tai'i*, 138.

25. Mutō, *Manshūkoku no Dammen*, 208.

CHAPTER 7 MANCHUKUO

1. Satō Shin'ichirō, *Manshū oyobi Manshūjin* [Manchuria and Manchurians] (Shinkyō: Manshū Jijo Annaijo, 1940), 1.

2. Hanson to Secretary of State, July 7, 1932, RG 59, 123.H194/379, Box 505, Folder 7.

3. Keimu Sōkyoku, "Jo ni Kaete," *in Daikan'en no Kaibō*, i.

4. Damian Harper, Steve Fallon, and Katja Gaskill, *China* (Victoria, Australia: Lonely Planet Publishing, 2005), 350; Hugh Thompson and Kathryn Lane, *DK Eyewitness Travel Guide: China* (London: DK Publishing, 2012), 438.

5. "No Dogs or Japanese, 70% of Chinese Agree," forum.mugen-infantry.net/ index.php?topic=131253.0 (accessed April 5, 2012).

6. Rikugun Shō Chōsahan [Army Ministry, Research Branch], *Haerbin Fukin no Sentō ni Tsuite* [Concerning the Battle in the Harbin Vicinity], February 8, 1932, Dalian City Library Archives, P 07311:112.

7. Manchukuo Bureau of Information and Publicity, Department of Foreign Affairs, *Manchukuo Handbook of Information* (Shinkyō: Manchukuo Yearbook Company, 1933), 16–18; Bureau of Information, *An Outline of the Manchukuo Empire, 1939* (Dairen: Manchuria Daily News, 1939), 42–47.

8. Amieto Vespa, *Secret Agent of Japan* (New York: Little, Brown and Company, 1938), 108–9; Edgar Snow, "Japan Builds a New Colony," *Saturday Evening Post*, February 24, 1934, 13.

9. Francis Clifford Jones, *Manchuria since 1931* (London: Royal Institute of International Affairs, 1949), 50; Tsukase Susumu, *Manshūkoku: "Minzoku Kyōwa" no Jitsuzō* [The True Nature of Manchukuo "Racial Harmony"] (Tōkyō: Yoshikawa Kōbunkan, 1998), 78.

10. Tsukase, *Manshūkoku: "Minzoku Kyōwa" no Jitsuzō*, 30.

11. Hanson to State, "Report of Consul General Hanson's Trip in Barga," February 4, 1933, RG 59, 123.H194/398, Box 505, Folder 7.

12. Report on Consul General G. C. Hanson's Trip from Harbin to Moscow, June 21, 1934, RG 59, 123.H194/460, Box 505, Folder 7.

13. Mutō Tomio, *Manshūkoku no Dammen* [Sketches of Manchukuo] (Tōkyō: Kindaisha, 1956).

14. Mutō, *Manshūkoku no Dammen*, 209.

15. Li Min, "Amakasu Masahiko yu Man'ei" [Amakasu Masahiko and the Man'ei Studios], in *Weiman Renwu* [People of Bogus Manchukuo], ed. Sun Bang. *Weiman Shiliao Congshu* [Collection of Historical Materials on Bogus Manchukuo] (Jilin: Jilin People's Publishing Company, 1993), 226.

16. Yamaguchi Yoshiko, aka Li Xianglan, aka Shirley Yamaguchi, was the star with top billing for the Manchurian Film Studios. After the war, she made films in Japan and Hollywood. Later she became a representative to the Japanese Diet. Her singing is still remembered as 1930s nostalgia. See Ian Buruma, *The China Lover* (New York: Penguin, 2008).

17. Zhang Yi, "Wo Suo Zhidao de Manying" [What I Remember about Manchurian Film], in *Weiman Wenhua* [Bogus Manchukuo Culture], ed. Sun Bang. *Weiman Shiliao Congshu* [Collection of Historical Materials on Bogus Manchukuo] 7 (Jilin: Jilin People's Publishing, 1993), 156–74.

18. Zhang, "Wo Suo Zhidao de Manying" 167.

19. Zhang, "Wo Suo Zhidao de Manying"; see also Hamano Kenzaburō, *Aa Manshū* [Ah, Manchuria] (Tōkyō: Akigen Shobō, 1970), 113–14.

20. Li Min, "Amakasu Masahiko yu Man'ei," in *Weiman Renwu*, 230.

21. Mutō, *Manshūkoku no Dammen*, 213–15.

22. Keimu Sōkyoku, "Shukuhakunin," in *Daikan'en no Kaibō*, 62. The dignified beggar is one who can demonstrate skills acquired from elite training to elicit money from the crowd. See Lu Hanchao, *Street Criers: A Cultural History of Chinese Beggars* (Stanford, CA: Stanford University Press, 2005).

23. Lu, *Street Criers*, 152.

24. Li Debin and Shi Fang, *Heilongjiang Yimin Gaiyao* [An Outline of Migration to Heilongjiang] (Harbin: Heilongjiang People's Publishing Company, 1987), 90–91.

CHAPTER 8 CONTROL

1. *Manshūkoku Keisatsu Shi* (Shinkyō: Chianbu Keimushi, 1942), unnumbered page in photograph section.

2. Katō Toyotaka, ed., *Manshūkoku Keisatsu Juyō Shashin Bunkei Shiryosei* [A Collection of Important Photographic Resources on the Manchukuo Police] (Matsuyama: Moto Zaigai Komuin Engokai, 1982), ii.

3. James A. B. Scherer, *Manchukuo: A Bird's-Eye View* (Tōkyō: Hokuseido Press, 1933), 74.

4. Makuuchi Mitsuo, *Manshūkoku Keisatsu Gaishi* [An Unofficial History of the Manchukuo Police] (Tōkyō: San Ichi Shobō, 1996), 23.

5. Hanson to Nelson Johnson, Consular Monthly Report, March 9, 1933, RG 59, 893.105 MANCHURIA/2, National Archives, Washington, DC.

6. Mou Jianbing, "Wei Andongxian Jingcha Tongzhi de Ji Jianshi" [A Few Incidents in the Phony Andong County Police], in *Zhimin Zhengquan* [Colonial Political Control], ed. Sun Bang (Jilin: Jilin People's Publishing Company, 1993), 315.

7. Hanson to State, "Memorandum," March 8, 1932, RG 59 893.1052/10.

8. Katō Toyotaka, *Manshūkoku Keisatsu Shōshi* [Short History of the Manchukuo Police], Vol. 1: *Manshūkoku Kenryoku no Jittai ni Tsuite* [Concerning the Actual Condition of Power in Manchukuo] (Matsuyama: Man-Mō Dōhō Engokai Ehime-ken Shibu, 1968), 139; Mou, "Wei Andongxian Jingcha," 315. Katō claims that the postwar Japanese organization benefited from modern improvements accomplished by the Manchukuo police. The *baojia* system created first a *pai*, an organization of ten families with one elder as guarantor. Ten *pai* (牌) became a *jia* (甲), and ten *jia* became a *bao* (保), each of which had a headman or guarantor responsible for the actions of his flock. Katō, *Manshūkoku Kenryoku no Jittai ni Tsuite*, 10, 98–99.

9. One nifty diagram shows details of the way a briefcase could conceal a radio transmitter. Makuuchi, *Manshūkoku Keisatsu Gaishi*.

10. Katō, *Manshūkoku Kenryoku no Jittai ni Tsuite*, 146; Katō Toyotaka, *Manshūkoku Keisatsu Shōshi* [Short History of the Manchukuo Police], Vol. 2: *Manshūkoku no Chika Sōshiki ni Tsuite* [On the Organization of Manchukuo Underground] (Matsuyama: Man-Mō Dōhō Engokai Ehime-ken Shibu, 1974), 13–15.

11. Rikugun Shō Chōsahan [Army Ministry; Research branch], *Ha'erbin Fukin no Sentō ni Tsuite* [Concerning the Battle in the Harbin Vicinity], February 8, 1932. Dalian City Library Archives, P 07311:112.

12. Amieto Vespa, *Secret Agent of Japan* (Boston: Little, Brown and Company, 1938), 26–29. When Vespa's autobiography first appeared in Manchukuo, it must have caused a negative reaction among the Japanese authorities with whom he worked. Frank Lockhart, the US consul at the time, reported to the State Department that the contents were accurate, although the situation that Vespa reported had improved by the time of publication. Lockhart to State, June 6, 1939, RG 59, 893.01MANCHURIA/1567, LM 182, Reel 51.

13. Manchurian Railroads Publicity Board, *Shinko Manshūkoku no Zeno* [The Rising New Nation of Manchukuo], black-and-white film, 1933 Record Group 242, National Archives Collection of Foreign Records Seized, 1675–1983, National Archives, College Park, Maryland.

14. Hanson to Secretary of State, March 14, 1932, RG 59, 893.105 MANCHU-RIAF/HS/116.

15. G. C. Hanson to Nelson T. Johnson, "Bandit Organization near Harbin," September 21, 1932, RG 59, 893.108/207.

16. Ji Fenghui, ed., *Huashuo Ha'erbin* [Tales of Harbin] (Harbin: Heilongjiang People's Publishing Company, 2002), 123.

17. Meng Lie, ed., *Huashuo Ha'erbin* [Harbin Told in Pictures] (Beijing: Hualing Publishing Company, 2002), 182–84.

18. Ji, *Huashuo Ha'erbin*, 184.

19. N. T. Johnson to State, August 16, 1932, RG 59, 893.48/592; Johnson to State, August 17, 1932, RG 59, 893.48/593; Johnson to State, August 19, 1932, RG 59, 893.48/597, LM 182, Reel 75.

20. G. C. Hanson, "Report," April 20, 1932, RG 59, 893.00P.R.HARBIN/49.

21. Hanson to State, "Attack by Japanese Gendarme," November 9, 1932, RG 59, 123.H194/388, Box 505, Folder 7.

22. H. G. W. Woodhead, *A Visit to Manchukuo* (Shanghai: Mercury Press, 1932), 97–99.

23. Woodhead, *A Visit to Manchukuo*, 67–70; Edgar Snow, "Japan Builds a New Colony," *Saturday Evening Post*, February 24, 1934, 81.

24. Tsukase, *Manshūkoku: "Minzoku Kyōwa" no Jitsuzō*.

25. Katō, *Manshūkoku Kenryoku no Jittai ni Tsuite*, 142–43.

26. Fan Guangming, "Dunhua Jige Weijingcha" [A Few Manchukuo Police in Dunhua], in *Weiman Shehui* [Manchukuo Society], ed. Sun Bang. *Weiman Shiliao Congshu* [Collection of Historical Materials on Bogus Manchukuo] (Jilin: Jilin People's Publishing Company, 1993), 373–74.

27. Fan, "Dunhua Jige Weijingcha," 374–75; G. C. Hanson, "Report," April 30, 1932, RG 59, 893.00P.R.HARBIN/49.

28. Walter Adams to Secretary of State, "Police Methods in Manchukuo," August 27, 1936, RG 59, 893.105 MANCHURIA/11, 4.

29. Walter Adams to Secretary of State, "Police Methods in Manchukuo," August 27, 1936, RG 59, 893.105 MANCHURIA/11, 4.

30. Snow, "Japan Builds a New Colony," 81. Snow called Hanson the "best-loved consul general anywhere."

31. Xiao Long and Wang Erwen, "Ha'erbin Riwei Jingcha Youguan Waizhi Fengmian" [The Japanese Police Foreign Section in Harbin], in Sun Bang, *Zhimin Zhengquan*, 709.

32. Xiao and Wang, "Ha'erbin Riwei Jingcha Youguan Waizhi Fengmian," 710–11.

33. Vespa, *Secret Agent of Japan*, 47.

34. Vespa, *Secret Agent of Japan*, 205–24.

35. Hanson to State, December 1933, RG 59 893.00P.R.HARBIN/62; January 1934, 893.00P.R.HARBIN/63; December 1934, 893.00.HARBIN/73; February 1935, 893.00P.R.HARBIN/76; Microfilm LM063, Reel 32.

36. Makuuchi, *Manshūkoku Keisatsu Gaishi*, 57–62; the quote is on p. 52. Four million is not a surprising number. Even the postwar Japanese government was obsessive about fingerprinting. This was an insult to the Japanese-born Korean

population. My prints are on record with the Japanese police. As a foreign resident in the 1980s, I was required to provide them.

37. Yue Ruheng, "Bayan Xiang Weijing Wuke Neimu" [The Inside Story of the Bayan County Police], in Sun Bang, *Zhimin Zhengquan*, 346.

38. Gao Yubi, "Weiman Jingcha Jigou de Ri" [Days in the Manchukuo Police Organization], in *Weiman Renwu* [People of Bogus Manchukuo], ed. Sun Bang. *Weiman Shiliao Congshu* [Collection of Historical Materials on Bogus Manchukuo] (Jilin: Jilin People's Publishing Company, 1993), 217–25.

39. Walter Adams to Secretary of State, "Police Methods in Manchukuo," August 27, 1936, RG 59, 893.105 MANCHURIA/11, 14.

40. Yue, "Bayan Xiang Weijing Wuke Neimu," in Sun Bang, *Zhimin Zhengquan*, 346–47. The Tucker Telephone, named for the Tucker Prison Farm in Arkansas where it punished disruptive prisoners, would become infamous in the United States in the 1960s, when its use here at home became public. Yue, the author, must have had a difficult time watching the torture. His description of the process is imprecise and confusing. A detailed description can be found in Seth B. Goldsmith, "The Status of Prison Health Care," in *Public Health Report* 89, no. 6 (November–December 1974): 569–75. Elaine Scarry, in her book *The Body in Pain: The Making and Unmaking of the World* (New York: Oxford University Press, 1985), describes the use of common household appliances as instruments of torture. Using everyday words and implements as tools of torture breaks down the victim's connection to the environment. To do so is to "make language and civilization participate in their own destruction" (40–44).

41. Yuki Tanaka, *Hidden Horrors: Japanese War Crimes in World War Two* (Boulder, CO: Westview Press, 1996).

42. Makuuchi, *Manshūkoku Keisatsu Gaishi*, 223.

CHAPTER 9   WORKING GIRLS

1. Quoted in Ruth Mazo Karras, "The Regulation of Brothels in Late Medieval Europe," *Signs* 14, no. 2 (winter 1989): 399–433.

2. Keimu Sōkyoku, "Seiyoku Rōdōsha" [Sex Workers], in *Daikan'en no Kaibō*, 84.

3. Keimu Sōkyoku, "Seiyoku Rōdōsha," in *Daikan'en no Kaibō*, 84–101.

4. Two films that depict upper-class Chinese courtesans are *Hai Shang Hua* [Flowers of Shanghai] (1998), directed by Hou Hsiao-hsien, and *Yenzhi Kou* [Rouge] (1987), directed by Stanley Kwan. Japanese geisha tradition has been made familiar by the film *Memoirs of a Geisha* (2005), directed by Rob Marshall. A more accurate portrayal of a geisha's life can be found in the autobiography of Mineko Iwasaki, *Geisha: A Life* (New York: Altria Books, 2002).

5. Catherine Vance Yeh, *Shanghai Love: Courtesans, Intellectuals, and Entertainment Culture, 1850–1910* (Seattle: University of Washington Press, 2006); Sue Gronewold, *Beautiful Merchandise: Prostitution in China, 1860–1936* (New York: Harrington Park Press, 1985); Christian Henriot, *Prostitution and Sexuality in Shanghai: A Social History, 1849–1949* (London: Cambridge University Press, 2001).

6. Gronewold, *Beautiful Merchandise*, 16.

7. Katō Toyotaka, "Daikan'en," *Shōsetsu: Daikan'en* [Novel: Garden of Grand Vision] (Matsuyama: Ehime Tsushinsha, 1974), 200.

8. Tang Xinwei, ed., "Lao Jiyuan" [Brothels], in *Shuohua Ha'erbin* [Tales of Harbin] (Harbin: Heilongjiang People's Publishing Company, 2002), 195.

9. Mi Dawei, *Heilongjiang Lishi—Fu Ha'erbin Chengshi Shi* [The History of Heilongjiang: The History of Harbin City Attached] (Harbin: Heilongjiang People's Publishing Company, 2012), 340.

10. Ji, "Lao Jiyuan," in *Huashou Ha'erbin*, 194–95.

11. Keimu Sōkyoku, "Seiyoku Rōdōsha," in *Daikan'en no Kaibō*, 4–7.

12. Keimu Sōkyoku, "Seiyoku Rōdōsha," in *Daikan'en no Kaibō*, 84.

13. Keimu Sōkyoku, "Seiyoku Rōdōsha," in *Daikan'en no Kaibō*, 83.

14. Keimu Sōkyoku, "Seiyoku Rōdōsha," in *Daikan'en no Kaibō*.

15. Keimu Sōkyoku, "Jo ni Kaete" [In Place of an Introduction], in *Daikan'en no Kaibō*, vii.

16. Margery Wolf, *Women and the Family in Rural Taiwan* (Stanford, CA: Stanford University Press, 1972), 98–99, 205–8; in an earlier work, *The House of Lim: A Study of a Chinese Farm Family* (New York: Appleton-Century Crofts, 1968), Wolf describes a prostitute daughter who was welcome by the villagers upon her return because whatever the girl did in the city was not reflected in her behavior in the countryside. Sheldon Garon found that 82 percent of prostitutes interviewed in a 1918 survey in Osaka, Japan, entered the profession to help impoverished families ("The World's Oldest Debate? Prostitution and the State in Imperial Japan, 1900–1945," *American Historical Review* 98 [June 1993]: 715).

17. Keimu Sōkyoku, "Seiyoku Rōdōsha," in *Daikan'en no Kaibō*, 59.

18. Keimu Sōkyoku, "Seiyoku Rōdōsha," in *Daikan'en no Kaibō*, 98; Horikawa Ryūjin, *Harubin Nikki* [Harbin Diary] (Nagoya: Shōtokudō, 1934), 29.

19. Zhang Xueliang was the warlord who controlled Manchuria from 1928, when his father, Zhang Zuolin, was murdered by a Japanese bomb, until the 1931 Mukden Incident deposed him. He was a playboy and an opium addict until events in Manchuria changed the direction of his life.

20. Keimu Sōkyoku, "Seiyoku Rōdōsha," in *Daikan'en no Kaibō*, 95.

21. Keimu Sōkyoku, "Seiyoku Rōdōsha," in *Daikan'en no Kaibō*, 95.

22. Keimu Sōkyoku, "Seiyoku Rōdōsha," in *Daikan'en no Kaibō*, 97.

23. Keimu Sōkyoku, "Seiyoku Rōdōsha," in *Daikan'en no Kaibō*, 87–88.

24. Keimu Sōkyoku, "Seiyoku Rōdōsha," in *Daikan'en no Kaibō*, 91–93.

25. Keimu Sōkyoku, "Seiyoku Rōdōsha," in *Daikan'en no Kaibō*, 99.

26. Keimu Sōkyoku, "Seiyoku Rōdōsha," in *Daikan'en no Kaibō*, 98.

27. Keimu Sōkyoku, "Seiyoku Rōdōsha," in *Daikan'en no Kaibō*, 86.

28. Keimu Sōkyoku, "Seiyoku Rōdōsha," in *Daikan'en no Kaibō*, 87.

29. Keimu Sōkyoku, "Seiyoku Rōdōsha," in *Daikan'en no Kaibō*, 96.

30. Keimu Sōkyoku, "Seiyoku Rōdōsha," in *Daikan'en no Kaibō*, 96.

31. Katō, "Daikan'en," *Shōsetsu: Daikan'en*, 188–89.

32. Keimu Sōkyoku, "Seiyoku Rōdōsha," in *Daikan'en no Kaibō*, 83.

33. Sabina Fruhstuck, *Colonizing Sex: Sexology and Social Control in Modern Japan* (Berkeley: University of California Press, 2003). On comfort women, see Yoshimi Yoshiaki, *Comfort Women: Sexual Slavery in the Japanese Military during World War Two*, trans. Suzanne O'Brien (New York: Columbia University Press, 2000); Yuki

Tanaka, *Japan's Comfort Women: Sexual Slavery and Prostitution during World War Two and the U.S. Occupation* (London: Routledge, 2002). A personal account is found in Maria Rosa Henson, *Comfort Woman: A Filipina's Story of Prostitution and Slavery under the Japanese Military* (Lanham, MD: Rowman & Littlefield, 1999).

CHAPTER 10   HARBIN VICE—DRUGS

1. Keimu Sōkyoku, "Ahen" [Opium], in *Daikan'en no Kaibō*, 115.
2. Lu Shouxin, "Ha'erbin de Yapian Yandu" [Opium Poison in Harbin], in *Weiman Shehui* [Manchukuo Society], ed. Sun Bang. *Weiman Shiliao Congshu* [Collection of Historical Materials on Bogus Manchukuo] (Jilin: Jilin People's Publishing Company, 1993), 444.
3. Keimu Sōkyoku, "Ahen," in *Daikan'en no Kaibō*, 115–44.
4. Kathryn Meyer and Terry Parssinen, *Webs of Smoke: Smugglers, Warlords, Spies, and the History of the International Drug Trade* (Lanham, MD: Rowman & Littlefield, 1998); John Jennings, *The Opium Empire: Japanese Imperialism and Drug Trafficking in Asia, 1895–1945* (Westport, CT: Praeger, 1997).
5. Norman Smith, *Intoxicating Manchuria: Alcohol, Opium, and Culture in China's Northeast* (Vancouver: University of British Columbia Press, 2012).
6. Lu, "Ha'erbin de Yapian Yandu," in Sun Bang, *Weiman Shehui*, 444–46.
7. Lu, "Ha'erbin de Yapian Yandu," in Sun Bang, *Weiman Shehui*, 146.
8. Lu, "Ha'erbin de Yapian Yandu," in Sun Bang, *Weiman Shehui*, 146.
9. Keimu Sōkyoku, "Ahen," in *Daikan'en no Kaibō*, 115.
10. Nelson T. Johnson to State, March 12, 1932, Telegram, RG 59 893.01. MANCHURIA/32; Johnson to State, March 14, 1932, Telegram, RG 59 893.01. MANCHURIA/39; Johnson to State, March 17, 1932, Telegram, RG 59 893.01. MANCHURIA/45; National Archives, Washington, DC, LM 182, Reel 46.
11. Myers to Nelson T. Johnson, May 12, 1933, RG 59 893.01.MANCHURIA/3 and Myers to Nelson T. Johnson, January 3, 1934, RG 59 893.01.MANCHURIA/26, LM 182, Reel 46. William R. Langdon to Nelson T. Johnson, Banditry in Manchukuo, December 1936, RG 59 893.01.MANCHURIA/54, LM 182, Reel 46.
12. John Joseph Considine, *When the Sorghum Was High* (New York: Longmans, Green and Company, 1941).
13. Hao Rangxian, "Lao Erge Jiehuo Wei Fei" [Old Second Brother Gathers a Band and Becomes a Bandit], in *Weiman Shehui* [Manchukuo Society], ed. Sun Bang. *Weiman Shiliao Congshu* [Collection of Historical Materials on Bogus Manchukuo] (Jilin: Jilin People's Publishing Company, 1993), 553–57.
14. William R. Langdon to Nelson T. Johnson, Banditry in Manchukuo, December 1936, RG 59 893.01.MANCHURIA/54, LM 182, Reel 46.
15. Keimu Sōkyoku, "Ahen," in *Daikan'en no Kaibō*, 116–17.
16. Opium smoking rituals are described and profusely illustrated in Peter Lee, *Opium Culture: The Art and Ritual of the Chinese Tradition* (Rochester, VT: Park Street Press, 2006); Keimu Sōkyoku, "Ahen," in *Daikan'en no Kaibō*, 117–18.
17. This system is described in Meyer and Parssinen, *Webs of Smoke*, and Jennings, *The Opium Empire*.

18. Keimu Sōkyoku, "Ahen," in *Daikan'en no Kaibō*, 120–25; for descriptions of the Japanese opium monopoly, see Meyer and Parssinen, *Webs of Smoke*; Ryū Meishū, *Taiwan Tōchi to Ahen Mondai* [Control of Taiwan and the Opium Problem] (Tōkyō: Yamakawa Publishing, 1983); Jennings, *The Opium Empire*.

19. Even the *Manchurian Yearbook*, which went out of its way to paint the puppet state in a positive light, admitted the infirmaries were inadequate. *Manchukuo Yearbook* (Shinkyō: Manchukuo Yearbook Company, 1942), 698.

20. Keimu Sōkyoku, "Ahen," in *Daikan'en no Kaibō*, 148–50.

21. Gao Zuozhi, "Rewei Fanyuan Dupin Duhai Haicheng Renmin Jishi—Ji Yapian Lingmaisuo" [The Situation of the Japanese Spreading Poison among the Haicheng People], in *Weiman Wenhua* [Bogus Manchukuo Culture], ed. Sun Bang. *Weiman Shiliao Congshu* [Collection of Historical Materials on Bogus Manchukuo] 7 (Jilin: Jilin People's Publishing Company, 1993), 436–38.

22. Makuuchi Mitsuo, *Manshūkoku Keisatsu Gaishi* [An Unofficial History of the Manchurian Police] (Tōkyō: San Ichi Shobō, 1996),

23. Keimu Sōkyoku, "Ahen," in *Daikan'en no Kaibō*, 115–44; Keimu Sōkyoku, "Sennin no Mohi Mitsubaisha" [Korean Narcotics Dealers], in *Daikan'en no Kaibō*, 144–56.

24. Cabot Coville to State Department, Consular Monthly Report, March 1934, RG 59, Internal Affairs of China, 893.00P.R.HARBIN/65.

25. Keimu Sōkyoku, "Ahen no Mitsuyu" [Opium Smuggling], in *Daikan'en no Kaibō*, 136–37.

26. Keimu Sōkyoku, "Ahen no Mitsuyu," in *Daikan'en no Kaibō*, 139.

27. Keimu Sōkyoku, "Ahen no Mitsuyu," in *Daikan'en no Kaibō*, 139–40.

28. Keimu Sōkyoku, "Ahen no Mitsuyu," in *Daikan'en no Kaibō*, 139–40.

29. Yamauchi Saburō, a heroin manufacturer, described this arrangement in his memoirs, "Mayaku to Sensō: Nitchū Sensō to Himitsu Heiki" [Narcotics and War: The Sino-Japanese War and Its Secret Weapon], *Jimbutsu Ōrai* [Affairs of Eminent Men] (September 1965): 165–69. Cabot Coville to State Department, Consular Monthly Report, March 1934, RG 59, Internal Affairs of China, 893.00P.R.HARBIN/65.

30. Katō Toyotaka, *Manshūkoku Keisatsu Shōshi* [Short History of the Manchukuo Police], Vol. 2: *Manshūkoku no Chika Sōshiki ni Tsuite* [On the Organization of Manchukuo Underground] (Matsuyama: Man-Mō Dōhō Engokai Ehime-ken Shibu, 1974), 83–84.

CHAPTER 11   HARBIN VICE—GAMBLING

1. Keimu Sōkyoku, "Tobaku, Buraikin" [Gambling, Villains], *Daikan'en no Kaibō*, 100–114; quote from 100–101.

2. Wang Xianwei, "Ha'erbin Taiheqiao Duchang de Guanfang Beijing" [Official Backing for Harbin's Peace Bridge Gambling Club], in *Weiman Shehui* [Society in Manchukuo], ed. Sun Bang (Jilin: Jilin People's Publishing Company, 1993), 518.

3. Even Osnos, "The God of Gamblers: Why Las Vegas Is Moving to Macau," *New Yorker*, April 9, 2012, 45–55. For vivid photos and interesting trivia about Macau casinos, see Jim Edwards, "These Casinos in Macau Make

Las Vegas Look Like a Dump," *Business Insider*, July 3, 2012, http://www.businessinsider.com/these-casinos-in-macau-make-las-vegas-look-like-a-dump-2012-7?op=1#ixzz2vgy3HdiO.

4. Keimu Sōkyoku, "Tobaku, Buraikin," in *Daikan'en no Kaibō*, 100; the thought is repeated in the section about prostitution, "Seiyoku Rōdōsha" [Sex Workers], 93.

5. Ji Fenghui, ed. "Lao Du Chang" [Gambling Halls], in *Huashuo Ha'erbin* [Tales of Harbin] (Harbin, Heilongjiang People's Publishing Company, 2002), 198–99; Ji Fenghui, ed., "Sai Ma Chang" [Race Track], in *Huashuo Ha'erbin*, 200–201.

6. Liu Shouyi, "Ha'erbin de Saimachang" [Harbin's Racetrack], in *Weiman Shehui* [Society in Manchukuo], ed. Sun Bang (Jilin: Jilin People's Publishing Company, 1993), 520–24.

7. Keimu Sōkyoku, "Tobaku, Buraikin," in *Daikan'en no Kaibō*, 101.

8. Keimu Sōkyoku, "Tobaku, Buraikin," in *Daikan'en no Kaibō*, 101.

9. Keimu Sōkyoku, "Tobaku, Buraikin," in *Daikan'en no Kaibō*, 100–101.

10. Keimu Sōkyoku, "Tobaku, Buraikin," in *Daikan'en no Kaibō*, 101–102.

11. Keimu Sōkyoku, "Tobaku, Buraikin," in *Daikan'en no Kaibō*, 102.

12. Keimu Sōkyoku, "Tobaku, Buraikin," in *Daikan'en no Kaibō*, 102,103.

13. Keimu Sōkyoku, "Tobaku, Buraikin," in *Daikan'en no Kaibō*, 108.

14. Keimu Sōkyoku, "Seiyoku Rōdōsha," in *Daikan'en no Kaibō*, 94.

15. Keimu Sōkyoku, "Tobaku, Buraikin," in *Daikan'en no Kaibō*, 110.

16. Keimu Sōkyoku, "Tobaku, Buraikin," in *Daikan'en no Kaibō*, 114.

17. Keimu Sōkyoku, "Tobaku, Buraikin," in *Daikan'en no Kaibō*, 111–12.

18. Keimu Sōkyoku, "Tobaku, Buraikin," in *Daikan'en no Kaibō*, 112.

19. Keimu Sōkyoku, "Tobaku, Buraikin," in *Daikan'en no Kaibō*, 112–13.

20. Keimu Sōkyoku, "Tobaku, Buraikin," in *Daikan'en no Kaibō*, 113.

21. Frederic Wakeman Jr. uses the term "casino economy" in *The Shanghai Badlands: Wartime Terrorism and Urban Crime, 1937–1941* (New York: Cambridge University Press, 1996).

22. Ji, "Lao Du Chang," in *Huashuo Ha'erbin*, 199.

23. Wang, "Ha'erbin Taiheqiao Duchang de Guanfang Beijing."

24. Wang, "Ha'erbin Taiheqiao Duchang de Guanfang Beijing," 516–19.

25. Wang, "Ha'erbin Taiheqiao Duchang de Guanfang Beijing," 517.

26. Wang, "Ha'erbin Taiheqiao Duchang de Guanfang Beijing," 518.

27. Wang, "Ha'erbin Taiheqiao Duchang de Guanfang Beijing," 519.

28. Wang, "Ha'erbin Taiheqiao Duchang de Guanfang Beijing," 519.

29. Wang, "Ha'erbin Taiheqiao Duchang de Guanfang Beijing," 519.

30. *Taveras v. Resorts International Hotel, Inc.*, Civil No. 07-4555 (RMB) 2008 U.S Dist. LEXIS 98451. I. Nelson Rose, "Compulsive Gambler Just Can't Win," Gambling and the Law, 2011, http://www.gamblingandthelaw.com/index.php/columns/288-compulsive-gambler-just-cant-win21 (accessed September 7, 2013).

CHAPTER 12   THE END OF THE ROAD

1. Keimu Sōkyoku, "Seikaku" [Character], in *Daikan'en no Kaibō*, 290.

2. Wang Ying, "Shuang Cheng de Yanguan" [Opium Shops of Shuangchen], in *Weiman Shehui* [Manchukuo Society], ed. Sun Bang. *Weiman Shiliao Congshu*

[Collection of Historical Materials on Bogus Manchukuo] (Changchun: Jilin Renmin Chubanshe, 1993), 455.

3. Keimu Sōkyoku, "Ishoku" [Clothes and Food], in *Daikan'en no Kaibō*, 200–201.

4. Keimu Sōkyoku, "Shakuhakunin no Matsuro" [The End of the Road for the Lodgers], in *Daikan'en no Kaibō*, 259–60.

5. Keimu Sōkyoku, "Shakuhakunin no Matsuro," in *Daikan'en no Kaibō*, 261–62.

6. Keimu Sōkyoku, "Shakuhakunin no Matsuro," in *Daikan'en no Kaibō*, 262–63.

7. Keimu Sōkyoku, "Shakuhakunin no Matsuro," in *Daikan'en no Kaibō*, 264–65.

8. Keimu Sōkyoku, "Shakuhakunin no Matsuro," in *Daikan'en no Kaibō*, 265–66.

9. Keimu Sōkyoku, "Shakuhakunin no Matsuro," in *Daikan'en no Kaibō*, 267–68. This kind of god money can be purchased at any Chinese temple or shrine. A large packet might cost a dollar or so. The exchange rate with heaven is quite generous.

10. Keimu Sōkyoku, "Shakuhakunin no Matsuro," in *Daikan'en no Kaibō*, 268.

11. Keimu Sōkyoku, "Shakuhakunin no Matsuro," in *Daikan'en no Kaibō*, 286.

12. Keimu Sōkyoku, "Shakuhakunin no Matsuro," in *Daikan'en no Kaibō*, 289–90.

13. Keimu Sōkyoku, "Shakuhakunin no Matsuro," in *Daikan'en no Kaibō*, 281.

14. Wei Yu, "Zongdu Zhengci de Benchi" [Opium Policy in Benchi], in *Weiman Jingji Liutao* [Economic Plunder], ed. Sun Bang. *Weiman Shiliao Congshu* [Collection of Historical Materials on Bogus Manchukuo] (Changchun: Jilin Renmin Chubanshe, 1993), 449.

15. Hao Rangxian, "Heishan Xiang Linshi 'Guoshi Diaocha' Jilu" [Recollections of the Heishan County Provisional Census], in *Weiman Shehui* [Manchukuo Society], ed. Sun Bang. *Weiman Shiliao Congshu* [Collection of Historical Materials on Bogus Manchukuo] (Changchun: Jilin Renmin Chubanshe, 1993), 271.

16. Lu Shouxin, "Ha'erbin de Yapian Yandu" [Opium Poison in Harbin], in Sun Bang, *Weiman Shehui*, 444–46.

17. Shen Wenming, "Weiman Xin Jing Gengsheng Xunliansuo Neimu" [The Inside Story of the Manchurian Reform Training Centers in Shinkyō], in Sun Bang, *Weiman Shehui*, 147–57.

18. Chi Rong, "Ridi Zai Fuxun Jianli de Jingcha Jigou ji qi Feixing" [The Japanese Imperialist Police Structure Established at Fuxun and Its Criminal Activities], in Sun Bang, *Zhimin Zhengquan*, 298–99; Katō Toyotaka, *Manshūkoku Keisatsu Shōshi* [Short History of the Manchukuo Police], Vol. 2: *Manshūkoku no Chika Sōshiki ni Tsuite* [On the Organization of Manchukuo Underground] (Matsuyama: Man-Mō Dōhō Engokai Ehime-ken Shibu, 1974), 170–71.

19. Li Chunsong, oral testimony, "Weiman Fudaoyuan Neimu" [The Inside Story of the Manchukuo Guidance Halls], in Sun Bang, *Weiman Shehui*, 125, 127.

20. Xiao Chongguang, "Renjian Diyu—Fulang Ying" [Hell on Earth—the Vagrant Barracks], in Bang, *Weiman Shehui*, 139–47.

21. Xiao, "Renjian Diyu—Fulang Ying," in Bang, *Weiman Shehui*, 139–47.

22. Keimu Sōkyoku, "Shakuhakunin" [Lodgers], in *Daikan'en no Kaibō*, 67.

23. Amieto Vespa, *Secret Agent of Japan* (Boston: Little, Brown and Company, 1938), 267–95.

24. Gerolamo Cardano, "James Bond d'Abruzzo in Cina," Il Barbiere della Serra, http://archive.is/85tj5 (accessed August 23, 2012).

25. Division of Far Eastern Affairs, "Memo," December 5, 1928, RG 59, 123. H194/259, Box 505, Folder 7.

26. Hanson to Secretary of State, April 16, 1934, RG 59, 123.H194/445, Box 505, Folder 7.

27. Roy Howard to Cordell Hull, December 13, 1934, RG 59, 123.H194/490, Box 505, Folder 7; Will Rogers to Cordell Hull, December 12, 1934, RG 59, 123. H194/488, Box 505, Folder 7; Karl Bickel to Cordell Hull, December 9, 1934, RG 59, 123.H194/485, Box 505, Folder 7.

28. "U.S. Names Envoy for Addis Ababa" and "Abyssinia Charges Italians Attacked," *New York Times*, February 13, 1935.

29. Troutman to Secretary of State, July 29, 1935, Telegram, RG 59, 123. H194/551, Box 505, Folder 7; Cordell Hull to Hanson, August, 6, 1935, Telegram, RG 59, 123.H194/560, Box 505, Folder 7; Troutman to Secretary of State, August 6, 1935, Telegram, RG 59, 123.H194/558, Box 505, Folder 7.

30. "Master's Report, at Sea," September 3, 1935, in Harold Fyfe, US Despatch Agent, to Herbert C. Hengstler, Division of Foreign Service Administration, Confidential, September 11, 1935, RG 59, 123.H194/622, Box 505, Folder 7.

31. "Hanson Laid Fall to Bank Meddling," *New York Times*, September 12, 1935; "G. C. Hanson's Body Here," *New York Times*, September 11, 1935.

32. "Suicide of a Consul," *Time*, September 16, 1935; Simms to Cordell Hull, September 4, 1935, Telegram, RG 59, 123.H194/575, Box 505, Folder 7.

33. "Cause of Consul General Hanson's Suicide Revealed," *Harbin Shimbun*, October 14, 1935, enclosure in Walter Adams to Secretary of State, "Editorial on Suicide of George C. Hanson," RG 59, 123.H194/688, Box 505, Folder 7.

34. Walter Adams to Secretary of State, "Transportation Expenses of Consul General George C. Hanson and Vice Consul T. L. Lilliestrom," June 8, 1937, RG 59, 123.H194/737, Box 505, Folder 7.

CHAPTER 13 PUNISHING THE POLICE

1. Katō Toyotaka, *Manshūkoku Keisatsu Shōshi* [Short History of the Manchukuo Police], Vol. 3: *Manshūkoku no Kaitai to Keisatsu* [The Dismantling of Manchukuo and Its Police] (Matsuyama: Man-Mō Dōhō Engokai Ehime-ken Shibu, 1976), 201–2.

2. Satō Shin'ichirō, *Satō Shin'ichirō Senshū* [Satō Shin'ichirō Selected Writings] (Tōkyō: Satō Shin'ichirō Senshū Kankōkai, 1994), 249.

3. Katō, *Manshūkoku no Kaitai to Keisatsu*, 113, 196.

4. Katō, *Manshūkoku no Kaitai to Keisatsu*, 77.

5. The final phase of the revolution in Manchuria is described in Steven L. Levine, *Anvil of Victory: The Communist Revolution in Manchuria, 1945–1948* (New York: Columbia University Press, 1987).

6. Louise Young, "Colonizing Manchuria: The Making of an Imperial Myth," in *Mirror of Modernity: Invented Traditions of Modern Japan*, ed. Stephen Vlastos (Berkeley: University of California Press, 1998), 95–109.

7. Katō, *Manshūkoku no Kaitai to Keisatsu*, 76–77; for maps and troop distribution, see 112–17.

8. Satō, *Satō Shin'ichirō Senshū*, 215–18.

9. Katō, *Manshūkoku no Kaitai to Keisatsu*, 116.

10. Katō, *Manshūkoku no Kaitai to Keisatsu*, 136.

11. Katō, *Manshūkoku no Kaitai to Keisatsu*, foldout insert after 201.

12. Katō Toyotaka, "Daikan'en," *Shōsetsu: Daikan'en* [Novel: Garden of Grand Vision] (Matsuyama: Ehime Tsushinsha, 1974), 233–36.

13. Katō, "Daikan'en," in *Shōsetsu: Daikan'en*, 242–43.

14. Katō, "Daikan'en," in *Shōsetsu: Daikan'en*, 243.

15. Katō Toyotaka, *Manshūkoku Keisatsu Shōshi* [Short History of the Manchukuo Police], Vol. 2: *Manshūkoku no Chika Sōshiki ni Tsuite* [On the Organization of Manchukuo Underground] (Matsuyama: Man-Mō Dōhō Engokai Ehime-ken Shibu, 1974), 171; Katō, *Manshūkoku no Kaitai to Keisatsu*, 196.

16. Katō, *Manshūkoku no Kaitai to Keisatsu*, 142.

17. Katō, *Manshūkoku no Chika Sōshiki ni Tsuite*, 170–71.

18. Katō Toyotaka, *Manshūkoku Keisatsu Shōshi* [Short History of the Manchukuo Police], Vol. 1: *Manshūkoku Kenryoku no Jittai ni Tsuite* [Concerning the Actual Condition of Power in Manchukuo] (Matsuyama: Man-Mō Dōhō Engokai Ehime-ken Shibu, 1968), 138.

19. Most likely *Roei no Uta* (露營の歌) [The Field Camp Song]. The Chinese source gives an attempt at the Japanese, but I did not recognize it. Zhang Yi, "Wo Suo Zhidao de Manying" [What I Remember about Manchurian Film], in *Weiman Wenhua* [Bogus Manchukuo Culture], ed. Sun Bang. *Weiman Shiliao Congshu* [Collection of Historical Materials on Bogus Manchukuo] 7 (Jilin: Jilin People's Publishing Company, 1993), 168–69.

20. Zhang, "Wo Suo Zhidao de Manying," in Bang, *Weiman Wenhua*, 168–69; Hamano Kenzaburō, *Aa Manshū* [Ah, Manchuria] (Tōkyō: Akigen Shobō, 1970), 113.

21. Satō, *Satō Shin'ichirō Senshū*, 173–77.

22. Satō, *Satō Shin'ichirō Senshū*, 213.

23. Satō, *Satō Shin'ichirō Senshū*, 186–87.

24. Satō, *Satō Shin'ichirō Senshū*, 191–93.

25. Satō, *Satō Shin'ichirō Senshū*, 187–90. Commissioner Lin Zexu was nobody's fool. He did not burn the opium. He mixed it with salt and lime, allowed it to fester, then drained it into the ocean. Satō must have heard an urban legend. He also gets the characters of the man's name wrong.

26. Satō, *Satō Shin'ichirō Senshū*, 186–90.

27. Satō, *Satō Shin'ichirō Senshū*, 194.

28. Satō, *Satō Shin'ichirō Senshū*, 205.

29. Satō, *Satō Shin'ichirō Senshū*, 213–15.

30. Satō, *Satō Shin'ichirō Senshū*, 229–32.

31. Satō, *Satō Shin'ichirō Senshū*, 233–37.

32. Satō, *Satō Shin'ichirō Senshū*, 245–46.

33. Satō, *Satō Shin'ichirō Senshū*, 293–94.

34. Satō, *Satō Shin'ichirō Senshū*, 294, 307.

35. Satō, *Satō Shin'ichirō Senshū*, 308.

CONCLUSION

1. Katō Toyotaka, *"Daikan'en no Kaibō* no Megutte" [Return to the Garden of Grand Vision], in *Manshūkoku Keisatsu Shōshi* [Short History of the Manchukuo Police], Vol. 2: *Manshūkoku no Chika Sōshiki ni Tsuite* [On the Organization of Manchukuo Underground] (Matsuyama: Man-Mō Dōhō Engokai Ehime-ken Shibu, 1974), 148–71; quote on p. 154.

2. Satō Shin'ichirō, *Satō Shin'ichirō Senshū* [Satō Shin'ichirō Selected Writings] (Tōkyō: Satō Shin'ichirō Senshū Kankōkai, 1994), 190.

3. Keimu Sōkyoku, "Seikaku" [Character], in *Daikan'en no Kaibō*, 290.

4. Keimu Sōkyoku, "Shakuhakunin" [Lodgers], in *Daikan'en no Kaibō*, 48–51.

5. Keimu Sōkyoku, "Seikaku," in *Daikan'en no Kaibō*, 294.

6. Keimu Sōkyoku, "Seikaku," in *Daikan'en no Kaibō*, 290–93.

7. Katō Toyotaka, *Manshūkoku Keisatsu Shōshi* [Short History of the Manchukuo Police], Vol. 1: *Manshūkoku Kenryoku no Jittai ni Tsuite* [Concerning the Actual Condition of Power in Manchukuo] (Matsuyama: Man-Mō Dōhō Engokai Ehime-ken Shibu, 1968), 317.

8. Katō, *Manshūkoku Kenryoku no Jittai ni Tsuite*, 317.

9. Katō, *Manshūkoku no Chika Sōshiki ni Tsuite*, 213.

10. Katō,"Daikan'en," *Shōsetsu: Daikan'en* [Novel: Garden of Grand Vision] (Matsuyama: Ehime Tsushinsha, 1974), 200.

11. Katō, "Daikan'en," *Shōsetsu: Daikan'en*, 196–97.

12. Satō, *Satō Shin'ichirō Senshū*, 64.

13. Satō, *Satō Shin'ichirō Senshū*, 261–63.

14. Steven L. Levine, in *Anvil of Victory: The Communist Revolution in Manchuria, 1945–1948* (New York: Columbia University Press, 1987), 123–74, gives descriptions of people in Changchun rooting through trash and people in Shenyang eating grass and bark. Paul Byrne, *The Chinese Revolution: The Triumph of Communism* (Minneapolis: Compass Point Books, 2007), 61–65, gives military details about the battle for Manchuria. A thorough study in English needs to be done.

15. Wang Yufei and Gotō Haruhiko, "Harubin shi Fujiadian Chi-iki no 'Dayuan' Shiki Kenchiku Airia ni Okeru Toshi Kūkan Keitai to Shūjū Keisei Ryōiki ni Kansuru Kenkyū" [On the Relation between Urban Space and Dwelling Territory in the "Dayuan" House Area of Fujiadian, Harbin, China], *Nihon Kenchiku Gakkai Keikakukei Ronbunshū* [Journal of Architecture and Planning Transactions of the Architecture Institute of Japan] 622 (December 2007): 113–20.

16. James Carter, "The Future of Harbin's Past," *Itinerario* 35, no. 3 (2011): 83.

Appendix A
Character List

Aisin Gioro Puyi	愛新覺羅．溥儀
Amakasu Masahiko	甘粕正彦
Anti-Japanese Save the Nation Association	抗日救國會
The Asia	アジア号
Autopsy of the Garden of Grand Vision	大觀園 の 解剖
Autumn Forest (Churin) Department Store	秋林公司
Backpackers	背搭子
Bai (Room 2)	滿人白
Bandit-suppressing operations	討匪作戰
Bandits	匪
Baojia	保甲
Baron Xu Street	許公路
Basket peddlers	挑筐子的
Beijing	北京
Beijing Labor Company	北京勞動公司
Big Belly Wang	汪大肚子
Big brother, father, or precious	哥哥; 爸爸; 心肝兒
Big fish	大物
Big Liver Li	李大胆子
Binjiang (Hinkō) County	濱江省

Binjiang Daily (Hinkō)	濱江日報
Black Dragon (Amur) River	黑龍江
Blind Man Wang (aka Sticky Bean Cake)	王大瞎 (粘豆包兒)
Border Pacification Constabulary	國境警察隊
Boxer Rebellion (Yihetuan)	義和團
Boy	ボーイ
Branch Office	別室
Braying Mule Wang (Room 3)	王大叫驢 (aka 王三)
Bright Sun Street	景陽街
Bungei Shunjū	文藝春秋 週刊文春
Changchun	長春
Chengde	承德
Chiang Kai-shek (Jiang Jieshi), 1887–1975	蔣介石
China *ronin*	支那浪人
Chinese baroque	中華巴洛克
Chinese Eastern Railway (North Manchuria Railway)	東清鉄路
Chun Fang	春芳
Circle, the	圈
Circle River Cemetery	圈河義地
Clean the Capital; Strengthen Public Safety	淨化首都; 強化治安
Close the door	關門兒
Cloud Fairy Pavilion	雲仙閣
Concordia Society	協和會
Continental Labor Company	大陸勞動公司
Courtyard style	大院式
Dadong Labor Company	大東勞動會社
Dalian	大連
In Japanese: Dairen	
In Russian: Dal'nii (meaning "distant" or "far away")	
Daoguang	道光
Daoli (inside the tracks)	道裏
Daowai (outside the tracks)	道外
Daqing oil fields	大庆油田
Deep-fried devil	油炸鬼
Dope	ヤク
Duan the Korean (Room 6)	鮮人段

East Rising Soup and Fry Shop 東昇湧燒鍋
Eastern Ocean devils 東洋鬼子

False devils 假鬼子
Fan Chuanzhong 范傳忠
Fatty Ding 丁胖子
Felt shop 格布房記
Feng Dàren or Feng Dǎren 馮大人 or 打人
Feng Dengdiao 馮登釣
Feng Desheng 馮德勝
Feng shui (geomancy) 風水
Fengtian Province (at times Liaoning 奉天省 (遼寧省)
　　Province)
Fifth Little Wang 王小五
Final war 最終戰爭論
First Emperor Island City 秦皇島市
Flower assembly 花會局
Flower Shop 花店
Flower Willow District 花柳地方
Flowers worship the staff 花子拜稈兒
Forest Constabulary 森林警察隊
Fragrant Mill 香坊
Fu Baoshan 傅寶善
Fu Zhenji 傅振集
Fujiadian 傅家甸 or 傅家店
Fujita 福田
Fuxin Mining group 阜新煤礦

Gao the Korean (Room 10) 鮮人高
Gao Zuozhi 高作智
Garden of Abundance 裕盛園
Garden of Grand Vision 大觀園
Ge Chunfang 葛春芳
General Affairs Office 總務所
Ghost King Hall 鬼王廟
Ghost market (thieves' market) 鬼市
Gimpy Sun 孫拐子
Gotō Reiji, ?–1949 後藤冷次警佐
Great East Pawnshop 大東當
Great New Department Store 大羅新百貨店

Great New Street 大新大街
Great Poison Conqueror 大敗毒
Guanyu, or the God of War 關老爺
Guarantee money 擔保金
Guidance halls 輔導院
Guiding across 引導を渡す
Guo Zhanshu 郭占忠

Halal (Muslim) 清真回回
Han Ziming 韓子明
Harbin 哈爾濱 or 哈尔滨
 In Japanese 哈爾濱
  or when spelled in katakana ハルピン (before 1945)
  or ハルビン (after 1945)
 In Russian: Kharbin
Harbin Assistant Chief of Police Maruta 偽合兒賓警察厅副長 圓田
Harbin City Police Central Administration 哈爾濱市警察局本部
Harbin City Police Department chief 偽合兒賓警察厅長
Harbin Land Office 濱江省公暑土地調察局
Harbin Opium Dispensary Number 哈爾濱三十四号管烟所
 Thirty-Four
Harbin Special Services Agency 合兒賓特務機關
Healthy-living centers 康生院
Healthy-Living Reporting Brigades 康生報國隊
Hebei Province 河北省
Heilongjiang Province 黑龍江省
Herding the Old Sheep 赶老羊
Heroin 海洛因
Hill of 10,000 Bodies 萬人坑
Hinkō provincial governor Yu Jingtao 賓江省長于鏡濤
Hosokawa Takuyoshi 長谷川德榮
House of Shang Soy Milk Shop 尚家醬汁館

Ikehata Satoshi 池端敏
Imbeciles 痴呆
Increase Fortune Food Shop 增發館
Information ネタ
Internal Guidance Policy 內面指導權
Inukai Kii (Tsuyoshi), 1855–1932 犬養 毅

Iron Jaw Liu	劉鐵嘴
Ishii Shirō	石井四郎
Ishiwara Kanji	石原 莞爾
Itagaki Seijirō	板垣 征四郎
Japanese living in Manchukuo	日系
Jehol (Rehe)	熱河
Jiaqing emperor	嘉慶帝
Jilin	吉林省
Jin Zhiyuan	金智元
Jurchen	女眞
Kagawa Tetsuzō	香川鐵蔵
Kang the Korean (Room 5)	鮮人康
Kang Youwei	康有為
Kangde emperor, 1934–1945	康德帝
Kangxi emperor	康熙帝
Kantō (Guandong, often written as Kwantung) Army	關東軍
Katō Kanji	加藤 完治
Katō Toyotaka, 1918–?	加藤豊隆
Kempeitai (military police)	憲兵隊
King of Hell loan	閻王利
King of Hell Sha	沙閻王
Kingly Way	王道
Kitaiskaia (or Kitaiskaya) Street	
In Japanese	キタイスカヤ通り
or	キタイエスカヤ通り
In Chinese	中央大街
Kodama Yoshio	児玉 誉士夫
Kōmoto Daisaku	河本大作
Kondō Kunijirō	近藤國治郎
Koo, V. K. Wellington, Gu Weijun	顧維鈞
Lush Flowers Lane	荟蕾芳里
Li Family Flophouse	李家大院
Li Kuiwu (aka Old Second Brother)	李魁武 (老二哥)
Li Runzhi (aka Sticky Skin Li)	李潤芝 (李大胶皮)
Li the Korean (Room 1)	鮮人李

Li Xiangchen	李相臣
Li Xuejing	李學敬
Li Ziming	李自明
Liao River	遼江
Liaoning Province (at times Fengtian Province)	遼寧省 (奉天省)
Lin Jitang	林繼唐
Lin Yuming	林玉明
Lin Zexu	林則徐
Ling jia'r	領家兒
Little Warrior's Storehouse	小武蔵
Liu Jinsheng	劉金生
Living style	主局
Long coat	大褂兒 長衣
Long Spring Street (Changchun Street, named for the city)	長春街
Lower bunkroom	下舖
Lu Family Charity Burial Ground	陸家義地
Lu Shouxin	卢守信
Lucky Street	太吉街
Lushun (Ryushin, Port Arthur)	旅順
Ma San	馬三
Ma the Old Beggar	馬老丐
Manchu Lodge	滿洲棧
Manchukuo, March 1932–August 1945 In Chinese: Manzhouguo In Japanese: Manshūkoku	滿洲國
Manchukuo Film Association In Chinese: Man'ei/Manying	滿洲映画協会 滿映
Manchukuoan	滿系 or 滿人
Manchurian (Mukden) Incident or 9/18 Incident	九•一八事變
Materials	料子
Matsumoro Takayoshi	松室孝浪
Merit	功 (いさおし)
Military comfort women	従軍慰安婦
Ming Dynasty, 1368–1644	明朝
Mizoguchi Yoshio	水口嘉夫

Model Waist Brand	模腰牌兒
Modern clothes	摩登服
Modern Hotel	モデルンホテル 馬迭爾賓館
Morals Society	道德會
Morikawa Yūko	森川遊子
Morphine	嗎啡
Mukden (pronounced "Hoten" in Japanese, "Fengtian" in Chinese; today, Shenyang)	奉天
Mukden Opium Processing Plant	禁煙總局奉天工廠
Mutō Nobuyoshi	武藤 信義
Mutō Tomio	武藤 富男
Nagao Yoshigorō	長尾吉五郎
Nakaii Hisaji	中井久兒
Nakamura Shintarō	中村震太郎大尉事件
Nangang (South Hill)	南 崗
Nangang Dayou Ward Pauper's Burial Ground	南崗大有坊市立貧民義地
Nanjing	南京
National (Japanese) Diet	国会議
Nationalist Party (Guomindang or KMT)	國民黨
New Capital, 1932–1945	新京
In Chinese: Xinjing	
In Japanese: Shinkyō	
New Jade Hair Dresser	新玉理髮館
New New Soy Milk Shop	新新醬汁館
New Town	新舖
Nimble Finger Company	快手公司
Ning Changhai (Room 7)	寧長海
Ningcheng County	寧城縣
Noble Treasure Hall	貴寶堂
North Manchuria Authority	北滿江運局
Northeast	東北
Nurhaci, the Taizu Emperor of the Qing Dynasty	努爾哈赤 清太組
Old Bean Curd Factory	老豆腐坊
Old Hairy	老毛子

Old Mrs. Cheng	老程
Old Woman Li (Room 8)	老李
Old Woman Huang	黃老婆
Operation Flash	光工作
Opium	鴉片
Opium paste	煙膏
Opium residue	煙灰
Opium addict smoking permit	吸煙証 or 吸吃鴉片通帳
Osaka	大阪
Ōsugi Sakae	大杉 栄
Paralyzed Wu	吳癱子
Peace Bridge	太平橋
Peace Bridge Gambling Club	太平橋賭場
Peace Preservation Bureau (Internal Security) in the Manchukuo Police Affairs Bureau	警務總局保安局保安局
Peach Blossom Alley	桃花巷
Pesky Mao	毛淘氣
Phony Manchukuo government	偽政府
Phony Manchukuo (*Wei Man*)	偽滿
Phony police force	偽警察部
Pilferer or pickpocket	搔拂う
Pingfang	平房区
Pingkangli (aka the Circle)	平康里 (圈里 or 圈樓)
Pledge song	宣誓歌
Poker	扑克
Poor Mouth Liu	劉貧嘴
Precinct	派出所
Present-day song	現世歌
Protected villages	集團部落
Provincial Police Chief Akiyoshi Toshiro	省警務厅秋吉威郎
Public Order and Enforcement Operation	治安肅正工作
Pull out the futon	拉舖
Pulling the tow rope	拉綷子
Puyi, Henry	愛新覺羅．溥儀
Qing Dynasty, 1644–1911	清朝
Qipao	旗袍
Qiqihar	齊齊哈爾

Rabbit piss	兔子尿
Raised by a stinking cunt	臭屄養的
Reform training units	更生訓練所
Rehe (Jehol)	熱河
Rich Brocade Street	富錦街
Rich Spring Pavillion	富春樓
Righteous Sun Street	正陽街 (today 靖宇街)
River Constabulary	水上警察署
Roulette	轉輪
Running tents	跑棚子
Russo-Japanese War	日露戦争
Safety valve	安全瓣
Saitō Taniyoshi	済藤潤吉
Satō Shin'ichirō	佐藤慎一郎
Satō Tarō	佐藤 太郎
Scroll	幅
September 18 History Museum	九一八歷史博物管
Sex workers	性慾勞働者
Shandong Province	山東省
Shang Youwen	尚有文
Shangdu	上都
Shanghai	上海
Shaobing youtiao	燒餅油條
Shenyang	沈阳市
Shibuya Saburō	澁谷三郎
Shimogaki Ka'ichirō	下垣嘉一浪
Shochu	燒酎
Shogun	將軍
Single room	單間兒
Sister, sweetheart, or wife	妹妹; 寶貝兒
Sitting in the square	坐方的
Smoke	烟
Soft	軟派
Songhua River	松花
In Russian: Sungari	
South Manchurian Railroad Company (Mantetsu)	南滿洲鐵道 株式会社
Special Service Agency	特務部
Special Service Organization	特務機關

Spring Forest Lodge   春林栈
Spring Swan Hall   鴻春院
Stolen Goods and the Distribution of   盗品と盗品處理
   Stolen Goods
Subprecinct police stations   分駐所
Sun Island   太陽島
Sun Jinzi   孫金子
Sun Yat-sen   孫中山 or 孫文
Swallow Green and Li Shishi   燕青和 李师师
Swan Ascending Lodge   鴻陞栈

Taiwan   台灣
Takeuchi Tokugai   竹內德亥
Tang Songshan   唐宋山
Temple of Extreme Joy   極樂寺
Ten Thousand Blossoms Lodge   萬發栈
Thread Street   埠頭區斜紋街禁煙工廠
Three Tō Group (San-tō guruupu)   三藤グループ
Three-Legs Guo   郭三腿
Thunder Asia Market   震亞商店
Ticks   ダニ
To go   走
To smoke   吸
Tōjō Hideki   東條 英機
Tonghua Incident   通化事件
Top of the staff   稈兒上的
Top secret   極祕
Tower of Loyal Souls   忠靈塔
Traitors to the Han Chinese   漢奸
Twelfth Street Benevolent Home   十二道街慈善舍

Unit 731   部隊
   Officially called Biological Research   関東軍防疫給水部本部
   and Water Purification Bureau
Unity first; resistance second   攘外必先安内
Upper bunkroom   上舖
Use poison to cure poison   用毒治毒

Vagrant camps   浮浪營
Vampires   吸血鬼

Variety shop or store	千貨舖
Village of Grand Vision	大觀里
Villain	無賴漢
Virtue	德
Wan	卍
Wang Huixiang	王惠鄉
Wang the Carpenter	王瓦匠
Wang Three the Villain	無賴漢王三
Wang Xianwei	王賢樟
Wang Xianzhou (Room 9)	王先洲
Warm Fragrance Alley	溫香里遊廓
Wealth, Prosperity, Long Life, Pine, Bamboo, Plum, Special Fir	富祿壽松竹梅特衫
Wei Jingchabu Phoney police bureau	偽警察部
Wei Man	偽滿
Welcoming Spring Hall	迎春院
White Flour (Face) Devil	白麵（面）鬼
Wild pheasants	野雞
World Red Swastika Society	世芥紅卍會
Wuhan	武漢
Xi'an Incident	西安事變
Xu Guodong (aka Big Gold Tooth)	徐國棟 (大金牙)
Xuantong emperor, 1909–1912	宣統皇帝
Yagi, Nikolai Nikolaievich	柳
Yamada Jun'saburō	山田純三浪
Yamato Hotel	大和旅館
Longmen Hotel (today)	龍門大廈
Yamauchi Saburō	山內三郎
Yanagida Momotarō	柳田桃太郎
Yang Yang	杨扬
Yang Zhongyin	楊忠印
Yellow County, Shandong Province	黃縣 山東省
Yellow River	黃河
Yihe Glue Factory	義和喫 膠房
Yingkou	營口
Yu Zhishan	于芷山

Yue Ruheng   岳如衡

Zhang (Room 4)   滿人張
Zhang En (aka Frozen Ghost Corpse)   張恩 (凍死鬼)
Zhang Fengshan   張鳳山
Zhang Jinghui   張竟惠
Zhang Junshan   張純山
Zhang the Idiot   張大傻瓜
Zhang Xueliang   張學良
Zhang Yi   張奕
Zhang Zuolin   張作霖
Zhao the Barbarian   趙老蠻子
Zhou Chengting   周成亭
Zhu Chengguang   朱成光
Zou Linchang (courtesy name: Xisan)   鄒琳昌 （鶸三）

Appendix B
Cursing

Gotō Reiji figured that curse words were a window into a culture. They flew out of a person's mouth in an unguarded moment of rage. Therefore he noted with interest the expressions of anger that passed all around him as he strolled through the garden. In China there were five forbidden words (not George Carlin's seven, but close). All of them refer to genitals or the ways in which genitals are used. These words are "cunt" (屄), "fuck" (肏), "screw" (幹), "penis" (雞巴), and "insert" (日). (Actually the character 日 reads "sun," but Gotō maintains it also indicates sex in Manchukuo.)

The most common phrase, one that can be heard on any Chinese street even today, is literally "his mother's" (他媽的)—the word "cunt" is usually left to the imagination, although not always. Gotō reported hearing people scream, "Your mother's stinking cunt" (媽了個臭屄).

Everyone in East Asia knows the story in which the mother of the sage Mencius moves three times to ensure her child will grow up in a proper atmosphere. Naturally the last move is to be near a school. Gotō reminds us of this tale before he reports hearing mothers in the Garden of Grand Vision call their children "you little cunt bean!" (你這小屄豆子). The children then, even first graders, use the same foul language.

Gotō gives us some of the choicest words from the block, starting with the old favorite: "his mother's" (他媽的). "His mother's cunt" comes with variations: his mother's (他媽的) big (大), small (小), smelly (臭), or bloody (血) cunt (屄). "Blood" in Chinese is a strong word; adding "blood" to a curse makes it all the more vile to Chinese ears, so Gotō tells us.

"Cunt eye" refers to the vaginal entrance: "big cunt eye" (大屄眼兒), "little cunt eye" (小屄眼兒), "bloody cunt eye" (血屄眼兒), "smelly cunt eye" (臭屄眼兒). "Cunt bean" (屄豆子) goes through all the permutations. A cunt bean, we are told, is the clitoris. It is used a lot to curse Japanese women.

Of course, the universal "fuck you" (肏你) makes the list, as do "fuck your mother" (肏你娘 or肏你媽), "fuck your grandmother" (肏你奶奶), "fuck your elder sister" (肏你姐姐), and "fuck your younger sister" (肏你妹妹). To express extreme bile there is always "fuck your ancestors" (肏你祖宗) or even "fuck your ancestors to the sixteenth generation" (肏你家十六輩祖宗). And, of course, "blood" (血) can always be added to any of the above as a modifier.

Penises get the same treatment as cunts, but with more euphemisms: "chicken" (雞子), "little chicken" (小雞子), "chicken tail" (雞巴), "calf" (牛子), "old two" (老二), "ladle" (杓兒). Chicken head (雞巴頭兒) or turtle head (龜頭) refers to the tip of the penis. It implies that the person's head looks like the tip of a penis.

The slang for pubic hair, chicken tail hair (雞巴毛兒) or calf hair (牛子毛兒), can be used as in the following examples: "Fucked by a chicken hair!" (雞巴毛兒肏的) or "Fucked by a calf hair!" (牛子毛兒肏的).

"King Eight" (王八) refers to a turtle. "Turtle" or "turtle egg" (王八蛋) is used to refer to a bastard. Gotō refers to the folk idea that because the turtle shell must hinder sex, a female turtle will rely on a snake for pleasure and offspring. *Wang ba* (王八), or "King Eight," can be written *wang ba* (忘八), meaning "forget eight." In other words, a turtle forgets the eight virtues: filial piety, obedience, loyalty, sincerity, ritual, duty, purity, and humility.

Gotō warns his readers not to greet a Manchukuoan by asking if it might rain. He or she will certainly get angry. Turtles are thought to know when rain is coming. They will all disappear into the water. A barometer is called a "turtle's office" (王八衙門) for this reason.

Gotō explained that the word "rabbit" (兔子) referred to a stupid fellow. A rabbit is a catamite (Gotō's word) or a gay man—specifically one being paid for sex. He further explains that a rabbit has long hind legs. When a male prostitute sells his body for anal sex, he must raise his rear end up like a rabbit—hence the origin of the curse word.

A rabbit leg (兔腿) is a police informant. "Selling the large kang" (賣大炕的) can be said to imply that a family earns money from prostituting its women. A *kang* is a heated platform for sleeping, the implication being that in your family, anyone can sleep with your mother, wife, or sister.

The terms "empty man" (乏人), "empty egg" (乏蛋), and "empty kid" (乏孩子) all describe a general nobody.

In my misspent youth, we called a "fart seed" (屁種) a "fartleberry" or a "dingleberry."

A person's intellect can be challenged with "crazy bug" (糊塗蟲), "crazy mixed-up egg" (混蛋), "imbecile" (傻子), "imbecile egg" (傻蛋), or "imbecile flower" (傻花子).

People can be told that they do not amount to all sorts of things: "not a person" (不是人), "not merchandise" (不是貨), "not a thing" (不是東西) (I was called this once and didn't realize how tame a curse it is at the time), "not material" (不是料).

"Chicken tail (penis) hits the drum" (雞巴打鼓) might be shouted at a poor musician.

Appendix C
Flophouse Names and Franchise Owners

Note: Flophouse names are given in the order that they appear in Gotō Reiji's text. They are arranged by building.

GARDEN OF GRAND VISION (大觀園)

Spring Forest Lodge (春林棧), lower floor, west hall
  Lin Jitang (林繼唐), forty-three, from Shandong, former boatman
Swan Ascending Lodge (鴻陞棧), lower floor, east hall, south corner
  Yang Kunshan (楊堃山), forty, from Shandong, former petty merchant
Ten Thousand Blossoms Lodge (萬發棧), lower floor, east hall
  Feng Yanming (馮延銘), forty-seven, from Mukden, former grain merchant
Manchu Lodge (滿洲棧), lower floor, east hall, north corner
  Man Xingzhou (滿興洲), forty-two, from Jinzhou, former variety shop owner
Prosper China Lodge (中興棧), upper floor, south hall, east corner
  Zhao Rongzhang (趙榮疆), forty-one, from Hebei, former variety store owner
Virtue Ascending Lodge (德陞棧), upper floor, south hall
  Yang Dehui (楊德惠), thirty-four, from Shandong, former Eighteenth Street Precinct police chief
Guanzhou Lodge (冠 洲棧), upper floor, south hall, west side
  Mei Guanzhou (梅冠洲), forty-five, from Shandong, former farmer

Peace Lodge (太平棧), upper floor, west hall, south corner
Yang Ziyuan (楊子元), forty-five, from Shandong, former Seventh Street Precinct police chief
Prosperity Lodge (興合棧), upper floor, west hall, toward the north side
Li Xinghe (李興合), thirty-seven, from Hebei, former employee in a noodle shop
Ten Thousand Riches Lodge (發福棧), upper floor, west hall, north end
Zou Naikun (鄒乃鯤), twenty-five, from Harbin, former warehouse manager
Zhizhong Lodge (致 中棧), upper floor, east hall, south corner
Yang Zhizhong (楊致 中), forty-five, from Hebei, former soldier
Rich Virtue Lodge (福德棧), upper floor, east hall, north side
Li Pinyan (李斌彥), thirty-eight, from Hebei, former carpenter
Rich Peace Lodge (福安棧), upper floor, east hall, north side
Liu Lean (劉樂安), fifty-one, from Beijing, former variety store owner

VILLAGE OF GRAND VISION (大觀里)

Gather Prosperity Lodge (福合棧), first floor, east hall
Zhang Shaoen (張紹恩), thirty-seven, from Jinzhou, former clerk in a shipping office
Western Shining Lodge (西盛棧), upper floor, west hall
Liu Shaotang (劉紹堂), forty-seven, from Hebei, former variety store employee
Eternity Lodge (永遠棧), upper floor, west hall
Zhao Qinghai (趙慶海), twenty-seven, from Jingtu, former High Noon Street police precinct officer
Double Prosperity Lodge (雙發棧), upper floor, west hall
He Ziyang (何子陽), fifty, from Jinzhou, former flour mill worker
Forest Rising Lodge (林陞棧), upper floor, west hall
Lin Gusheng (林殿陞), fifty, from Jinzhou, former Harbin tax office clerk
Triple Surplus Lodge (三餘棧), upper floor, over the Da Guan Li north gate
Wang Hualong (王化龍), fifty-six, from Yingkou, former tenant farmer

FLOPHOUSES IN THE NEIGHBORHOOD

Spring Peace Lodge (春和棧), upstairs in the building east of the Village of Grand Vision
Li Changxiang (李長相), fifty-six, from Mukden, former city clerk, in business since 1936

Establish Justice Lodge (義成棧), upstairs in the building east of the Village of Grand Vision

> Song Huaren (宋豁然), forty-four, from Hebei, former grain merchant who arrived 1931, owner of the business since 1936

Having Wealth Lodge (富有棧), upstairs in the building east of the Village of Grand Vision

> Zhang Dianyou (張殿有), fifty-four, from Jinzhou City, former coolie boss in a gold factory, owner of the business since 1936

Hebei Lodge (河北棧), upstairs in the building west of the Village of Grand Vision

> Li Junxiu (劉俊秀), twenty-eight, from Hebei Province, former worker in a ready-made clothes shop on Fourth Street, arrived in 1936

Spring Ascending Lodge (春陞棧), upstairs in the building east of the Village of Grand Vision

> Sun Zhenhua (孫振華), fifty-five, proprietor, from Shandong Province, formerly ran a used clothing store and managed an inn, arrived in 1912

LI FAMILY GRAND HALL (李家大院)

All Ascending Lodge (全陞棧), first floor at the entrance

> Zong Fu (宗福), fifty-three, proprietor, from Jilin City, former odd jobs man, in business since 1938

Double Shelter Lodge (雙蔭棧), first floor

> Quan Yungchang (全永昌), thirty-five, from Mukden, former policeman from Righteous Sun Street, owner of the business since 1938

Harbin Spring Lodge (濱源棧), first floor

> Feng Zhaoxiang (馮兆鄉), forty-nine, proprietor since 1936, from Mukden, former silver shop manager

All Prospering Lodge (全興棧)

> Wei Quanxing (韓全興), fifty-six, from Mukden, former Seventh Street innkeeper, lodge owner since 1938

Swan Ascending Lodge (鴻陞棧), second floor

> Wei Pinyi (魏品一), sixty-three, from Jinzhou, former peasant and innkeeper, owner of the business since 1936

Sincere Peace Lodge (信和棧), second floor

> Lin Xishan (林錫山), thirty-four, from Jinzhou City, former variety store owner, owner of the business since 1937

Preserve Happiness Lodge (振祥棧), second floor

> Zhao ZhenYang (趙振样), forty-three, from Julan City, formerly in the Manchukuo military, owner of the business since 1938

Triple Greatness Lodge (三泰棧), second floor

> Yang Chunxiu (楊春秀), forty-five, from Shandong Province, former police patrolman on Righteous Sun Street, owner of the business since 1936

Profit Expands Lodge (利發棧), second floor
  Li Hongxiu (李鴻秀), sixty-one, from Hulan City, former odd jobs man,
  owner of the business since 1936

VIRTUE HAMLET (義村里)

Together Happiness Lodge (同樂棧)
  Li Yuemo (李悅謨), forty-five, from Shandong Province, former a clerk
  in the Diplomatic Office, owner of the business since 1936

Source: Keimu Sōkyoku, "Kichinyado no Kōsei," in *Daikan'en no Kaibō*,
22–25.

Appendix D
Currency

After the creation of Manchukuo, Japanese authorities executed a needed currency and banking reform. They consolidated three official banks, prohibited private banknote issue, and replaced fifteen different circulating banknotes with a unified currency. By 1940 the Manchurian yuan, or dollar, was pegged to the Japanese yen and traded internationally at the following rates:

100 Manchurian yuan [M$] = US$23.44
1 Manchurian yuan [M$] = £3.64
1 Manchurian yuan [M$] = ¥1

For a better sense of real value:

Gotō Reiji probably earned M$300 per month.
Li Xianglan, the film star, earned M$250 per month.
Lin Jitang, landlord of the Spring Forest Lodge, earned M$20 per month when he worked as a crewman on a riverboat.
A package of heroin cost M$0.50.
A night in the upper dorm cost M$0.10.
A bowl of rice cost M$0.10.
An orange cost M$0.02.
Soymilk cost M$0.06.
An hour with a prostitute cost M$0.40 to M$0.60.

Appendix E

Cost of Scavenged Goods

Item	Unit of Sale	Value (M$)
Daily-use items		Variable
Clothing		Variable
Furniture		Variable
Food		Variable
Dead rats	Per corpse	0.02
Dead cats	Per corpse	0.10–0.15
Dead dogs	Per corpse	0.05–0.10
Rotten fish or fruit	10 jin*	0.03
Bones: human, mammal, or bird	10 jin	0.20
Waste hemp	10 jin	0.50
Waste paper	10 jin	0.20
Waste string or matting	10 jin	0.05
Cotton rags	10 jin	2.00
Rags	10 jin	0.03
Rag cloth	10 jin	0.10–1.0
Coal embers	10 jin	0.05
Coal	10 jin	0.15
Charcoal	10 jin	0.30
Pig bristles and hair	10 jin	15.00
Pig bristles	10 jin	45.00
Old tiles	Apiece	0.02
Tiles	Apiece	0.05
Scrap glass	10 jin	0.25
Makeup vials, empty	10 jin	0.03
Scrap pottery	10 jin	0.03
Scrap earthenware	10 jin	0.02
Bricks	10 jin	0.25
Empty cans	10 jin	0.25
Needles	10 jin	0.25
Old electrical equipment	10 jin	2.00
Scrap iron	10 jin	0.50
Boards	10 jin	0.10
Cigarette butts	1 jin	0.60

* 1 jin (斤) = 1.33 pounds.

Appendix F
Smuggling Costs

Item	Expense (¥)	Income	Remarks
Purchase price of opium	13,250		$5 per tael*, 2,650 taels purchased
Peasant's traveling expenses	360		$0.15 per tael, twelve peasants
Shipping permit	189.25		$0.05 per tael handling charge
Bribes	189.25		$0.05 per tael to the official making out the shipping permit
Trucking fees	757		$0.20 per tael shipping from Miyun to Beijing shops
Bribes	189.25		$0.05 per tael to the Beijing police
Taxes	757		$0.20 per tael
Handling charge	1,703.25		$0.45 per tael
Selling price		68,130	$18 per tael
Total costs	17,395		Traveling expenses included
Profit		50,735	

* A tael (兩) is a Chinese ounce, or 1.33 ounces avoirdupois.

Bibliography

ARCHIVES AND GOVERNMENT REPORTS

Assessor to the Commission of Enquiry into Sino-Japanese Dispute. *Memoranda Presented to the Lytton Commission by V. K. Wellington Koo, Assessor*. New York: Chinese Cultural Society, 1932–1933.

Japanese Chamber of Commerce. *Manchukuo: The Founding of a New State in Manchuria*. New York: Japanese Chamber of Commerce, 1933.

Keimu Sōkyoku [Police Affairs General Office], Hinkōshō Chihō Hōan Kyoku [Hinkō Prefecture Regional Public Safety Bureau]. *Daikan'en no Kaibō* [Autopsy of the Garden of Grand Vision]. *Kanminzoku Shakai Jittai Chōsa* [Investigation into the Social Conditions of the Chinese Race]. Unpublished report. Tōkyō: National Diet Library, 1942.

League of Nations, Commission of Enquiry into the Sino-Japanese Dispute. *Appeal by the Chinese Government. Report of the Commission of Enquiry Signed by the Members of the Commission on September 4th, 1932, at Peiping*. Geneva: Geneva Research Center, 1932.

Manchukuo Bureau of Information and Publicity, Department of Foreign Affairs. *Manchukuo Handbook of Information*. Shinkyō: Manchukuo Yearbook Company, 1933.

———. *An Outline of the Manchurian Empire, 1939*. Dairen: Manchuria Daily News, 1939.

Manchukuo Yearbook. Shinkyō: Manchukuo Yearbook Company, 1934–1942.

National Archives and Records Administration, College Park, Maryland, General Records of the Department of State (Record Group 59); National Archives Collection of Foreign Records Seized (Record Group 242).

Sun Bang, ed. *Jingji Lueduo* [Economic Plunder]. *Weiman Shiliao Congshu* [Collection of Historical Materials on Bogus Manchukuo]. Jilin: Jilin People's Publishing Company, 1993.

———. *Weiman Junshi* [Manchukuo Military Affairs]. *Weiman Shiliao Congshu* [Collection of Historical Materials on Bogus Manchukuo]. Jilin: Jilin People's Publishing Company, 1993.

———. *Weiman Renwu* [People of Manchukuo]. *Weiman Shiliao Congshu* [Collection of Historical Materials on Bogus Manchukuo]. Jilin: Jilin People's Publishing Company, 1993.

———. *Weiman Shehui* [Society in Manchukuo]. *Weiman Shiliao Congshu* [Collection of Historical Materials on Bogus Manchukuo]. Jilin: Jilin People's Publishing Company, 1993.

———. *Weiman Wenhua* [Manchukuo Culture]. *Weiman Shiliao Congshu* [Collection of Historical Materials on Bogus Manchukuo]. Jilin: Jilin People's Publishing Company, 1993.

———. *Zhimin Zhengquan* [Colonial Political Control]. *Weiman Shiliao Congshu* [Collection of Historical Materials on Bogus Manchukuo]. Jilin: Jilin People's Publishing Company, 1993.

PUBLISHED SOURCES

Bakich, Olga. "Do You Speak Harbin Sino-Russian?" *Itinerario* 35, no. 3 (2011): 23–36.

———. "Émigré Identity: The Case of Harbin." *South Atlantic Quarterly* 99, no. 1 (winter 2000): 51–73.

———. "Origins of the Russian Community on the Chinese Eastern Railway." *Canadian Slavic Papers* 27, no. 1 (March 1985): 1–14.

Bayat, Asef. "Un-civil Society: The Politics of the 'Informal People,'" *Third World Quarterly* 18, no. 1 (1997): 53–72.

Bello, David. "The Cultured Nature of Imperial Foraging in Manchuria." *Late Imperial China*, 31, no. 2 (December 2010): 1–33.

Boo, Katherine. *Behind the Beautiful Forevers: Life, Death, and Hope in a Mumbai Undercity.* New York: Random House, 2012.

Boyle, Danny, dir. *Slumdog Millioniare.* Fox Searchlight Pictures, 2008.

Brynner, Rock. *Empire and Odyssey: The Brynners in Far East Russia and Beyond.* Hanover, NH: Steerforth Press, 2006.

Buruma, Ian. *The China Lover.* New York: Penguin, 2008.

Carter, James. "A Tale of Two Temples: Nation, Region, and Religious Architecture in Harbin, 1928–1998." *South Atlantic Quarterly* 99, no. 1 (winter 2000): 97–115.

———. *Creating a Chinese Harbin: Nationalism in an International City, 1916–1932.* Ithaca, NY: Cornell University Press, 2002.

———. "The Future of Harbin's Past." *Itinerario* 35, no. 3 (2011): 73–85.

Chen, Janet Y. *Guilty of Indigence: The Urban Poor in China, 1900–1953.* Princeton, NJ: Princeton University Press, 2012.

Condidine, John Joseph. *When the Sorghum Was High.* New York: Longmans Green and Company, 1941.

Courtwright, David. *Forces of Habit: Drugs and the Making of the Modern World.* Cambridge, MA: Harvard University Press, 2001.

Davis, Mike. *Planet of Slums*. London: Verso, 2006.

Drea, Edward J. *Japan's Imperial Army: Its Rise and Fall, 1853–1945*. Lawrence: University of Kansas Press, 2009.

Dreyer, Edward L. *China at War, 1901–1949*. London: Longman Press, 1995.

Duara, Prasenjit. *Sovereignty and Authenticity: Manchukuo and the East Asian Modern*. Lanham, MD: Rowman & Littlefield, 2003.

Dubois, Thomas David. "Rule of Law in a Brave New Empire: Legal Rhetoric and Practice in Manchukuo." *Law and History Review* 26, no. 2 (summer 2008): 285–316.

Ferrell, Jeff. *Empire of Scrounge: Inside the Urban Underground of Dumpster Diving, Trash Picking and Street Scavenging*. New York: New York University Press, 2006.

Fogel, Joshua. "Integrating into Chinese Society: A Comparison of Japanese Communities of Shanghai and Harbin." In *Japan's Competing Modernities: Issues in Culture and Democracy, 1900–1930*, edited by Sharon A. Minichiello, 45–69. Honolulu: University of Hawaii Press, 1998.

Garon, Sheldon. "The World's Oldest Debate? Prostitution and the State in Imperial Japan, 1900–1945." *American Historical Review* 98 (June 1993): 715.

Garrett, Valery M. *Chinese Clothing: An Illustrated Guide*. Hong Kong: Oxford University Press, 1994.

———. *Mandarin Squares: Mandarins and Their Insignia*. Hong Kong: Oxford University Press, 1990.

Gee, Nathaniel Gist. *A Class of Social Outcasts: Notes on the Beggars in China*. Peking Leader Reprints 1. Peking: Peking Leader Press, 1925.

Gernet, Jacques. *A History of Chinese Civilization*. Cambridge: Cambridge University Press, 1987.

Gielgud, Val Henry. *Outrage in Manchukuo*. London: Rich and Cowan, 1937.

Gold, Hal. *Unit 731 Testimony: Japan's Wartime Human Experimentation Program*. Singapore: Yen Books, 1996.

Goldsmith, Seth B. "The Status of Prison Health Care." *Public Health Report* 89, no. 6 (November–December 1974): 569–75.

Gottchang, Thomas R., and Diana Lary. *Swallows and Settlers: The Great Migration from North China to Manchuria*. Ann Arbor, MI: Center for Chinese Studies, 2000.

Gronewold, Sue. *Beautiful Merchandise: Prostitution in China, 1860–1936*. New York: Harrington Park Press, 1985.

Ha'erbin Kōtsū Kabushiki Kaisha. *Harupin Kankō Annai* [Harbin Sightseeing Guide]. Special-276/535. Tōkyō: National Diet Library, 1939.

Hall, Robert Burnett. "The Geography of Manchuria." *Annals of the American Academy of Political and Social Science* 152 (November 1930): 278–92.

Hamano Kinzaburō. *Ah, Manshū* [Ah, Manchuria]. Tōkyō: Akigen Shobō, 1970.

Hammer, Joshua. *Yokohama Burning: The Deadly 1923 Earthquake and Fire That Helped Forge the Path to World War II*. New York: Free Press, 2006.

Harper, Damian, Steve Fallon, and Katja Gaskill. *China*. Victoria, Australia: Lonely Planet Publishing, 2005.

Hershatter, Gail. *Dangerous Pleasures: Prostitution and Modernity in Twentieth Century Shanghai*. Berkeley: University of California Press, 1997.

Horikawa Ryūjin. *Ha'erbin Nikki* [Harbin Diary]. Nagoya: Shotokudō, 1934.

Hoshi Ryōichi. *Manshū Rekishi Kaidō: Maboroshi no Kuni o Tazunite* [The Roads of Manchuria: A Visit to a Dreamlike Country]. Tōkyō: Kōjinsha, 2000.

Hou Hsiao-hsien, dir. *Hai Shang Hua* [Flowers of Shanghai]. 3H Productions/Shochiku Company, 1998.

House, William J. "Priorities for Urban Labor Market Research in Anglophone Africa." *Journal of Developing Areas* 27 (October 1992): 49–68.

Hsu, Carolyn. *Creating Market Socialism: How Ordinary People Are Shaping Class and Status in China.* Durham, NC: Duke University Press, 2007.

Hussy, Harry. *"Manchukuo" in Relation to World Peace: Things Not Told in the Report of the Commission of Enquiry.* Geneva: n.p, 1932.

Iwasaki, Mineko. *Geisha: A Life.* New York: Altris Books, 2002.

Jansen, Marius B. *Sun Yat-sen and the Japanese.* Cambridge, MA: Harvard University Press, 1954.

Jennings, John. *The Opium Empire: Japanese Imperialism and Drug Trafficking in Asia, 1895–1945.* Westport, CT: Praeger, 1997.

Ji Fenghui, ed. *Huashuo Ha'erbin* [Tales of Harbin]. Harbin: Heilongjiang People's Publishing Company, 2002.

Jones, Francis Clifford. *Manchuria since 1931.* London: Royal Institute of International Affairs, 1949.

Jowett, Philip. *Rays of the Rising Sun: Armed Forces of Japan's Asian Allies, 1931–1945.* Solihull, England: Helion, 2004.

K'ang-hsi, *Emperor of China: Self-Portrait of K'ang-hsi.* Translated by Jonathan Spence. New York: Knopf, 1975.

Kagawa Tetsuzō. *Manshū de Hataraku Nihonjin* [Japanese Working in Manchuria]. Tōkyō: Diamond Publishing, 1941.

Katō Toyotaka. "Daikan'en." In *Shōsetsu: Daikan'en* [Novel: Garden of Grand Vision]. Matsuyama: Ehime Tsushinsha, 1974.

———. ed. *Manshūkoku Keisatsu Juyo Shashin Bunkei Shiryosei* [A Collection of Important Photographic Resources of the Manchukuo Police]. Matsuyama: Moto Zaigai Komuin Engokai, 1982.

———. *Manshūkoku Keisatsu Shōshi* [Short History of the Manchukuo Police]. Vol. 1: *Manshūkoku Kenryoku no Jittai ni Tsuite* [Concerning the Actual Condition of Power in Manchukuo]. Matsuyama: Man-Mō Dōhō Engokai Ehime-ken Shibu, 1968.

———. *Manshūkoku Keisatsu Shōshi* [Short History of the Manchukuo Police]. Vol. 2: *Manshūkoku no Chika Sōshiki ni Tsuite* [On the Organization of Manchukuo Underground]. Matsuyama: Man-Mō Dōhō Engokai Ehime-ken Shibu, 1974.

———. *Manshūkoku Keisatsu Shōshi* [Short History of the Manchukuo Police]. Vol. 3: *Manshūkoku no Kaitai to Keisatsu* [The Dismantling of Manchukuo and Its Police]. Matsuyama: Man-Mō Dōhō Engokai Ehime-ken Shibu, 1976.

Kingly, W. Dean. "Japan's Discovery of Poverty." *Journal of Asian History* 22, no. 1 (1988): 1–24.

Kōmoto Daisaku. "Watakushi wa Chō Sakurin o Koroshita" [I Murdered Zhang Zuolin]. In *Bungei Shunjū ni Miru Showa Shi* [Showa History as Seen through the Bungei Shunjū Magazine], edited by Bunge Shunjū, 1:44–52. Tōkyō: Bungei Shunjū Ltd., 1988.

Koshizawa Akira. *Harubin no Toshi Hattatsu Shi* [History of the Growth and Development of Harbin]. Tōkyō: Nittchu Kaishizai Kyokai Kaiho, 1986.

Kwan, Stanley, dir. *Yenzhi Kou* [Rouge]. Golden Harvest Company/Golden Way Films Ltd., 1987.

Lahusen, Thomas. "A Place Called Harbin: Reflections on a Centennial." *China Quarterly*, no. 154 (June 1998): 400–410.

———. "Dr. Fu Manchu in Harbin: Cinema and Moviegoers of the 1930s." *South Atlantic Quarterly* 99, no. 1 (winter 2000): 143–61.

Larsen, Erik. *In the Garden of Beasts: Love, Terror, and an American Family in Hitler's Berlin*. New York: Crown, 2011.

Lee, Peter. *Opium Culture: The Art and Ritual of the Chinese Tradition*. Rochester, VT: Park Street Press, 2006.

Li Debin and Shi Fang. *Heilongjiang Yimin Gaoyao* [An Outline of Migration to Heilongjiang]. Harbin: Heilongjiang People's Publishing Company, 1987.

Lindt, A. R. *Special Correspondent: With Bandit and General in Manchuria*. London: Corben-Sanderman, 1933.

Linebarger, Paul. *The Political Doctrines of Sun Yat-sen: An Exposition of the San Min Chu I*. Baltimore: John Hopkins University Press, 1937.

Lo Cheng-Pang. "The Fight against Opium." *Pan-Pacific* 34 (October–December 1939): 71–72.

Lu Hanchao. *Beyond the Neon Lights: Everyday Shanghai in the Early Twentieth Century*. Berkeley: University of California Press, 1999.

———. *Street Criers: A Cultural History of Chinese Beggars*. Stanford, CA: Stanford University Press, 2005.

Mackinnon, Stephen, and Diana Lary. *China at War: Regions of China, 1937–1945*. Stanford, CA: Stanford University Press, 2007.

Makuuchi Mitsuo. *Manshūkoku Keisatsu Gaishi* [An Unofficial History of the Manchukuo Police]. Tōkyō: San-Ichi Shobō, 1996.

Manshūkoku Keisatsu Shi [History of the Manchukuo Police]. Shinkyō: Chianbu Keimushi, 1942.

Marshall, Rob, dir. *Memoirs of a Geisha*. Columbia, 2005.

Matsuoka Yoshihisa. *Making of Japanese Manchuria, 1904–1932*. Cambridge, MA: Harvard University Press, 2003.

Mehta, Suketu. *Maximum City: Bombay Lost and Found*. New York: Alfred A. Knopf, 2005.

Meng Lie, ed. *Huashuo Ha'erbin* [Harbin Told in Pictures]. Beijing: Hualing Publishing Company, 2002.

Meyer, Kathryn, and Terry Parssinen. *Webs of Smoke: Smugglers Warlords, Spies, and the History of the International Drug Trade*. Lanham, MD: Rowman & Littlefield, 1998.

Mi Dawei. *Heilongjiang Lishi—Fu Ha'erbin Chengshi Shi* [The History of Heilongjiang: The History of Harbin City Attached]. Harbin: Heilongjiang People's Publishing Company, 2012.

Mimura, Janis. *Planning for Empire: Reform Bureaucrats and the Japanese Wartime State*. Ithaca, NY: Cornell University Press, 2011.

Mitter, Rana. *The Manchurian Myth: Nationalism, Resistance and Collaboration in Modern China*. Berkeley: University of California Press, 2000.

Miyasaki Ichisada. *China's Examination Hell: The Civil Service Examination of Imperial China*. Translated by Conrad Schirokauer. New York: Weatherside, 1976.

Morikawa Hatsuno. *Aa, Harupin: Morikawa Hatsuno Shuki; kōtei hoki Komiyama Noboru* [Ah, Harbin: the diary of Morikawa Hatsuno; revised by Komiyama Noboru]. Tōkyō: Katakura Shoten, 1984.

Mutō Tomio. *Manshūkoku no Dammen* [Sketches of Manchukuo]. Tōkyō: Kindai-sha, 1956.

Nagano Sei'ichi. *Kitaman Fūdo Zakki* [Notes on the Topography of North Manchuria]. Tōkyō: Zuyuho Publishing Company, 1938.

Neuwirth, Robert. *Shadow Cities: A Billion Squatters, a New Urban World*. New York: Routledge, 2005.

Nishizawa Yasuhiko. *Zusetsu "Manshū" Toshi Monogatari: Harubin, Dairen, Shen'yō, Chōshun* [Illustrated tales from the cities of Manchuria: Harbin, Dalian, Shenyang, Changchun]. Tōkyō: Kawade Shobō, 1996.

Ogata, Sadako N. *Defiance in Manchuria: The Making of Japanese Foreign Policy, 1931–1932*. Berkeley: University of California Press, 1964.

Okamoto, Shumpei. *Impressions of the Front: Woodblock Prints of the Sino-Japanese War, 1894–1895*. Philadelphia: Philadelphia Museum of Art, 1983.

———. *The Japanese Oligarchy and the Russo-Japanese War*. New York: Columbia, 1970.

Orwell, George. *Down and Out in Paris and London*. New York: Harcourt, Brace and World, 1961.

Osnos, Evan. "The God of Gamblers: Why Las Vegas Is Moving to Macau." *New Yorker*, April 9, 2012, 45–55.

Paine, S. C. M. *The Wars for Asia, 1911–1949*. Cambridge: Cambridge University Press, 2012.

Peattie, Mark. *Ishiwara Kanji and Japan's Confrontation with the West*. Princeton, NJ: Princeton University Press, 1975.

Puyi, Henry. *The Last Manchu: The Autobiography of Henry Pu Yi, Last Emperor of China*. New York: Putnam, 1967.

Qu Wei and Li Shuxiao, eds. *The Jews in Harbin*. Beijing: Social Sciences Documentation Publishing House, 2003.

Remick, Elizabeth J. "Police Run Brothels in Republican Kunming." *Modern China* 33, no. 4 (October 2007): 423–61.

Ryū Meishū. *Taiwan Tōchi to Ahen Mondai* [Control of Taiwan and the Opium Problem]. Tōkyō: Yamakawa Publishing, 1983.

Sano Shinichi. *Amakasu Masahiko, Ranshin no Kōya* [Amakasu Masahiko, Field of Ambition]. Tōkyō: Shinchōsha, 2008.

Satō Shin'ichirō. *Manshū oyobi Manshūjin* [Manchuria and Manchurians]. Shinkyō: Manshū Jijō Annaijo, 1940.

———. *Satō Shin'ichirō Senshū* [Satō Shin'ichirō Selected Writings]. Tōkyō: Satō Shin'ichirō Senshū Kankōkai, 1994.

Scarry, Elaine. *The Body in Pain: The Making and Unmaking of the World*. New York: Oxford University Press, 1985.

Scherer, James A. B. *Manchukuo: A Bird's-Eye View*. Tōkyō: Hokuseido Press, 1933.

Schiffrin, Harold Z. *Sun Yat-sen and the Origins of the Chinese Revolution*. Berkeley: University of California Press, 1968.

Sevine, Steven L. *Anvil of Victory: The Communist Revolution in Manchuria, 1945–1948*. New York: Columbia University Press, 1987.

Sims, Richard. *Japanese Political History since the Meiji Renovation, 1868–2000.* New York: Palgrave, 2001.

Sipkov, Philip J. *Escape from Destiny: A Biographical Sketch of George E. Prujan.* Washington, DC: Printed by author, 1986.

Smith, Norman. "Hibernate No More! Winter, Health, and the Great Outdoors." Paper presented at the "The Manchurian Environment: Natural Resources, Climate and Disease" workshop, University of British Columbia, May 18, 2013.

———. *Intoxicating Manchuria: Alcohol, Opium, and Culture in China's Northeast.* Vancouver: University of British Columbia Press, 2012.

Snow, Edgar. "Japan Builds a New Colony." *Saturday Evening Post*, February 24, 1934.

Song Hongyan. *Dongfang Xiao Bali* [The Little Paris of the East] (Harbin: Heilongjiang Kexue Zhishu Chubanshe, 2001).

South Manchurian Railroad Company. *Harubin Annai* [Harbin Guide]. Special 276/594. Tōkyō: National Diet Library, 1923.

Spence, Jonathan. *Gate of Heavenly Peace: The Chinese and Their Revolution, 1895–1980.* New York: Viking, 1981.

Strasser, Susan. *Waste and Want: A Social History of Trash.* New York: Henry Holt, 1999.

Suleski, Ronald. *Civil Government in Warlord China: Tradition, Modernization and Manchuria.* New York: Peter Lang, 2002.

Sumino Yukihiro. "Yamato Hoteru Junrei" [Yamato Hotel Pilgrimage], *SD* (February 1996): 97–100.

Takafusa Nakamura. "Recession, Recovery, and War, 1920–1945." In *The Interwar Economy of Japan: Colonialism, Depression, and Recovery, 1910–1940*, edited by Michael Simka, 99–143. New York: Garland Publishing, 1998.

Tamanoi Mariko. *Crossed Histories: Manchuria in the Age of Empire.* Honolulu: University of Hawaii Press, 2005.

Tanaka Yuki. *Hidden Horrors: Japanese War Crimes in World War Two.* Boulder, CO: Westview Press, 1996.

Taveras v. Resorts International Hotel, Inc., Civil No. 07-4555 (RMB) 2008 U.S Dist. LEXIS 98451.

Thompson, Hugh, and Kathryn Lane. *DK Eyewitness Travel: China.* London: DK Publishing, 2012.

Tsukase Susumu, *Manshūkoku: "Minzoku Kyōwa" no Jitsuzō* [The True Nature of Manchukuo "Racial Harmony"]. Tōkyō: Yoshikawa Kōbunkan, 1998.

———. "The Penetration of Manzhouguo Rule in Manchuria." In *China at War: Regions of China, 1937–1945*, edited by Stephen R. Mackinnon, Diana Lary, and Ezra Vogel, 110–33. Stanford, CA: Stanford University Press, 2007.

Tsunoda Fusako. *Amakasu Tai'i* [Captain Amakasu]. Tōkyō: Chūō Kōronsha, 1975.

Venkatesh, Sudhir. *Gangleader for a Day: A Rogue Sociologist Takes to the Streets.* New York: Penguin, 2008.

Vespa, Amieto. *Secret Agent of Japan.* Boston: Little, Brown and Company, 1938.

Wakeman, Frederic, Jr. *The Shanghai Badlands: Wartime Terrorism and Urban Crime, 1937–1941.* New York: Cambridge University Press, 1996.

Waley, Arthur. *The Opium War through Chinese Eyes.* Stanford, CA: Stanford University Press, 1958.

Wang Yufei and Gotō Haruhiko. "Harubin shi Fujiadian Chi-iki no 'Dayuan' Shiki Kenchiku Airia ni Okeru Toshi Kūkan Keitai to Shūjū Keisei Ryōiki ni Kansuru Kenkyū" [On the Relation between Urban Space and Dwelling Territory in the "Dayuan" House Area of Fujiadian, Harbin, China]. *Nihon Kenchiku Gakkai Keikakukei Ronbunshū* [Journal of Architecture and Planning Transactions of the Architecture Institute of Japan] 622 (December 2007): 113–20.

Wells, Audrey. *The Political Thought of Sun Yat-sen: Development and Impact.* London: Palgrave, 2001.

Williams, Peter, and David Wallace. *Unit 731: Japan's Secret Biological Warfare in World War Two.* New York: Free Press, 1989.

Wolf, Margery. *The House of Lim: A Study of a Chinese Farm Family.* New York: Appleton-Century Crofts, 1968.

———. *Women and the Family in Rural Taiwan.* Stanford, CA: Stanford University Press, 1972.

Wolff, David. "Bean There." *South Atlantic Quarterly* 99, no. 1 (winter 2000): 97–120.

Woodhead, H. G. W. *A Visit to Manchukuo.* Shanghai: Mercury Press, 1932.

Xu Xueshi. "Organization and Grassroots Structure of the Manzhouguo Regime." In *China at War: Regions of China, 1937–1945,* edited by Stephen Mackinnon, 134–47. Stanford, CA: Stanford University Press, 2007.

Yamamura Shinichi. *Manchuria under Japanese Domination.* Translated by Joshua A. Fogel. Philadelphia: University of Pennsylvania Press, 2006.

Yamauchi Saburō. "Mayaku to Sensō: Nitchu Sensō to Himitsu Heiki" [Narcotics and War: The Sino-Japanese War and Its Secret Weapon]. *Jinbutsu Ōrai* [Affairs of Eminent Men] (September 1965): 165–69.

Yanagida Momotarō. *Harubin no Zanshō* [Harbin Afterglow]. Tōkyō: Hara Shobō, 1986.

———. *Harupin Tsuioku* [Remembering Harbin]. Tōkyō: Self-published, 1974.

Yoshimoto Yoniko. *Manshū Ryukoki* [Notes on a Journey through Manchuria]. Tōkyō: Tōhaku Hakkojo, 1934.

Young, A. Morgan. *Imperial Japan, 1926–1939.* New York: William Morrow and Company, 1938.

Young, Louise. "Colonizing Manchuria: The Making of an Imperial Myth." In *Mirror of Modernity: Invented Traditions of Modern Japan,* edited by Stephen Vlastos, 95–109. Berkeley: University of California Press, 1998.

———. *Japan's Total Empire: Manchuria and the Culture of Wartime Imperialism.* Berkeley: University of California Press, 1998.

Index

About the Author

Kathryn Meyer is associate professor of history at Wright State University. She received her BA from the University of Vermont and her PhD from Temple University. Her time in Asia includes two years studying Chinese language at the Stanford Center at Taiwan University in Taipei and a year teaching Japanese history for Temple University in Japan. She returned to Japan while researching her previous book, *Webs of Smoke*: *Smugglers, Warlords, Spies, and the History of the International Drug Trade* (Rowman & Littlefield, 1998), which led to her discovery of the police report that became the basis for *Life and Death in the Garden*. When not traveling or working in Asia, she lives in Dayton, Ohio, where she teaches classes on Asian history and the history of drugs and crime and rides her horse Ghandi [*sic*].

STATE AND SOCIETY IN EAST ASIA

Series Editor: Elizabeth J. Perry